The Resilience Economy

A PRACTICAL & PROVEN FRAMEWORK FOR ECONOMIC DIVERSIFICATION AMONG NEWLY INDUSTRIALIZED ECONOMIES

Dr. Eng. Ahmed Saeed Al-Nayeli Al-Shamsi

PASSIONPRENEUR® PUBLISHING

Publishing information
Publishing, design, and production facilitated by Passionpreneur Publishing, A division of Passionpreneur Organization Pty Ltd, ABN: 48640637529

www.PassionpreneurPublishing.com
Melbourne, VIC | Australia

*To my father and mother who sacrificed
a lot to take care of our family, and to my wife
who has been patient with me from day one
and has overlooked my faults.*

Table of Contents

Acknowledgement vii

Preface ix

List of abbreviations xiii

Chapter 1: A Wake-Up Call 1

Chapter 2: The Wheel of Economic Diversification and Development 13

Chapter 3: Financial Funding/Natural Resources 29

Chapter 4: Human Development 53

Chapter 5: Governance, Institutions, and Policies 93

Chapter 6: Infrastructure 127

Chapter 7: Export Orientation 157

Chapter 8: Innovation 185

Chapter 9: Entrepreneurship 215

Chapter 10: Private Sector 241

Chapter 11: State-Owned Enterprises 265

Chapter 12: Final Thoughts and Recommendations 291

Conclusion: Beyond the Wheel 321

Acknowledgments

I would like to express my deep appreciation to my professor, Dr. Arijit Sikdar, who guided me through my doctoral research at the University of Wollongong in Dubai (UOWD). My thesis forms the basis of this book.

A very special note of gratitude goes to my coach, mentor, and friend, Dr. David Dombkins, for all his support and for believing in me.

Thanks for all your encouragement!

Preface

National economic development is a complex process in which nations confront many hurdles throughout the journey and only a small number are successful in reaching their goals. During the second half of the twentieth century, many nations gained independence from Western colonial powers and engaged in the national development movement, trying to pull their people out of poverty and misery. Most started on a sound, initial footing but lost direction during the journey because of the complexity and lack of clarity on what is required to succeed.

The "wheel" of economic diversification and development is a framework to guide nations to reach their economic and social goals through factors that strengthen the development process and improve the quality of the process outcomes. Many nations work to enhance these factors but do not pay sufficient attention to the quality of the outcome and the importance this holds for long-term sustainable development. Any one of these factors can support economic development, produce high-quality outcomes, or can present obstacles and create issues that can negatively affect the other factors.

These factors do not exist in a vacuum. They are interrelated, where success in one factor will lead to success in other factors, and vice versa. These factors need to function in a system of systems setup to provide flexibility for execution and alignment. The system of systems arrangement has the ability to manage the effect of all factors within, and outside, the wheel.

There are many other factors that affect economic diversification and development but in this wheel I have selected those that are the most influential on other factors. All nations, irrespective of the conditions of development, will need to produce strong outcomes when applying these factors in order to promote the other factors and to advance.

Who is this book for?

This book is for state leaders who wish to advance their nation in the face of obstacles. The wheel provides guidance to the factors that work together as the vehicle for the economy, moving forward with the view to overcoming all bumps in the road.

This book is also for ministers and senior officials who are involved directly or indirectly in the planning and execution of national advancement strategies. The wheel provides them with the requisite tools to review and understand before planning strategies.

The wheel of economic diversification and development is for anyone who seeks to build their nation and enhance its capabilities to position itself among the advanced nations. While easy to understand, the wheel is difficult to execute, and requires implementation by those that are truly patriotic and altruistic to achieve the necessary outcome.

How is this book structured?

The content of this book is arranged around key factors that are easy to understand and directly accessible when needed. The wheel was built by structuring nine factors into three core parts. The 'outer circle' includes the factor of financial funding, resembling the tire and tube that makes the movement of the wheel smoother. Then there are the three factors that resemble the rim of the wheel: human development, infrastructure, and governance, policies, and institutions. The last part, the inner circle, forms the bolts that connect the wheel to the vehicle allowing it to move. This contains five factors: export orientation, innovation, entrepreneurship, the private sector, and state-owned enterprises.

Each factor is discussed as a separate chapter, with examples applied to the success story of Singapore, then applied to Abu Dhabi and the Gulf Cooperation Council countries to identify the shortfalls. A comparison of factors is then presented at the end of each chapter.

The book also offers some recommendations for those seeking to use this wheel to advance their nations. These recommendations can be used as steps to achieve sound outcomes when implementing the factors and can ultimately lead to national advancement.

The content of this book is based on Thesis was submitted to University Of Wollongong in Dubai in partial fulfillment of the requirements for Doctorate in Business Administration (DBA) by the author, thesis title is "Strategies to Diversify and Develop the Economy of Abu Dhabi and GCC Countries: Application of "Wheel of Diversification" model".

List of Abbreviations

ACE	Action Community for Entrepreneurship
ACTVET	Abu Dhabi Centre for Technical and Vocational Education and Training
ADEC	Abu Dhabi Education Council
ADGAS	Abu Dhabi Gas Liquefaction Company
ADIA	Abu Dhabi Investment Authority
ADIC	Abu Dhabi Investment Company
ADIO	Abu Dhabi Investment Office
ADNOC	Abu Dhabi National Oil Company
ADPC	Abu Dhabi Ports Company
ADQ	Abu Dhabi Holding
ADVETI	Abu Dhabi Vocational Education and Training Institute
ADWEA	Abu Dhabi Water and Electricity Authority
AED	UAE Dirham
AMP	Accredited Mentorship Partner
AOs	Administrative Officers
ASEAN	Association of South East Asian Nations
A*STAR	Agency for Science, Technology and Research
ATRC	Advanced Technology Research Council
BMRC	Biomedical Research Council
BP	British Petroleum
CEF	ComCare Enterprise Fund
CEO	Chief Executive Officer
CI	Corruption Index
COAD	Competitiveness Office of Abu Dhabi

CPF	Central Provident Fund
CPTE	Council for Professional and Technical Education
CSF	Centre for Strategic Futures
DED	Department of Economic Development
DPM	Department of Urban Planning and Municipalities
EAIG	Emirates Advanced Investments Group
EDB	Economic Development Board
EDIC	Emirates Defence Industries Company
EIA	Energy Information Administration
ENEC	Emirates Nuclear Energy Corporation
EPZ	Export Processing Zones
ESC	Economic Strategic Committee
ESVF	Early Stage Venture Capital
ETPL	Exploit Technologies Pte Ltd
EWI	Environment & Water Industry Program
FDI	Foreign Direct Investment
FTAs	Free Trade Agreements
FTZ	Free Trade Zone
GASCO	Abu Dhabi Gas Industries
GCC	Gulf Cooperation Council
GCI	Global Competitiveness Index
GDP	Gross Domestic Product
GEE	Global Entrepreneur Executives
GEM	Global Entrepreneurship Monitor
GII	Global Innovation Index
GIP	Global Investor Program
GLC	Government-Linked Companies
GNP	Gross National Product
GPFG	Government Pension Fund Global
GPFN	Government Pension Fund Norway
HD	Human Development

HDB	Housing Development Board
HDI	Human Development Index
HHP	Human Health and Potential
HMDP	Healthcare Manpower Development Programme
H–O	Heckscher and Ohlin theory
IAT	Institute of Applied Technology
ICAD	Industrial City of Abu Dhabi
ICT	Information, Communication and Technology
IDA	Infocomm Development Authority
IDB	Industrial Development Bureau
IDMPO	Interactive Digital Media Program Office
IE	International Enterprise
IIF	Institute of International Finance
IMD	International Institute for Management Development
IMF	International Monetary Fund
INSEAD	Institut Européen d'Administration des Affaires
IP	Intellectual Property
IPIC	International Petroleum Investment Corporation
JODCO	Japan Oil Development Company
JTC	Jurong Town Corporation
KFED	Khalifa Fund for Enterprise Development
KIZAD	Khalifa Industrial Zone Abu Dhabi
KPI	Key Performance Indicators
KPFTZ	Khalifa Port Free Trade Zone
KRIVET	Korea Research Institute for Vocational Education and Training
KSA	Kingdom of Saudi Arabia
KUSTAR	Khalifa University of Science, Technology And Research
LIUP	Local Industry Upgrading Program
MAIP	Market Access Incubation Program
MAP	Management Associates Programme

MA	Management associates
MDA	Media Development Authority
MEXT	Ministry of Education, Culture, Sports, Science and Technology (Japan)
MINDEF	Ministry of Defence
MNC	Multi-National Corporation
MTC	Manufacturing, Trade and Connectivity
NCB	National Computer Board
NFIE	National Framework for Innovation and Enterprise
NIC	National Innovation Committee
NIE	National Institute of Education
NRF	National Research Foundation
NSTB	National Science and Technology Board
NTU	Nanyang Technological University
NTUC	National Trades Union Congress
NUS	National University of Singapore
NVPC	National Volunteer and Philanthropy Center
OECD	Organization for Economic Cooperation and Development
OEM	Original Equipment Manufacturers
PCT	Patent Cooperation Treaty
PEI	Precision Engineering Institute
PERC	Political Economic & Risk Consultancy
PISA	Program for International Student Assessment
POC	Proof-of-Concept
PPP	Public–Private Partnership
PSA	Port of Singapore Authority
PSB	Productivity and Standards Board
PwC	PricewaterhouseCoopers
QCC	Quality and Conformity Council
QFCA	Qatar Financial Centre Authority
RAHS	Risk Assessment and Horizon Scanning

RCE	Research Centers of Excellence
R&D	Research and Development
RIE2020	Research, Innovation and Enterprise 2020 Plan
RIEC	Research, Innovation and Enterprise Council
S&T	Science & Technology
SCAD	Abu Dhabi Statistics Center
SDF	Skills Development Fund
SEEDS	Startup Enterprise Development Scheme
SERC	Science and Engineering Research Council
SIFS	Small Industry Finance Scheme
SingStat.	Singapore Statistics
SIPRI	Stockholm International Peace Research Institute
SMEs	Small and Medium-Sized Enterprises
SNDE	Smart Nation and Digital Economy
SOEs	State-Owned Enterprises
SoS	System of Systems
SP+	Scenario Planning Plus
SPO	Scenario Planning Office
SPRING	Standards, Productivity and Innovation Board
SSA	Sector Specific Accelerator Program
SSP	Singapore Science Park
STB	Singapore Tourism Board
STEM	Science, Technology, Engineering and Mathematics
STTI	Singapore Technical Training Institute
SWFI	Sovereign Wealth Fund Institute
TAQA	Abu Dhabi National Energy Company
TDB	Trade Development Board
TDIC	Tourism Development and Investment Company
TEA	Total early-stage Entrepreneurial Activity
TECS	Technology Enterprise Commercialization Scheme
TIS	Technology Incubation Scheme

TRIPS	Paris Convention, and the Trade Related Aspects of Intellectual Property Rights
TVET	Technical and Vocational Educational Training
Twofour54	Media free zone
UAE	United Arab Emirates
UIF	University Innovation Fund
UN	United Nations
UNCTAD	United Nations Conference on Trade and Development
UNDP	United Nations Development Programme
UNECE	United Nations Economic Commission for Europe
UOWD	University of Wollongong in Dubai
URA	Urban Redevelopment Authority
URD	Urban Redevelopment Department
USS	Urban Solutions and Sustainability
VC	Venture Capital
WB	World Bank
WDI	World Development Indicators
WEF	World Economic Forum
WHO	World Health Organization
WIPO	World Intellectual Property Organization
WTO	World Trade Organization
YSEP	Youth Social Entrepreneurship Program
ZADCO	Zakum Development Company
ZonesCorp	Higher Corporation for Specialized Economic Zones

CHAPTER 1

A Wake-Up Call

Learning from Mistakes

*"Sit down before fact as a little child, be prepared to give
up every conceived notion, follow humbly wherever and
whatever abysses nature leads, or you will learn nothing."*

— THOMAS HUXLEY, ENGLISH BIOLOGIST (1825–1895)

Every few years Abu Dhabi and the United Arab Emirates (UAE)
face the effects of falling petroleum prices. When the oil price
is high, the government spends generously; when the oil price is low,
spending is tightened. For as long as I can remember, there has been
talk about the importance of economic diversification and how this
will support the financial security of the nation when oil prices drop
as well as prepare the nation for the period following oil and gas deple-
tion. Yet, none of the efforts to diversify the economy has succeeded,
and there have always been obstacles stopping the UAE and Gulf
Cooperation Council (GCC) from achieving a general recovery plan.

Many will ask why I am writing about economic diversification,
when great economic minds have discussed this subject many times
and come up with key theories and won international recognition

and awards. The subject has been a field of theory for the past 200 years, since Adam Smith wrote on it. What can I possibly add? In this chapter, I will provide a brief account of what happened to me and what places me in a position to write about this subject and create a new framework of economic diversification suited to my country, the GCC and similar countries.

I was born in 1968, two years after the late Shaikh Zayed became ruler of Abu Dhabi and three years before the independence of the United Arab Emirates. The founding fathers had to tackle a lot of problems to transfer the nation from a land with no unified concept of statehood, no infrastructure, with people still living in tents, and no friendly nation willing to take us by the hand, except for Kuwait.

Petroleum revenue was our lifeline, and the government used this revenue to transfer the country into one of the most advanced nations globally. In the 1970s, the government started to build housing for people to settle down and stop moving around in tents. The government created schools and motivated parents to let their kids attend, and created roads to connect cities and make travel easier within the country. My father used to spend ten days traveling between Al-Ain and Dubai. I can now travel the distance in one hour.

The people were Shaikh Zayed's first priority and how to use the wealth received from oil to help the people take the nation to the next level, to have a life better than what their parents had. Shaikh Zayed grew up during difficult times and did not want his people to experience such hardships. He knew that oil reserves were depleting and needed to think beyond the "oil age". For this, he created many investment arms such as the Abu Dhabi Investment Authority.

In 1986, the oil price fell to less than US$10 a barrel. As a result, many financial benefits were withheld and many government projects were stopped due to a tightening of funds. That was the first time I started to hear about the need for diversification and how it would be useful for the nation to confront falling oil prices and prepare for the period after depletion. The government started to think seriously about how to diversify the economy, but there was no coordinated strategy that was devised. When prices start to rise again at the end of 1990, there was no discussion about economic diversification and it seemed that there was no problem to consider. In 1998, the issue of economic diversification arose again and is repeated every time oil prices drop.

In the late 1980s, I was sent to the United States to study aerospace engineering as part of the UAE's efforts to create an aerospace industry, including an air force and airlines. I was happy to be part of such efforts, and when I finished my studies I returned to my country filled with hopes and passion to apply what I had learned and to create a new industry. But I found out that the plans had changed over a short period, and that the government was pursuing new ideas to advance the economy. This was a shock for me as I had spent all this time studying a field of research that was no longer required.

So, I decided to concentrate my attention on a military career, especially since Shaikh Mohammad Bin Zayed was Chief of Staff in the army and was rebuilding the military to be among the best in the region. His actions were motivated especially by recent events in which Iraq had attacked Kuwait. Shaikh Zayed and his son did not want the same thing happening to the UAE.

For the next 12 years, I was busily engaged in military training and missions, and in self-development. In 2008 I received a master's degree in International Business from the University of Wollongong in Dubai, which provided a different perspective on looking at and analyzing economic and political activities.

Since the 1980s, many initiatives were developed to find solutions to problems in Abu Dhabi and the UAE in relation to the economy, population balance (15–20% of the UAE are citizens),

Emiratization, and many other issues, but none were realized because most of the time the solution was not logical, could not be applied, or there was no continuous process of implementation. I was monitoring the initiatives at the time and wondering when the government would finally have a good strategy with an implementation plan.

Shaikh Muhammad bin Zayed Al Nahyan started his involvement in diversifying the economy at the end of the 1990s – he focused on tourism and real estate. In 2004, he assumed the position of Crown Prince of Abu Dhabi, which allowed him to create and execute plans for economic diversification. To support his strategy, the Executive Affairs Authority was created and enhanced his flagship Mubadala (sovereign wealth fund). Shaikh Muhammad encouraged industry chiefs to focus on the development of the domestic economy.

In the mid-2000s, learning from the unsuccessful attempts to diversify the economies in the UAE and other GCC countries, Abu Dhabi developed the "Abu Dhabi Economic Vision 2030" with long-term goals and considerations. The emirate wanted to establish a variety of economic sectors to diversify away from the petroleum sector. The government is committed to supporting the establishment of these sectors until they can stand alone. The new sectors need to have the ability to resist global recessions and make use of the region's market to create strong and advanced industries.

In 2008, Vision 2030 was launched intending to reduce dependency on oil and gas and stimulate a knowledge-based economy. Since then, the emirate has made important strides towards securing its growth plans against global and regional risks and ensuring wealth for future generations. The aim of the vision is to create an environment that will allow industries and sectors to develop using policies, human capital, and the private sector to support the development of industry, innovation, and entrepreneurship.

As stated in the vision, the goal is to develop "Abu Dhabi as a sustainable, diversified, high-value-added economy that encourages enterprises and entrepreneurship and is well-integrated in the global economy". Through this plan, which is scheduled to last approximately twenty years, Abu Dhabi has committed itself to improving the depth and stability of the economy, diversifying its financial revenue sources, and reducing its dependency on unstable oil revenues, while concurrently ensuring the emirate's foundations for competitiveness are enhanced.

The vision sets specific targets for the period leading up to 2030, including a four-fold increase in gross domestic product (GDP), an increase in the non-oil sectors' share of GDP from 42% to 64%, and an 8.6% annual growth rate for the non-oil sectors. An essential component of Vision 2030 is to shift Abu Dhabi into high-tech industries with greater emphasis on low-energy manufacturing. The sectors are earmarked for long-term sustainable growth, with the idea that they will be developed and enhanced to survive the recessions and crises of the global economy. Abu Dhabi aims to execute its vision by developing and enhancing twelve economic sectors:

1. Energy (oil and gas)
2. Petrochemicals
3. Aviation, aerospace and defense
4. Metals
5. Pharmaceuticals, biotechnology and life sciences
6. Healthcare equipment and services
7. Tourism
8. Transportation, trade and logistics
9. Education
10. Media
11. Financial services
12. Telecommunication services

The developers of Vision 2030 surveyed the economic environment and identified the factors to be enhanced and areas for improvement to strengthen the competitiveness of Abu Dhabi both regionally and internationally. Specifically, the developers reviewed labor policy, monetary policy, fiscal policy, and business legislation as key devices that should be improved to enhance the business environment.

Importantly, Vision 2030 acknowledges the importance of infrastructure and the need to improve it for the vision to be successful, with the human development factor also recognized as a key component for the success of the economic strategy.

Abu Dhabi has made progress in recent years to diversify and develop the economy. However, the strategy of economic development and diversification is exposed to external shocks, especially drops in the oil price. The current oil crisis has shown the government that it is still vulnerable to such volatility. Because of the dropping oil price and its subsequent negative effect on the economy, the government unofficially put Vision 2030 on hold. One of the objectives of the vision is "Diversified Fiscal Revenue Sources" which is not met when government revenue is still dependent on petroleum revenues (see Table 1.1). It is essential that a strategic implementation plan is designed for the effective execution of Vision 2030. It is critical for Abu Dhabi to take corrective steps to ensure the success of the initiative and to diligently pursue it.

Table 1.1 Percentage distribution of government revenues (%)

Item	2005	2006	2007	2008	2009	2010	2011	2012	2013	2014	2015
Petroleum Royalties and Tax Revenue	85.9	92.3	91.6	92	89.2	82.6	90.6	89.6	93	91	79.6
Department Collections Revenue	11.6	5.8	6.5	6.4	8.1	7.3	6.5	6.7	6.1	7.9	18.8
Capital Revenue	2.5	1.9	1.9	1.6	2.7	10.1	2.9	3.7	0.9	1.1	1.6

source: SCAD reports

Like all those in Abu Dhabi, I was happy that finally, after 40 years, there was a strategy to diversify the economy away from petroleum. For everybody knows that the economy depends on petroleum revenues and every time the petroleum prices drop the government squeezes budgetary spending.

In 2009, I was seconded from the Armed Forces to a company responsible for developing the defense industry, which gave me a chance to participate in the execution of Vision 2030. Defense and aviation are one of the economic sectors highlighted in the vision, and my original dream of being part of the effort to develop the aerospace industry in Abu Dhabi was being realized.

As with all government companies in Abu Dhabi at this time, mine was engaged with an international consultancy to define the strategy of our company as part of Vision 2030. A few joint committees were created with the consultancy to create strategies supported by the staff. The consultancy gathered all the data and our ideas, and came up with a strategy which they said was proven, having been used in similar companies. This meant applying a pre-fixed strategy that was trimmed to become our new strategy. I raised many questions about the new strategy and the ability to execute it, but received pushback and was told that coming from a military background I did not know how things worked in the civilian arena. I told them that it was precisely because of this that I can see the weaknesses of the new strategy. The Chief Executive Officer (CEO) of our company decided to proceed in any case, as he wanted to demonstrate that he was implementing a strategy that supported Vision 2030.

At the same time, I was representing my company in meetings of the Executive Committee in the Executive Council as well as those held by the Department of Economic Development (DED). I thought these meetings would focus on creating an implementation plan to actualize the overall vision, but the meetings involved collecting data on the activities of different entities which fed into realizing the vision instead. I tried to talk to the committees to discuss an implementation plan, but was told that each entity should have its own implementation plan.

For years I was monitoring the implementation of the vision to see if it would be realized or not. There were many new projects and new announcements from different entities to support the vision. Among these, I noticed the following:

- Many projects were announced supporting the vision to gain media exposure.
- Most of these projects were not completed or ran over budget.
- Many entities used the vision to acquire a larger budget.
- Most key personnel used the vision to raise their status and advance their career.

Considerable amounts of money and time were lost as there was no implementation plan. This continued until the Executive Council stopped all projects in 2013 and decided to review them following the announcement by Shaikh Hazza Bin Zayed.[1]

However, it is now almost thirteen years since the vision was announced, and a number of questions should be asked. Is the vision still on track to completion? Has it met its periodic targets?

It is difficult to answer these questions, as no evaluation has yet been produced. Leading (2013) the effort to evaluate and re-prioritize projects in Abu Dhabi, Shaikh Hazza Bin Zayed Al Nahyan, Vice-Chairman of the Abu Dhabi Executive Council, stated "… given the challenging environment, the government has decided to carry out an extensive review of Abu Dhabi's capital projects to ensure the Emirate's resources were being optimized".[2] This statement is an indication that the government of Abu Dhabi is not fully following through on Vision 2030. While the initiative offers a sound approach to developing and enhancing the twelve economic sectors, there is a pressing need to review the approach, correct some of the mistakes, and modify the strategic plans.

The Abu Dhabi government recognizes factors that affect the advancement of the economy, and those that are weak and should be strengthened, which was made clear in the economic field of Vision 2030. The government has invested considerable effort into diversifying the economy, especially in the first five years after announcing Vision 2030. Even though the government has spent considerable time and money on each of the factors, the outcome from these factors has not been as impactful as expected. For example, human development remains a priority of

---

1   *The National Newspaper* (2013) "Abu Dhabi: 2013 report puts second five-year plan in spotlight." Economic Section, Staff. 11 March, p. 1.

2   Ibid

the government, with the promise of creating a skilled workforce as one of the objectives. The government has created educational institutes and has tried out many types of curriculum and ideas for schooling – such as the American, British, and Singaporean models – over the last fifteen years. Yet, these actions have not helped human development become a strong factor, with the quality of outcomes remaining poor. This same approach has been repeated for most factors, and despite the huge effort and costs, the outcomes have been poor.

Regardless of all the efforts, Abu Dhabi's economy remains non-diversified, with oil and gas accounting for 41.7% of the GDP and 56.4% of revenue in 2018.[3] A drop in oil price by about 40% since 2014 has resulted in delays to major projects such as the metro system, which was scheduled to open in 2018, and the urban planning component of Vision 2030. There are, nonetheless, determined efforts to diversify the economy through the advancement of high-tech industries, with innovation, entrepreneurship, and the private sector playing a central role.

In Abu Dhabi, innovation and entrepreneurship are weak and research and development (R&D) expenditure is low. The outputs of innovation such as publishable articles or patents are very low. Abu Dhabi is not competitive globally in any high-tech field. Entrepreneurship, on the other hand, has the potential to be a strong factor with some policy changes to enhance it, especially as many young people are now looking at the private sector as the best way to build a rewarding career, rather than through employment in the public sector. This will support the growth of a strong entrepreneurial private sector.

One of the main issues limiting Abu Dhabi in realizing Vision 2030 is that the government departments have no clear and obvious

---

3   SCAD (2020), *Statistical Yearbook of Abu Dhabi 2020*, Statistics Centre Abu Dhabi, May.

strategy or implementation plans aligned with the initiative; the same applies also to state-owned enterprises (SOEs).

Overall, similar to the other GCC countries, the lack of strategies, implementation plans, key performance indicators (KPIs), and performance reporting allows the entities the chance to come up with their own goals, which are not aligned with what the government wants. It enables them to keep changing directions and aims, and jump from one project to another, which results in wasting time and wasting billions of dirhams for poor outcomes or no outcomes at all.

In 2017, a new foreign expert was brought in to evaluate SOEs in Abu Dhabi's defense industry. It was then decided that he would lead the restructuring of the defense industry. Because of my position as Director of Business Development and Marketing in my previous company, I met him a few times and two or three of these instances were one-on-one meetings. It was clear to me that he was not the right person for the task, and that he would destroy the defense industry and set it back to square one.

I raised my concerns to the CEO of my company and he replied that this was not our problem and others should worry about it. I raised my concerns to other government figures in the military and civilian arenas, trying to warn them of how dangerous this expert was for the defense industry. Some of them shared my concerns, but no one did anything. Then I decided to take the matter to the highest possible level. I knew this was risky, so I prepared a short presentation on how to develop the defense industry in Abu Dhabi. I made sure not to offend anyone and highlighted the need to get rid of the foreign expert because of his lack of capability to lead Abu Dhabi's defense industry.

My presentation reached the level that I intended and was referred to the right people. I don't know what happen after that, but the foreign expert continued his career in the Abu Dhabi defense industry. As I predicted, within two years he had destroyed most of the industry's capabilities, especially the local human capabilities, and terminated many of projects that could have been successful. After two years it was very clear how bad things had become and he was fired but only after the damage was done.

As for me, I was punished by having my secondment cancelled. I was overlooked for promotion three times, before retiring on my existing rank. Someone did not like that I raised concerns about this matter, which proved that I was right.

I decided to finish my doctoral studies with a thesis on the strategies of economic diversification, so maybe in future when I tell leaders that their strategy is not working, they will listen.

In 2019, a new economic diversification initiative called Ghadan 21 was announced as Abu Dhabi's AED 50 billion, three-year accelerator programme. And the same mistakes were repeated in the initiative: no execution plan, no targets for certain sectors, no clear roles and responsibilities for different entities leading to the success of the initiative. As the programme nears completion some important questions need to be asked. Has any evaluation been conducted on the programme? Was it successful? What were the criteria for success?

Ghadan 21 faces the same issues that Vision 2030 faced, in which factors that can guarantee successful outcomes are weak and need to be strengthened first. It is very important to enhance these factors to make sure their outcome is of high quality. Strong factors lead to a successful strategy of economic diversification and development.

In this book, our discussion will focus on these factors, what they are, and how they can be strengthened to support economic strategies. The discussion will take us to other countries that used these factors and benefited from them.

CHAPTER 2

The Wheel of Economic Diversification and Development

Why this framework is different to the other models

"Every country should conduct its own reforms, should develop its own model, taking into account the experience of other countries, whether close neighbors or far away countries."

— MIKHAIL GORBACHEV, FORMER USSR LEADER
(1931–PRESENT)

"We must not rely on oil alone as the main source of our national income. We have to diversify the sources of our revenue and construct economic projects that will ensure a free, stable and dignified life for the people."

—SHAIKH ZAYED, FOUNDING FATHER OF THE UAE (1918–2004)

$\mathcal{W}$ hile all newly industrialized nations pursue economic development and diversification, only those that apply their capabilities and manage their expectations will succeed. Countries are complex and adaptive organisms that cannot be fixed along a predetermined route but work mostly as a network of systems where all the actions and activities in different systems affect each other. In pursuing economic growth and diversification, nations set strategies including a series of policies and actions based on foresight and vision, where the results lead towards the desired outcomes.

For a country to have a diversified economy, it should develop different sectors (industries), increase its export products portfolio, develop regulations and policies to support trade practice, create institutions to enforce regulations and policies, and above all develop the human capital and workforce.

Countries seeking diversification of their economy to pursue economic development need to have guidelines to follow and frameworks to apply in order to succeed as they develop their own approach. Economic diversification is affected by many factors, the total of which has not been integrated into one framework.

In this book, you will learn the nine factors of the model, divided into three components of the wheel. The *outer* wheel is represented by the natural resources and financial funding factor, necessary for economic growth. The *middle* wheel is represented by three factors: human development, policy, institutions and governance, and infrastructure. These factors are critical to building the economic capability to develop and diversify. The *inner* wheel is represented by five factors: export orientation, innovation, entrepreneurship, the private sector, and state-owned enterprise. These factors are the ones that support the transfer of the capabilities from the factors of the outer wheels into products or services that can compete globally and maintain their competitive advantage and thus lead to the diversification of the economy.

Using Singapore as a case study of successful economic diversification, the model was applied to evaluate how the factors need to be used to create successful diversification efforts. The model was subsequently used to evaluate the progress of Abu Dhabi's economy in relation to these factors, highlighting the weaknesses that constrain the emirate from diversifying its economy. Similarly, the model was also used to evaluate the progress of GCC countries in their diversification efforts, also identifying any weaknesses that present themselves. An impact evaluation methodology was used to assess the effects of each factor on the diversification and development of the economy in the cases of Singapore, Abu Dhabi and the GCC countries.

Why countries need to diversify

The first question to raise is why diversify the economy? Why try to move away from a sector with a strong comparative advantage? In his 2011 study, *Economic and Institutional Reforms in the Arab Gulf Countries*, Martin Hvidt outlined some of the benefits from economic diversification:

- Reduced exposure to external economic shocks.
- Improved productivity and competitiveness.
- Reduced growth volatility and economic cycles.
- Enhanced economic stability and sustainability.

Countries differ from each other in many respects such as labor force, skill levels of workers, location, levels of income, natural resource reserves, infrastructure and culture. These features will affect strategies, priorities, and policies for diversification. For example, providing employment is a major goal for many countries seeking diversification, however, the motivation for GCC countries, besides employment, is to protect the economy against oil price swings and create assets and resources of income for the long run.

While most countries diversify their economies for growth and employment purposes, some seek technology advancements while others similar to those of the GCC aim to shield their economy against oil price fluctuations. These responses also impact the selection of the diversification strategies. For example, in some cases the priority of the diversification strategy is to create labor-intensive manufacturing; in other cases, it is to create technologically advanced industries that need a highly skilled workforce. In some cases, the aim is to diversify only in the services sector or in the natural resources sector (e.g., in areas of oil, gas, diamonds, and copper).

GCC-depleted wealth

An International Monetary Fund (IMF) report published in 2020 indicates that the wealth of certain GCC countries will be depleted as early as 2034 if there is no change in the economic structure of these countries followed by a reduced dependency on oil and gas. Soaring oil prices during the periods of 2002–2007 and 2010–2014, reinforced the dominant presence of oil revenues in the GCC economies. As noted in the 2008 and 2016 reports by the Institute of International Finance (IIF), the share of oil revenues in the GCC economy increased from 30.8% of the GDP in 2002 to 40% in 2006, and 45% in 2013. Oil revenue, which constituted, on average, 77.4% of total government revenue in 2002 for GCC governments, increased to an average of 86% and 88% in 2006 and 2013, respectively. The share of oil in exports also increased from 61% in 2002 to 67% in 2006, falling back to 61% in 2013. These figures suggest that, despite efforts at diversification to enhance the non-oil sectors, the GCC countries are still dependent on petroleum for revenues, and therefore are continuously vulnerable to falls in oil price. It should be noted that these numbers only present the *direct* involvement of oil revenue in the local economy. If the indirect involvement of oil revenue with the industrial and services sectors is factored in, the overall input of oil on the GDP will be higher, thus further underlining the significance of this product to the economy.

The GCC countries are still facing the same challenges they faced in previous periods. Past efforts to reduce the high dependency on oil and diversify the economy did not lead to significant improvements in the structure of the economy despite the diversification efforts these countries were pursuing.

Every time a drop in oil prices occurred, GCC countries' financials and budgets became strained, projects were delayed and much of the governments' spending stopped. The GCC countries have sensed the need to diversify their economies and have created visions and strategies for the diversification of the economy. However, their attempts to diversify their economies over the past decades have met with little success.

In this book, a framework will be developed to help countries that are seeking to develop and diversify their economy and pursue national and financial growth. There are many existing models and frameworks that are sometimes implemented, as well as many factors analyzed in the literature that have been proven to have a substantial effect on economic diversification and growth.

This book develops an integrated framework based on the main factors that countries should focus on to drive economic development and diversification. These factors provide the pillars for nations to develop their own specific strategies for economic diversification and growth.

To develop this model, many factors were evaluated that affect the economy including fiscal policies, population, foreign direct investment (FDI), geographic location, regional economic cooperation, technology, productivity, competitiveness, and so forth. The book identifies factors that have evidentiary support for the idea that they play a major part in economic diversification. The subsequent discussion will analyze each factor and explain its role in the economic development and diversification of countries, thereby supporting its necessary inclusion in economic diversification.

Models for economic development

The relationship between economic development and public policies can be traced back to the time of mercantilism in the seventeenth century. Mercantilism viewed trade as a zero-sum game, where a trade surplus for one nation meant a trade deficit for another. Adam Smith, in his famous book *The Wealth of Nations*, viewed trade as positive for all trading partners, with the benefit coming to nations that specialize in the production in which they hold an absolute advantage. Ricardo's comparative advantage theory, on the other hand, does not require nations to have an absolute advantage in the production of goods, but rather, that different nations will benefit from international trade. At the beginning of the twentieth century, Heckscher and Ohlin explained that comparative advantage arises from variances in many factors among different nations, not only in labor and capital as Ricardo indicated. Because the Heckscher–Ohlin model faced application difficulties in the real-world context, other theories have been introduced including product cycle, country similarity, and economies of scale.

Countries have used different approaches for economic development throughout history. Since the Second World War, theories of economic development have fallen mostly into four schools: (1) Linear stages of growth; (2) Structural change; (3) Neo-Marxist (international dependence theory), and; (4) Neoclassical revival of the 1980s (see Table 2.1 for descriptions).

These theories evolved from previous theories (classical, neoclassical and Marxist). However, these theories could not address the economic issues of the Third World countries and newly industrialized nations, and how these countries can transform into developed nations. Each one of these schools of thought was applied by one or more countries and each theory, while initially succeeding, failed in the long term.

All these theories were promoting the involvement of the government except the neoclassical revival of the 1980s, which was promoting a total free market and a market-led approach.

Table 2.1. Description of economic theories

Theory	Description
Linear stages of growth	Economies must go through a number of development stages toward greater economic growth. These stages follow a sequence, each of which is reached through the completion of the previous stage. The stages are: 1. Traditional society: no access to technology; agricultural subsistence. 2. Pre-take-off: some manufactured products and investment in education. 3. Take-off: major changes in manufacturing and industrialization; greater urbanization and human capital buildup. 4. The drive to maturity: industry becomes more diverse with more sectors; income per capita increases. 5. Mass consumption: high-level consumption and luxuries; many industries involved in mass production.
Structural change	A mechanism by which underdeveloped economies transform from traditional and agriculture economies to modern, urbanized, industrial drivers in manufacturing and the services economy.
Neo-Marxist (international dependence theory)	Resources flow from poor to rich countries where both benefit from the trade, but does not advance the poor nations.
Neoclassical revival of the 1980s	Development is a result of the market forces, not strategic state action. The theory stresses the beneficial role of the free market, open economies, and privatization of public enterprises.

During the second half of the twentieth century, economic development and diversification were the ultimate goals for governments seeking prosperity for their nations. Many nations, especially the advanced ones (i.e., Western nations), had the foundations and the capital (finance), mostly through international funds or the Marshall Plan to support the development initiatives. This also led to the creation of many models and frameworks explaining the development processes and presenting them as solutions for nations seeking advancement.

Based on the economic development of Western countries, different models were developed. The linear stages of growth and structural change models were proposed to explain the different stages of economic growth. In 1990, Michael Porter came up with the National Diamond model to explain the rise of competitiveness involving a country's industry in the global market. Based on Porter's model, other models extended the explanation of the rise of international competitiveness for nations, such as Double Diamond and General Double Diamond models.

All of these models have tried to explain some aspects of a nation's economic development, e.g., international competitiveness. However, none of these models has explained in a holistic manner how an economy should diversify. Moreover, these models of economic development were developed based on the context of European nations, and thus were found to be less applicable to facilitate the economic progress of developing and newly industrialized nations.

Why economic models don't work

No specific model or framework for economic diversification exists that can guide a newly industrialized nation (or nation with only one main natural resource that dominates the economy), on how to diversify successfully and establish an economy that is resilient and not susceptible to the price fluctuations of natural resources or economic downturns.

GCC countries and many developing countries have been through experiences of trying to develop and diversify their economies. Many studies and models have been presented to the countries' governments but none have proved successful as they were not designed for these types of countries.

Many studies have analyzed the economic framework of the GCC countries and the need to diversify the economy away from petroleum, but none have come up with a practical pathway for member countries or newly industrialized nations to follow in order to successfully diversify their economies. The significance of this study is to come up with a framework that GCC members and similar countries can implement to diversify and develop their economies successfully.

GCC countries have actively tried to diversify their economies and have executed many projects, some of which have been successful and some less so. For most of the time, the GCC countries did not have a systematic approach for diversification, applying a trial and error approach instead. The diversification activities present the following challenges:

1. The economic visions of the GCC countries were driven by consultancy agencies with no implementation plans.
2. The industrial activities were based on petroleum and were energy-dependent.
3. The manufacturing and technology activities ranged from low to medium-complexity levels, which creates a challenge for generating advanced knowledge.
4. The diversification activities were negatively effected by non-efficient, state-owned enterprises.
5. SOEs have played a primary role in the economy in general and economic diversification in particular.
6. The private sector relies on the government and is not a risk-taker since there is no strong base for innovation and industry activities; the private sector is not pursuing industrial activities.

For these countries to be successful in diversification they need to have strong factors to support the efforts for economic diversification and development. Such factors will serve the economy and help the nation to build its capabilities, making sure the diversification efforts are a success. The wheel of diversification and development was created as a framework that can be used by governments to diversify their economies. The model has identified factors that are essential to the diversification of the economy and without the proper output of these factors successful diversification is difficult to achieve.

The wheel of economic diversification and development

This model is designed to serve countries that are pursuing economic development through the path of diversification. For a country to succeed in the diversification of the economy it is not enough to have the factors present, but the outcomes of the factors have to be of high quality, work systemically, and be both robust and resilient.

For each one of these factors to be effective, the nation should raise the quality of the output of that factor to ensure its robustness. It is not enough to have the setup and policies in place, each factor needs to have a high-quality and substantial outcome, and to have a significant positive effect on the economy. For example, having the private sector in the GCC countries set up to get involved in the economy and having many regulations created to support it, is not sufficient. By contrast, the private sector in the GCC countries is connected to the governments and depends on government contracts to do business, with the result that it cannot survive without this funding avenue. In GCC countries, effectively no private business deals directly with the market, other than a few services. That is one of the reasons that the private sector currently has great difficulty in contributing to the diversification efforts.

The model is designed as a wheel (Fig. 2.1) and is divided into three components: the outer circle (base factor) which is analogous to the tire in a wheel, provides the smoothness to the movement of the vehicle. The middle circle (enabler factors) is the strong disk that carries the load of the vehicle (the economy) and needs to be strong and tough for the wheel to hold together and perform as required. The inner circle (driver factors) are the bolts that connect the wheel to the vehicle and provide the propulsion to ensure that the activities are transferred between the factors and the economy.

1. Outer circle (base factor)
   i. Natural resources/financial fund

2. Middle circle (enabler factors)
   i. Human development
   ii. Governance, institutions, and policies
   iii. Infrastructure

3. Inner circle (driver factors)
   i. Export orientation
   ii. Innovation
   iii. Entrepreneurship
   iv. Private sector
   v. State-owned enterprise

The outer circle includes the base factor necessary to start the journey of economic diversification. Natural resources/capital form the main factor to start any movement, as without proper funding a country will not be able to establish or improve the other factors. Specifically, most of the developing or underdeveloped countries are lacking the resource factor and need funding. So, most of the developing and underdeveloped countries are thus provided funding through the World Bank and IMF to implement their economic growth.

The middle circle includes three factors, which form the enablers of any economic growth through diversification and development: human development, governance, institutions, and policies, and infrastructure. A country might have growth but without these factors being strong, the economy will be unable to face crises and advance.

The inner circle has the five driver factors that act just like the bolts on the wheel of a car, where they guarantee the connection and the best use of the wheel in order to serve the car (economy). These are export orientation, innovation, entrepreneurship, the private sector, and state-owned enterprise. The driver factors provide the power to enable each of the other factors to serve the economy and support the smoothest ride in the journey of economic diversification and development.

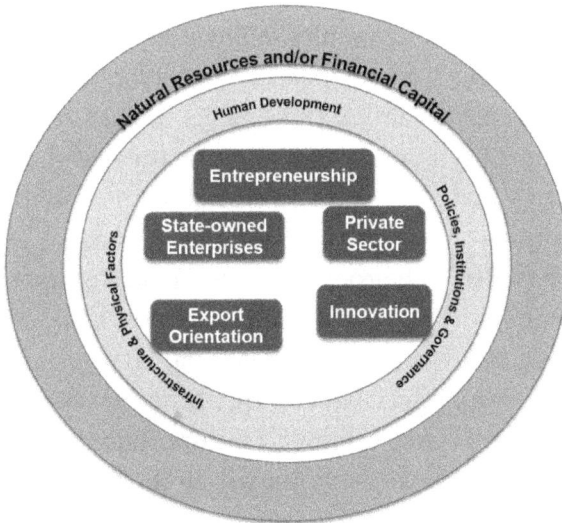

Fig. 2.1. The wheel of economic diversification and development

Each factor operates as an independent system that works together within a bigger system to drive economic diversification. The factors function like a system of systems that enable the country to take advantage of the current environment, to have foresight, and to adapt and change as the environment changes.

To have a significant impact, each individual factor works as a system by itself, and the overarching system of systems must be robust and resilient. A system must be robust to be effective and operate against unknowns and in unpredictable environments. Robustness is about functionality, not systems structure and components. Resilience is the ability of the systems and the over-arching system of systems to recover quickly and continue operating even when there has been a failure within a part of the system.

While countries need both resilience with robustness in implementing these factors, resilient and complex adaptive systems also need to possess the ability to be innovative. Innovation is required to maintain resiliency in complex systems and to create new structures and dynamics following system failures. As the environment changes, so must the factors evolve. Complex adaptive systems have a core capability that enables the factors and the over-arching system of systems to undergo fundamental change.

The factors and the overarching system of systems are drivers in evolutionary economics. The ability to adapt and change requires the factors to be robust and resilient. Resilience requires sufficient redundancy to survive and adapt over time, especially in times of crisis and when transformational changes are required. Systems that are too specialized or fine-tuned are often lacking in redundancy, fragile and subject to failure. Equally, systems that are fragile may survive or even flourish in the good times but will falter and may fail in times of crisis or when transformational change is required.

Over time, the country will experience deep changes in the environment that range from boom conditions to international financial crises. The robustness and resilience of each factor and how they work together as a system of systems will determine how effective the country is in dealing with the good and bad times.

In the following chapters, you will see how applying the factors of the model correctly to produce high-quality outcomes leads to a sustainable and growing economy that can resist different types of economic shock. Each factor will be discussed and applied to Singapore, Abu Dhabi and the GCC collective, before a comparison of results is presented to highlight the gaps needed to be tackled by the GCC countries and Abu Dhabi to be successful in economic diversification and development.

CHAPTER 3

Financial Funding / Natural Resources

Managing natural resources and financial efficiency

"I don't think anyone can speculate what will happen with respect to oil prices and gas prices because they are set on the global economy."

— KEN SALAZAR, US FORMER SECRETARY OF THE INTERIOR (1955–PRESENT)

For a country to pursue economic development and growth, it needs to fund different strategies for social and economic development. Funding can be generated in different ways. It may be obtained from international entities through loans, FDIs, grants, or local savings; or it could be through revenues generated from economic activities or natural resources (e.g., oil, diamonds, copper, and so forth).

Natural resources can provide funds for the development of the country and its economy if managed well. Many countries have natural resources but have not managed the generated funds properly for the development of the economy. Sachs and Warner's (2001) study provides good examples. The study shows that for a country to have a sustainable and growing economy it needs to diversify away from a dependence upon natural resources to become less susceptible to price swings or drops in the market demand of the commodity, and to avoid getting the 'Dutch disease' (curse of natural resources). Countries blessed with natural resources should manage these resources to increase their revenues and properly use them to finance economic development and diversification as well as social development.

Countries that have no revenue from natural resources need to find ways to fund development; these ways can be internal and external. Internal funding through savings by citizens, local funds such as pension funds and taxation as well as efficient spending of the government on projects can all be sought. External funding depends on attracting FDI and obtaining loans from international organizations and banks.

This chapter will enable you to understand the true effects of funding on economic diversification and how this can smoothen the process. It will also show that good management of natural resources will lead to a nation's greater wealth.

Natural resources and national development

The wealth extracted from natural resources makes up a substantial percentage of the wealth of many nations. Therefore, properly managing natural resources is a key factor for economic development. Many nations have seen, in general, an increase in revenue from natural resources because of the increase of commodity prices, regardless of fluctuations in pricing. Natural resources such as oil and gas have remained a major player in resource-abundant nations. But non-renewable resources (such as petroleum) are running out, so nations with these resources should manage their supplies wisely to maximize the gain from current extraction and still keep a sufficient level for future generations.

In resource-abundant nations, the design of policies managing the resources should encompass many aspects. The policies should ensure the gaining of maximum revenue while preserving natural resources for future generations. Also, the policies have to manage the use of the revenues from the natural resources to develop the nation, socially and economically. Social development includes upgrading the quality of life of the people as well as government services such as infrastructure, education, medical assistance, and housing. Economic development involves investing in fiscal diversification so as to be ready for when the natural resources run out. To support economic diversification, investment is required to develop new sectors, infrastructure, education, and so forth. Recent studies by the World Bank – *Where is the Wealth of Nations?* (2006) and *Overview of State Ownership in the Global Minerals Industry* (2011) – indicate that the main issue for low- and middle-income nations is to grow and enhance their tangible and intangible assets. Investing in infrastructure, health, education, and governance is, therefore, essential. In such nations, natural resource revenues play an important role as a source of funding for such investments. In the same studies, the World Bank indicates that in many cases the revenues from natural resources did not serve this role, because these revenues were not managed well and were misspent. Hence, the effective management of natural resources can contribute to the advancement of a nation in its efforts to develop the economy and play an essential part in its economic diversification.

Managing natural resources

As presented in the Organisation for Economic Co-operation and Development's (OECD) report *Natural Resources and Pro-Poor Growth* (2008), the reason for poor economic performance in natural resource-rich countries is the lack of efficient institutions to manage resources. Certainly, the strength of institutions is decisive in either avoiding the resources curse or falling into it. Sachs and Warner (2001) stressed that transparency and accountability are at the heart of policy prescriptions to cure the resources curse.

Because most natural resources are non-renewable, many resource-rich countries start planning for a post-depletion economy through diversification and shifting from exporting only the primary commodities to exporting manufactured products. Instead of exporting the resources as raw materials, which supports manufacturing in other countries, the exporting countries should gain more from the economic advantage of the resources and develop their own domestic manufacturing. But this needs investment and takes time and needs key conditions such as developing appropriate education and skills training, as well as policies supporting entrepreneurs, innovation, and local enterprises. To increase the value of revenue received from natural resources due to dropping commodity prices, many nations have created entities to collect part of these revenues and invest them locally and internationally to create a financial cushion when the prices of the natural resources drop resulting in the government's revenue fall. But these entities should be transparent and should protect the funding source they manage from internal politics and corruption. Many nations create sovereign wealth funds to manage their current wealth and to create future financial safety nets. Table 3.1 shows the four largest sovereign wealth funds in the world, three of which used the revenues from natural resources (petroleum) to support creating and enlarging the funds (Sovereign Wealth Fund Institute, 2021).

Table 3.1. The top sovereign wealth funds in the world (2021)

Country	Sovereign wealth fund	Assets (US$ bn)
Norway	Government Pension Fund Global	1.364
China	China Investment Corporation	1.046
Kuwait	Kuwait Investment Authority	693
UAE – Abu Dhabi	Abu Dhabi Investment Authority	650

source: Sovereign Wealth Fund Institute.

But some countries have no natural resources so how can they fund their development activities? How can they support the social projects to support their people? Each country should find ways to create financial funds for its activities. Most countries proceed the easy way by obtaining loans from international organizations or banks and become entrenched in the cycle of borrowing and settlement. Many countries have no natural resources but are creative in finding ways to support development. One country that had no natural resources but created an internal finance scheme to the point it was viewed as over-saving is Singapore.

Singapore: saving and funding

The scarcity of financial resources was a major challenge for Singapore on its path to development. When Singapore gained independence in 1965, it did not have natural resources or other key products for export to generate funds. Singapore's most important natural resource was its location and deep-water seaport, which made it a strategic maritime trading hub and provider of entrepot services. These activities were the principal source of funds at that time. Singapore took advantage of its location and deep-water seaport, and it became active in maritime maintenance, repair and shipbuilding activities, and services. As the economy was sensitive to the fluctuations of prices and export revenues, Singapore decided to detach itself from such an economic pattern.

The government of Singapore was not paralyzed by the scarcity of funds as were many newly independent states who were waiting for the international organizations to support them. Singapore had to be creative to provide funds to support its development strategies to build and advance the nation. Like many other governments, Singapore used local methods to generate funds such as taxes, duties, charges, and domestic savings. As the government's strategy was to diversify and develop the economy, it used two methods to reach its goals:

1. Generate funds locally through creating a saving scheme to serve both the people and the government, so the Central Provident Fund was created.
2. Attract foreign direct investment through multinational corporations, so the Singaporean Economic Development Board was created.

Central Provident Fund

Due to the lack of funds, the government of Singapore created a saving scheme to encourage people to save and use those savings to support the government initiatives to develop the nation. Subsequently, the government reorganized the social security fund as the Central Provident Fund (CPF). In addition to retirement savings, the new CPF encouraged people to use their savings to pay for education, insurance, property, and investments. The CPF was reformed from a traditional pension fund to become a saving scheme that supports enhancing the life of the beneficiary. The members are able to use the saved money to purchase houses and invest in many areas such as the stock market or gold. The government uses the money saved in the CPF to finance activities such as infrastructure and human development, and to create new industries to support the development of the nation and diversify the economy.

Compared to the social security programs operating in some Western countries, the concept of the CPF is different. Instead of the younger (working) generation paying for the program, while the retired generation withdraws from it, the CPF guarantees the return of the money with interest to depositors. Therefore, the CPF savings assure the government of funds to finance the public-sector development and economic development and diversification through enhancing the capability and attractiveness of the nation and investment in new economic sectors.

The saving scheme supported the development of the nation and cleared all external debt by 1994. In 1984, the saving rate reached 41% of the GDP. In 1986, the Economic Strategies Committee acknowledged that there was over-saving in the nation. The saving rate in 2012 was 49.2% of the GDP[4]. This high saving is due to the level of trust that the government forged with its people, where the CPF acts not only as a retirement fund, but also a saving fund for the people where each individual has the privilege to use their fund in the CPF to support their way of living.

---

4   World Bank (2015) Data for Singapore. World Bank, Washington D.C.

Economic Development Board

Another way for Singapore to generate funds was to attract foreign direct investment, and the government established the Economic Development Board (EDB) to create the environment necessary to attract multinational corporations. The FDI was directed to invest in targeted industries which led to the diversification of the economy. Table 3.2 shows the industries that the EDB was directing the investment to during the second decade of the twenty-first century. Currently, there are about twenty-five industries or sectors that the EDB is working with to ensure they are strong contributors to the economy and its diversification.

Table 3.2. The EDB's existing and new emerging industries as of 2017

Existing Industries	Emerging Businesses
Aerospace Engineering – Chemicals – Cities, Infrastructure & Industrial Solutions – Clean Energy – Consumer Business – Content and Media – Electronics – Energy – Environment and Water – Healthcare – Infocomm Products – Infocomm Services – Logistics and Supply Chain Management – Marine and Offshore Engineering – Medical Technology – Pharmaceuticals and Biotechnology – Precision Engineering – Professional Services	Automotive Lifestyle Products and Services Natural Resources Robotics Safety and Security Singapore: Real-Time Space

source: EDB

Financial management and capital formation

Prioritizing the use of available funds was an issue. As a startup nation, Singapore was facing many problems such as the poor standard of living (many people were still living in slums), high unemployment, low skill levels of workers, poor education, and a weak economy. The government had to prioritize the funding and find ways to finance the key activities and then enhance them over time.

To manage the scarce funds, Singapore controlled the budget spending closely. The government knew that efficient financial management was necessary to support all initiatives and solve the issues that the nation was facing from the start. The fiscal and monetary policies generated a high savings level, which allowed the government to spend money on human development and infrastructure, as well as supporting small to medium-sized enterprises (SMEs), SOEs, innovation, and entrepreneurs, and the export-orientation strategy.

To keep financial funds flowing to support the diversification of the economy, the government created sovereign wealth funds to invest internationally and use the returns to invest in supporting the government's initiatives. In addition, Singapore created government-linked companies (GLCs), which were allowed to create business abroad and expand their operations to grow their profits. These activities ensured funds were available for investment in the country and to create new economic sectors when needed, such as electronics in the 1970s, computers in the 1980s, and biomedical products in the 1990s.

How Singapore managed its savings

The government of Singapore played a strong role in the saving and investment process, as the coordinator between savers and investors – a role that no other country is performing.

During the period 1965–1999, Singapore had S$1.22 trillion available for investment purposes, with a third of it coming from abroad. Hopf also stressed that the government, through its financial institutions and incentive schemes, was able to influence 40% of the voluntary private saving[5]. The government created incentives for the private savings and for FDI to invest in the targeted industries and sectors. Table 3.3 shows that the government and its financial institutions control 54.3% (S$661 billion) of the total investment pool.

Table 3.3. Total saving and investment pool 1965–1999 (in S$ million)

Category	Amount / percentage
Government saving S$ million	360,113
Forced private saving S$ million	181,729
Voluntary private saving S$ million	284,990
Total gross national saving	**826,831**
Government-controlled (national saving) percentage	65.5%
Gross Foreign Inflows	**391,155**
TOTAL GROSS INVESTMENT FUND	**1,217,986**
Government-controlled of the Total Inv. Fund	661,384
Government-controlled percentage	54.3%

source: Hopf (2009)

The control of the government over such large funds allowed it to channel these funds into different economic sectors. For example, in promoting and developing its biotechnology industry, Singapore invested hundreds of millions of dollars into the sector for infrastructure and laboratories, to fund research and development and to recruit top international scientists.

The Singaporean government was involved in channelling the FDI into different sectors to support its diversification strategy through different incentive schemes to make these sectors economically feasible for the international investors. Table 3.4 shows the

---

5   Hopf, G. (2009) *Saving and investment: the economic development of Singapore 1965–99.* Saarbrücken: VDM Verlag Dr. Müller, pp. 241–318.

amount of FDI invested in different sectors of the economy, which is part of the private investments.

Table 3.4. Distribution of FDI by industry (1995–2015) in S$ billion

Sector	1995	2000	2005	2010	2015
Financial & Insurance Services	34.7	74.0	119.1	316.8	625.9
Manufacturing	35.5	69.5	103.6	139.8	170.3
Wholesale & Retail Trade	12.2	31.0	48.8	121.7	231.7
Transport & Storage	2.9	8.7	16.8	30.3	40.0
Professional & Technical, Admin. & Support Services	1.6	7.4	9.6	44.5	106.8
Real Estate, Rental & Leasing Services	4.4	5.9	8.1	25.6	35.0
Information & Communications	0.56	1.9	3.4	7.0	20.7

source: Statistics Singapore yearbooks

The financial fund that the government created supported economic and social activities in the country. The financial fund allowed the government to create the infrastructure necessary for the economy in general and for specific industries, for example, by creating labs for different technological industries such as electronics, high-tech engineering, and biomedical products. The impact of different strategies/policies to create financial funds on economic diversification is shown in Table 3.5.

Table 3.5. Impact of financial fund's strategies/policies on diversification

Strategies / policies	Outcome	Impact on economic diversification
Creation of EDB	• Attracts FDI • Provides investments and funds in different sectors	• Uses foreign investors to develop different economic sectors • Provides government funds when needed
Creation of CPF	• Creates large financial capital locally • Large savings	• Finances different factors and activities such as HD, infrastructure, SOEs, innovation, etc.
Sovereign funds	• Creates stream of international revenues for the nation • Imports foreign technology and talent	• Imports technology • Market for global customers
GLCs (SOEs)	• Provides the investment needed in new industries when the private sector would be reluctant to invest • Creates cooperation with international companies	• Invests and develops new economic sectors where the private sector was hesitating to start • Attracts new technologies to support different economic sectors through cooperation with foreign partners
Creation of sectorial statutory boards	• Provides government funds when needed • Enhances the attractiveness of a sector for the MNC	• Supports the development of economic sectors • Attracts MNC to bring production and technology to the country

This was how did Singapore could create and manage funds to support its development progress. But how did Abu Dhabi and the other GCC countries manage their natural resources funds to support development?

Natural resources in Abu Dhabi

The prosperity of Abu Dhabi and its transformation from tribal villages in the 1960s into a booming state and economy has been possible because of revenues from petroleum. Oil revenues have funded the establishment of every part of Abu Dhabi from infrastructure, hospitals, schools, and houses at the beginning of its development, to acquiring advanced technology and creating new economic sectors in the later stage.

Crude oil production started in 1962, however, a significant development in Abu Dhabi occurred after the sharp increase of oil prices in 1973. Before oil, Abu Dhabi's economy was dependent on the pearl trade and agriculture. Since oil exports started, the economy has transformed. Shaikh Zayed used oil revenues to develop Abu Dhabi and fight poverty, and channeled the revenues into sectors like healthcare, houses, and infrastructure. According to the findings of the Statistics Center of Abu Dhabi (SCAD), Abu Dhabi's GDP has grown from about AED 3.3 billion in 1970, to just above AED 931 billion in 2018.

Unlike other developed economies, Abu Dhabi sped through the developmental stages. High oil returns facilitated the path for Abu Dhabi to fast-track its development and supported the diversification efforts that the government had been pursuing. Nevertheless, fluctuations in oil prices and the global financial crisis have sharply reminded policy-makers that structural challenges must be addressed and a plan for a post-oil income era must be in place and executed.

Oil and gas industry

Abu Dhabi's share of global oil reserves stands at about 7%, around 94 billion barrels (Bb), which represents about 96% of the UAE's total reserve (98 Bb). Production in 2019 averaged three million barrels per day and was set to exceed 3.5 Mb/d by 2022. Abu Dhabi's reserve will last for about 70 years, assuming no further discoveries.

Abu Dhabi, unlike the other Gulf states, allowed the former concessionaire companies to be equity holders in the operating firms. It did not, as elsewhere, remove foreign ownership entirely. The Abu Dhabi National Oil Company (ADNOC) was established as a holding company with majority and minority equity stakes in all the producing companies. The government desired to energize oil production and exploration during the 1960s and 1970s, and at that time Abu Dhabi was lacking the capabilities in people and technology.

By contrast to certain other countries in the region, several international companies hold shares in Abu Dhabi's oil industry, including Shell, Total, British Petroleum (BP), ExxonMobil and the Japan Oil Development Company (JODCO). As noted by Davidson (2009), Abu Dhabi National Oil Company holds a controlling stake, not exceeding 60%.

Abu Dhabi owns roughly 3.4% of the world's natural gas, about 200 trillion cubic feet as per the Energy Information Administration (EIA) Country Analysis. Similar to the oil industry, ADNOC holds the majority stake (70%) of the Abu Dhabi Gas Liquefaction Company (ADGAS), with the remainder distributed between Total, BP and Mitsubishi Gas. As for the Abu Dhabi Gas Industries (GASCO), ADNOC owns 68% and the rest is distributed between Total, Royal Dutch Shell and Partex.[6] Income from oil exports is shown in Table 3.6.

---

6   Davidson, Christopher M. (2009), *Abu Dhabi: Oil and Beyond*. New York: Columbia University Press.

Table 3.6. Export of Crude Oil

Year	Crude Oil		
	Daily (1,000 barrels)	**Annual** (1,000 barrels)	**Av. Price** (US$ per barrel)
2000	1,770	647,820	27.4
2005	2,052	749,080	51.9
2010	2,040	744,525	78.6
2015	2,444	892,230	51.0
2019	3,058	1,116,109	64.0

source: SCAD reports

Other sources of income

Abu Dhabi has sought to invest its income from natural resources into different economic sectors and different countries. To achieve this, Abu Dhabi has created different investment bodies (sovereign wealth funds) to diversify its investment. Since the 1970s, Abu Dhabi has channeled its surplus oil revenues into long-term overseas investments as a way to buffer the domestic economy during oil price fluctuations. Most of these investments have been made through government-owned entities with their combined assets exceeding US$1 trillion. This investment places Abu Dhabi far ahead of other Gulf investors, such as Saudi Arabia and Kuwait, with about US$700 billion each, and Qatar with around US$320 billion.

The most important fund body in Abu Dhabi is the Abu Dhabi Investment Authority (ADIA). Since its establishment in 1976, ADIA's task has been to invest the oil revenue surplus to create a substantial financial income for the government and provide a buffer for the government when the oil prices drop. According to the Sovereign Wealth Fund Institute (SWFI), ADIA is ranked as one of the largest sovereign wealth funds in the world. In 2016, ADIA was ranked the second-largest sovereign wealth fund in the world with assets worth US$828 billion. In 2021, it was still one of the largest funds with assets worth US$650 billion.

Another important fund is the International Petroleum Investment Corporation (IPIC), which was established in 1984 as a joint venture between the Abu Dhabi National Oil Company and the Abu Dhabi Investment Company (ADIC). Its objectives are defined as investing globally in energy, energy-related industries and the chemicals sector. IPIC has built its worldwide oil-related investment portfolio to about US$55 billion.

Mubadala was founded in 2002 and is the third largest and fastest-growing of all fund bodies in Abu Dhabi. Mubadala has invested in many sectors and has created a diversified portfolio, including a variety of domestic and international investments that are worth over US$60 billion. In 2017, IPIC was acquired by Mubadala to become the fourteenth-largest sovereign wealth fund in the world with investments of US$125 billion, reaching US$230 billion in 2021.

Although dwarfed by the big investment entities, many other sovereign wealth funds are operated by Abu Dhabi. For example, the Abu Dhabi National Energy Company (TAQA), which was founded in 2005 as a public joint-stock company and in which the government of Abu Dhabi owns a 51% stake. TAQA's main foci of investments are power generation, water desalination, and the production and storage of oil and gas. In addition, it has invested in mining, metal, and the services sector. As of 2020, TAQA had built up about US$40 billion in assets since its establishment.

Table 3.7 shows the importance of petroleum revenues in the government's budget. In 2018, the petroleum revenue accounted for 56.1% of government revenue for Abu Dhabi. Even though the government is working to diversify the economy, petroleum remains the major revenue contributor. This can be seen in recent years when the oil price dropped from above US$100 per barrel in 2013, to less than US$50 per barrel in 2019. In response, Abu Dhabi and the other GCC governments had to either stop or slow down many of their initiatives and projects.

Table 3.7. Percentage distribution of government revenues (%)

Item	2005	2010	2015	2018
Petroleum royalties and tax revenue	85.9	82.6	79.6	56.1
Department collections revenue	11.6	7.3	18.8	3.9
Capital revenue	2.5	10.1	1.6	40

Source: SCAD reports

Exports are largely dominated by oil, gas, and oil products, and in 2017 they formed 21% of the GDP at AED 174.9 billion. Non-oil exports were valued at AED 22.3 billion and re-exports were valued at AED 21.8 billion, equating to 4% and 2.4% of GDP, respectively.

Table 3.8. Abu Dhabi's export volumes (2010–2017) by AED billion

Year	Total exports	Export of gas and oil products	Non-oil exports	Re-exports
2010	300.71	278.11	11.61	10.99
2011	445.53	422.49	11.48	11.57
2012	481.61	451.45	15.41	14.74
2013	522.90	490.46	15.99	16.45
2014	372.74	328.46	18.96	25.32
2015	235.5	185.9	30.8	18.9
2016	192.9	140.1	28.0	24.8
2017	219.0	174.9	22.3	21.8

Source: SCAD reports

The impact of revenue from natural resources on economic diversification

Despite growth in the non-oil sector over recent years, it is important to point out that Abu Dhabi's oil export earnings and budget surpluses have served as an essential source of funding for the development of infrastructure, human capital and other development projects that have transformed the emirate into what it is today. The revenues are also used to support the plans for diversification of the economy, even though many questions have been raised on how successful the diversification strategy remains. In comparing Abu Dhabi's approach to this factor with Singapore, the following points are noted:

- Single-source revenue: the Abu Dhabi government depends strongly on the revenue from petroleum and when the price of oil drops the government faces financial constraints. Singapore does not have such a problem because it does not depend on one major source of revenue.
- Internal savings: Abu Dhabi did not establish an internal saving scheme because it did not see the need for it. This left the government depending on revenue from petroleum to fund its projects and initiatives. Singapore, on the other hand, felt the need to create an internal saving system to create funds for its development strategies.
- Sovereign wealth funds: Abu Dhabi and Singapore both created sovereign wealth funds to invest in the international markets to provide government funding when needed. Both states own two of the largest funds globally.
- FDI and MNCs: Abu Dhabi attracts FDI and MNCs to invest in the country, but this investment has not enhanced local capabilities, nor has it created local suppliers or sufficient export

products. There has been a lack of planning on how to channel and use the FDI to support new industries or create capabilities. Singapore, however, created clusters for different industries to benefit from FDIs and MNCs by creating competitive export products, and local suppliers and capabilities.

GCC countries: natural resources/financial fund

Petroleum revenues have enabled the GCC countries to build their economies and to develop them continuously, to build and enhance social infrastructure, to accomplish one of the fastest urbanization rates in the world by transferring desert transects into modern cities, and to progressively become part of the global connections and networks.

Despite efforts to steer the economy away from petroleum, this still accounts for most of the GCC economies. In 2018, oil and gas still amounted to an average 40% direct share of the GDP for the Gulf States, not counting the many other diverse streams that derive from economic activities supported by oil and gas. Oil income remains the main source of revenue for GCC countries, and in 2018 it accounted for about 70% of the total GCC revenue, as reported by the World Bank.

Natural resources need to be treated as an industrial sector and not only as a fund generator. The petroleum industrial sector should contain upstream and downstream activities, technology transfer and acquisition, local capabilities building, and local private sector development. GCC governments need to enhance the capabilities in this sector to become competitive globally in order to export local capabilities and be part of the global economy.

Sovereign wealth funds are very important for the GCC states as a buffer during periods of lower oil prices. Each one of the GCC states has at least one sovereign wealth fund that is providing revenue to their government. The combined assets of the GCC's sovereign wealth funds was about US$2.3 trillion in 2018. These international investments provide income flows from abroad.

A good governance and monitoring process should be in place to ensure greater efficiency in these entities and to be accountable to the public for the effective use of their money. The head of these entities must be accountable for their mistakes and no political cover should be available for them.

Similar to Abu Dhabi, other GCC countries are dependent on oil and gas and did not work to create internal saving schemes or use FDIs to create genuine local industries. Norway is a very good example for the GCC members to follow in managing its natural resources revenue. Norway worked to develop a local supply of certain competitive goods and services required by the petroleum industry and not to demand an indiscriminate use of local suppliers. Norway's success in achieving high local content is largely due to government policies, which encouraged partnerships between foreign and domestic companies, and made research programs mandatory.

In 1972, the Norwegian Petroleum Directorate was established. Also, a preference policy for Norwegian goods and services was introduced, accompanied by a policy of knowledge transfer and research cooperation. The Ministry of Industry established a goods and services office as a watchdog to control the oil companies' contracting and procurement activities: prior to tender invitations, the operator had to announce the tender schedule and companies were to be invited. The ministry's role was to ensure that qualified Norwegian companies were included on the bidders' lists.

At the contract awarding stage, the operator was required to inform the ministry of its evaluation, along with the recommended supplier, price, country of origin and Norwegian content. The Norwegian content was calculated as value-added in Norway both in manpower and monetary terms. Ownership of the company was of less interest; what mattered was where the work was to be carried out, that is, locally or abroad.

The role of the ministry was to ensure that a Norwegian bidder was awarded the contract, if competitive in terms of price, quality, delivery time, and service. If the ministry was not convinced, consent could be withheld.

The emphasis placed on the Norwegian content made it an essential factor for all oil companies, and indeed, the ministry used this as one of the criteria when evaluating companies competing for new acreage. The ministry's policy was to be transparent and predictable in respect to the enforcement of the procurement policy. Moreover, as an observer in all license groups, the ministry secured insight into all the operators' contracting activities.

Norway's experience shows clearly that access to petroleum resources can be used as a bargaining tool, especially to obtain benefits that are of common interest. The GCC states still can use petroleum as leverage to enhance their technological capabilities. The GCC's advantage is the availability of huge proven oil reserves at low cost, which provide an ongoing attraction for the oil industry. To its disadvantage is the absence of a manufacturing base and skilled labor force, as well as the technological experience and scientific research.

With a modicum of participation, it would be possible not only to require foreign oil companies to train locals and transfer knowledge, but also to help develop some local supply and service industries and even bring them along to markets in other oil provinces. The Norwegian experience could provide a useful example, positive as well as negative.

Regional cooperation is an important element. The diversity of the GCC states contributes to the complementarity of their economies and labor markets. Regional cooperation aimed at common economic diversification would be able to draw on larger markets, more human resources, and more capital than individual efforts.

The logical step would be to diversify within petroleum by developing a local supply industry. Prospects for the oil market indicate a need to maintain and eventually expand capacity. Today, there is little local content in the deliveries. Developing a local or regional oil service industry could mean diversifying income sources and, at the same time, creating jobs.

Norway also created a fund to manage some of the petroleum revenues as a reserve and protection against the down effect of the price fluctuations. The fund acts as a buffer that provides greater flexibility in economic policy should oil prices or activity in the mainland economy decline, and serves as an instrument for dealing with the financial challenges presented by an ageing population and the prospect of declining oil and gas volumes.

The fund was established by parliament in 1990. To guarantee good governance, the Ministry of Finance holds the overall responsibility for the management of the Government Pension Fund which includes the Government Pension Fund Global (GPFG) and the Government Pension Fund Norway (GPFN). The operational management of the GPFG and GPFN is carried out by independent entities (Norges Bank and Folketrygdfondet, respectively), under mandates laid down by the ministry. The framework for the Government Pension Fund and the management of fund assets are outlined in an Act of Parliament and guidelines with supplementary provisions. The fund operates under the provision of the parliament to reduce the potential of manipulating fund decisions by politicians and opportunistic parties.

Conclusion

Funding is a major factor in the development of nations, both socially and economically. Natural resource-rich nations are blessed with this gift but need to manage it well, otherwise, it might become a curse. These countries need to create entities to oversee and manage the use of their natural resources – from the time the resources are still underground to the time revenues are collected – keeping in mind the benefits of current and future generations, as well as how to use these revenues for the wellbeing of the nation, socially and economically, as was done by Norway.

For some natural resource-rich countries it was not enough to create funds for future protection. Instead, it was necessary to use revenues from natural resources to create manufacturing and new economic sectors to diversify the economy away from a one-commodity economy, and invest part of the revenue into generating income for when the economy declines.

Countries lacking the natural resources to generate revenue need to create their own way of obtaining financial funds. Many nations have no natural resources and have succeeded in creating a stream of funds through attracting international investors and creating a system to increase and manage the local savings. Good examples of these have been the East Asian countries and regions such as Hong Kong, Taiwan, South Korea, and Singapore.

The natural resources/financial funds factor has had a significant impact on Singapore's economic diversification and development. Despite having no natural resources, Singapore created a sovereign wealth fund that has played a vital role and attracted FDI to different economic sectors. On the other hand, Abu Dhabi has obtained revenue through oil exports to fund its economic diversification and development. Abu Dhabi has established sovereign funds that are primarily used to supplement oil income during periods marked by low oil prices.

Natural resources/financial funds have had mixed effects on the GCC's economic diversification and development. Most GCC countries have significant oil reserves that have funded their development. While most GCC countries have established sovereign wealth funds, they have not used them effectively to drive economic diversification and development.

CHAPTER 4

Human Development

How can human development make or break an economy?

*"Wealth is not in money. Wealth lies in men. This is where
true power lies, the power we value.
This is what has convinced us to direct all our resources to
build the individual, and to use the wealth which God has
provided us in the service of the nation."*

— SHAIKH ZAYED, FOUNDING FATHER OF THE UAE (1918–2004)

Human development is a very important factor for any pathway to national development. Humans are the baseline for
all development. Creating a productive and innovative labor force is
not an easy task. In this chapter, the discussion will cover the role of
human development in economic progress and how some nations –
such as Japan, Singapore, and most of the East Asian countries –
could flourish depending on ways of planning and enhancing the
capabilities of human capital.

Human development is a major factor in economic development and diversification. The miracle in East Asia is due to many

factors, one of which is human development, which took place systemically alongside the other developments. Since the beginning, these countries established a good education and training system to have an active workforce and attract FDI. A good health system was established to take care of the people and to maintain a healthy and active workforce to build and develop the country.

Modern economic development is characterized by the development of human capabilities, which play an important role in economic growth. The importance of improving people's wellbeing for national development and growth was only been determined during the twentieth century. Also, there have been improvements in human capabilities associated with education, training and skills development.

Economic diversification is considered to be a factor that helps to achieve economic development and growth. However, one of the major factors that facilitate economic development and diversification is human development. Human development through education and continuous training along with the acquisition of knowledge, helps the economy to diversify by realizing new techniques of production, improving the quality of products, discovering new industries, and marketing and selling the products.

Human development can be determined by many elements, most of which cannot be captured by regular measures of the economy. For example, the effects of providing good healthcare and education are often revealed through long-term patterns and cannot be measured with simple numbers similar to GDP per capita. The contributions of health and education to the economy are mostly measured by the expenditure and cost of buildings and establishment of medical facilities and schools. This gauges the inputs associated with these activities rather than the outputs, and is different from other types of goods produced in an economy, since both are goods that contribute to all aspects of the economy and industry.

What is human development?

Human development refers to the policies, strategies, and activities that governments execute to raise the quality of life for their citizens through education, health, housing, and infrastructure. Human development can also be referred to as the process of increasing opportunities for people and enhancing the quality of their lives. In its *Human Development Report 2015*, the United Nations Development Programme (UNDP) defines human development as a practice that provides more choices for the people, which allows them to be educated and choose their profession and enjoy a good standard of living and a healthy lifestyle.

Thus, human development supports the building and enhancement of capabilities and skills so that individuals have a better chance to make proper lifestyle decisions for themselves. Through human development, states empower individuals to pursue life paths and to be part of the nation's development as a worker, leader, entrepreneur, investor, or innovator.

What is the relationship between human development and economic diversification?

For a nation to achieve the goal of economic diversification, a strategy should be created according to its resources and needs. For economic diversification, countries need to define strategies to decrease dependence on revenues from one natural resource and to increase job creation for their citizens.

Nations need inspiring and skilled people to absorb incoming global technologies and to create new ones. Competent people are required to create entities that are globally competitive and innovative and can enhance the productivity of the nation. Workers' skills stand as the main element to support diversification. The existence of a skilled labor force, which has the foundation to be able to move from an old sector to a new sector with minimal training, reduces the hurdles for companies to pursue new industries.

All components of human development have an impact on economic development and diversification. Education and training, for instance, has a strong effect on labor productivity and the ability of a worker to develop their skills. For example, in her paper "Social Development is Economic Development", Nancy Birdsall (1993) used data from Ghana, Peru and Malaysia to show that every additional school year of a farmer increases output annually by 2–5%. In her study on Indonesia, "The Medium Run Effects of Educational Expansion", Esther Duflo (2001) estimated an increase in wages of 1.5–2.7% for each school built.

Education has a major effect on innovation, technological improvements and entrepreneurship. In their study on India, "Technical Change and Human Resources and Investments: Consequences of the Green Revolution", Foster and Rosenzweig (1994), demonstrated that the increase in education level is associated with technology acquisition and adaptation. Similarly, the level of education and training increased entrepreneurship and technological change in businesses in Sri Lanka as demonstrated in Sorali Deraniyagala's (1995) study "Technical Change and Efficiency in Sri Lanka's Manufacturing Industry".

Educated, trained, and skilled human resources are the main force for the economic development and diversification of a nation.

Good education sets the foundation for individuals to pursue different paths and work in different industries from which they are enabled to develop their skills accordingly. Training workers to enhance their skills will support companies in achieving better performance, while allowing for the development of new businesses and new sectors.

Skilled individuals have the ability to face challenges, take advantage of opportunities and gain benefits for themselves and their nation. In their study "Economic Diversification for Sustainable Development in Nigeria", Anyaehie and Areji (2015) remarked that if people emphasize the development of market-oriented skills, their chances of growth, improved productivity, and opportunities increases to the higher end. Employees will contribute to diversification from their employment position by diversifying the activities of the organization they are working in, and by enhancing the capabilities of these organizations.

Self-employed individuals are entrepreneurial and innovative, and seek unique and new ideas, which contribute to economic development and diversification. The high performance of innovators, entrepreneurs, policy-makers, and leaders is influenced by education and training. Many skilled and educated individuals are innovative and create entrepreneurial activities that support economic diversification. Educated and skilled businesspeople benefit from opportunities and innovativeness to create new businesses and new industries. Thus, skilled and educated individuals perform better in their jobs and pursue new opportunities and challenges. Moreover, the investment decision, the size of inbound FDI, and the productivity level will undoubtedly be better when the outcome of human development is high.

Health also has effects on economic development and diversification. There are many studies that show the effects of health on the productivity of individuals and, by extension, the economy in general. Strauss and Thomas (1998), in their study "Health, Nutrition, and Economic Development", documented how productivity was improved as a result of health improvement. Many studies have observed that labor productivity increases in association with an increase in health quality. This is the case for many nations as shown, for example, in studies on Guatemalan sugar workers[7], Kenyan construction workers[8], and farmers in Sierra Leone[9]. In these studies, the increase of labor productivity appears to be correlated with the increase in health quality. From the studies mentioned above, it appears that healthy individuals will be more productive, which means a positive effect on the economy and the development of a nation, while also contributing to diversification efforts.

How did human development help South Korea to diversify its economy?

One of the main characteristics of South Korea is the accumulated stock of an educated workforce at a very high rate that no other nation could reach, which has contributed to the nation's economic development and diversification over the past five decades.

South Korea was successful in connecting the outcomes of education and training with the demand for industrial skills. The developments and changes in the education and training system were aligned

7   Immink, M., and Viterri, F. (1981) "Energy Intake and Productivity of Guatemalan Sugar-cane Cutters: An Empirical Test of the Efficiency Wage Hypothesis." *Journal of Development Economics*, Vol. 9 (2), pp. 273–287.

8   Wolgemuth, J.C., M. C. Latham, A. Hall, A. Chesher, and D. W. Crompton (1982) "Worker productivity and the nutritional status of Kenyan road construction laborers." *American Journal of Clinical Nutrition*, Vol. 36, pp. 68–78.

9   Strauss, J. (1986) "Does Better Nutrition Raise Farm Productivity?" *Journal of Political Economy*, Vol. 94 (2), pp. 297–320.

with economic advancement. Since the 1990s, the focus has been on developing a knowledge-based economy by moving from low-skilled labor to advanced-skilled labor, and to researchers and scientists.

Due to the Japanese occupation and the Korean War, the social system in Korea was destroyed. Following this, a new social system was established. In this new system, education became the key for social and economic progress as indicated by Heo et al. (2017) in their comparison study "Exploring Learning Culture in Finnish and South Korean Classrooms". So, a good education was key to gaining a good job, which would guarantee a good lifestyle and economic and social rewards. As a result of a focus on education, the number of students in schools (at all levels) increased sharply in the early years, which fueled an economic boom. In addition, this eagerness to have higher education led to the production of researchers, scientists and engineers[10], who formed a major part of the technology development that South Korea had established over the past two decades.

Building skills and capabilities for workers in South Korea was the result of an export-oriented approach for the economy. South Korea's exports were dependent on production processes using low-skilled labor, especially in the 1960s. Production then shifted to advance manufacturing at the beginning of the 1970s, which required more skilled labor. Also, the labor market became flexible and responsive to the global demand for skilled workers. In addition, competitiveness in the labor market created incentives for individuals to acquire more training and skills.

Since the South Korean government adopted the export-oriented approach to remain competitive in the global market, it started human development training programs to provide the skills

---

10   Heo, H., Leppisaari, I., and Lee, O. (2017) Exploring learning culture in Finnish and South Korean classrooms. The Journal of Educational Research, April.

required for current and potential industries. In the 1960s and 1970s vocational training in technical secondary school was initiated to provide workers with skills sufficient for industry engagement.

In the 1980s, when the industries started to move to more advanced technologies, there was a need for more skilled workers. The government encouraged universities and colleges to add curriculums to supply an advanced and highly skilled workforce for different industries. There are hundreds of institutes for higher education in South Korea – 350 are private institutes, 19 are industrial universities, and 145 are junior colleges – which mostly work very closely with local firms to provide training and education in the requisite skills.

In 1997, the South Korean government established the Korea Research Institute for Vocational Education and Training (KRIVET) under the prime minister's office. KRIVET supervises the vocational training system and its coordination to provide qualified skills to workers required for the different industries.

The technical training in South Korea is managed and coordinated by the government and the private sector is taking a major role in it. The public polytechnic and vocational institutes were integrated to form eleven colleges nationwide; there are more than 700 vocational high schools as well, which provide all industries with the skills required to develop human capital for the knowledge-based economy. In addition, the government encourages private firms to perform vocational training for their workers. Chaebols (large firms in Korea) are involved in the education and training system by creating institutes to serve skill needs and to prepare workers (i.e., technicians, engineers, and scientists) to absorb the incoming technologies and create ingenious technology.

After the financial crisis of the 1990s, South Korea took a strategic decision to transform itself into a knowledge-based

economy and create its own industrial innovations and technologies. The government encouraged the private sector to play
a major role in this transformation by taking the lead in innovation activities, enhancing its efficiency and productivity, and
creating its own technologies.

The example of South Korea shows how the process of human
development, moving from basic skills to more advanced skills,
facilitated the economic diversification of the nation from an
exporter of low-skill manufactured products to advanced manufacturing and technological innovation.

Human development in Singapore

So, how did Singapore create a capable workforce? How did it transform its people from a state of impoverishment to being socially
and economically advanced? To answer this question and many
others there are many factors, but human development is one of
the key factors that advanced Singapore.

Human development in Singapore has played the role of both
driver and enabler for the development of the nation:

- *Driver*: The nation's goals of employment for its people and
  raising their standard of living drives the government to develop
  the country and economy and to continue looking for ways to
  sustain growth.
- *Enabler*: One of the main factors for economic development is
  workforce skills and health. This connection, between human
  development and economic development and growth, was
  pursued simultaneously by the government. It did not prevent
  one from impacting the other.

Since independence, Singapore has worked on the development of both its people and the economy. The work on human development has proceeded along three paths: housing, health, and education (training).

Over the past five decades, Singapore has transformed the quality of life for its people from a Third World country into a developed nation. Previously, most Singaporeans were living in the slums and the education system was weak. By 2020, about 88% of Singaporeans owned houses. The health system covers the population and the quality of the hospitals attracts patients from other countries. The health system has become an industry in itself. The education and training system is strong and covers everyone and is sufficiently flexible to react to new trends or catastrophes in the economy.

Singapore's Human Development Index (HDI) value for 2019 was 0.938, which positions it eleventh out of 189 countries. Between 1990 and 2019, Singapore's HDI value increased from 0.718 to 0.938. Human development has underpinned the transformation of the nation as it has become a developed country and global economic force.

Education and training

At the time of independence, Singapore's education system was weak. The school infrastructure was poor, the curriculum was inappropriate, and there was no connection between the outcomes of the education system and the market needs. There was no training for workers and, additionally, there were no proper training facilities for teachers.

For Singapore, the major resource of the nation, besides its location, was its people. So, it needed to utilize the people effectively and synergize their activities and capabilities to serve its goals of prospering and advancing. From the start, the Singaporean leadership understood that human development paves the way to success and increasing the capabilities and skills of the citizens would contribute to economic development and diversification.

In order to diversify and develop the economy, the government of Singapore needed to improve its national workforce skills. Subsequently, it invested in workforce improvement through training and education to raise the skill levels of employees. Singapore was depending on attracting FDI, so it developed the skills of its workers to attract FDI among other incentives and emphasized the importance of improving the output quality of workers to meet its needs.

How was education revolutionized in Singapore?

Singapore has successfully and continuously upskilled its workforce to support economic development and diversification. Countless articles and studies have discussed the contribution of the skills development system to Singapore's prosperity. These articles highlight the close connection between economic diversification and development and skills development policies. Singapore's government was able to frame the system to provide the necessary skills to align with the new trends in the global economy. The notable feature is that upskilling efforts is a collaboration between public and private entities.

Since the end of the 1980s, and because of the new direction for the innovation and entrepreneurial economy, the focus has been on enhancing creativity and entrepreneurial behavior. The education system was revised to include projects and research papers to encourage students to think creatively and be more entrepreneurial in their approach. In 1996, the thinking skills program was launched, which was designed to tackle the lack of creativity within Singaporean graduates.

Since Singapore wanted to be a "knowledge-based economy" and regional center for research and development, the education and training system had to be reformed. The restructuring led to the diversification of the economy since innovation and entrepreneurship led to the creation of new economic sectors, such as biotechnology, chemical engineering and aerospace, while existing sectors, such as electronics, were expanded.

Singapore did not just educate small children, but trained its entire workforce!

In the period from 1965 to 1979, export-oriented industrialization was adopted in Singapore, which meant attracting FDI to manufacture products locally for the international market. With this new strategy, one of the incentives of attracting foreign investment was to provide a low-cost technically trained workforce. To generate more highly skilled personnel, local training institutions were established, such as the Singapore Technical Training Institute (STTI). The Economic Development Board was responsible for economic development and providing trustworthy technicians and used two ways to generate such skills: one method was to establish local institutions in cooperation with institutions and companies from advanced countries; the second method was to send selected workers overseas for training.

In the period from 1979 to 1990, Singapore transferred its production to more advanced and value-added products, which required skillsets suitable to the new and growing industries.

Three initiatives were created. First, the Vocational and Industrial Training Board was established in 1979 with jurisdiction over all technical, vocational, and commercial training institutions with the view to supplying technicians with general skills. The second initiative was to encourage foreign companies to take on the training of Singaporean workers, while the third initiative was to reform the education system. This was supported by reform of the curriculum at the National University of Singapore and the creation of Nanyang Technological University.

The national efforts to develop workers' skills involved the private sector and employers. The Skills Development Fund (SDF) was created in 1984 to encourage all firms to be part of the program. The SDF requires employers to contribute 1% of the gross salary of all employees to the fund. Up to 80% of their contribution can be requested to fund training for skills development. The companies that continue to use low-skilled manpower are penalized.

The key features of the education and training system in Singapore are the centralized planning of skills' development needs, government and private cooperation to integrate foreign investment, and technology transfer to provide the necessary skills to an emerging sector. The SDF guarantees business investments in skills foundation and advancement. The education and training system is regularly re-evaluated as the needs for national skills change. The system is set up to provide skilled labor for the existing economic sectors and can prepare skilled labor for emerging economic sectors in a relatively short time.

The SDF and EDB work together to provide skilled labor for new economic sectors. The work of both organizations oversees the availability of skilled workers for companies in different sectors to be ready with skilled personnel for when a new economic sector emerges and requires a specialized set of skills.

Who is involved in the workforce training?

The education and training system in Singapore is a network of government bodies and institutions. The Ministry of Education supervises and monitors the overall activities with a focus on strategic human resource development. The EDB focuses on skills to meet investors' skills needs, while the Council for Professional and Technical Education (CPTE) focuses on overall coordination between different entities to meet the needs of the market. In addition to these bodies, there is a range of other specialized institutions that concentrate on short and medium-term needs.

The Economic Development Board's main role is attracting international investors and meeting their demands for skilled manpower. The EDB established the link between economic development and skills, and works with other agencies, such as the Council for Professional and Technical Education (CPTE), the Productivity and Standards Board (PSB), and industry-specific bodies such as the Precision Engineering Institute (PEI), to meet the required skills of investors.

The Council for Professional and Technical Education is an independent body responsible for matching skilled personnel with the demands of the economy. The CPTE provides a skilled workforce for existing demands and projected future requirements. It works with different bodies in the education system such as schools, universities, institutions and polytechnics, to ensure the availability of workers with the required skills for each industry.

The main role of the Productivity and Standards Board is to improve productivity in all industries and firms. The PSB supports firms to acquire appropriate skills training for their workers. The PSB concentrates on developing the skills of existing workers and not on new workers or those re-entering the firm.

The government of Singapore created institutes for different skills training such as the PSB academy and it is mandatory for companies to train their workers for the required skills and to do so repeatedly. The PSB and different institutes and companies organize their training programs and schedules to benefit employees and companies.

Communication across the education and training system in Singapore is critical to achieving its goals. The channels of communication and cooperation between all institutions at different levels guarantee the translation of skillset demands into achievable goals for all institutions.

High-quality teachers and principals

Since human development starts from childhood, Singapore designed and delivered a strong foundation of education for its children. Competent teachers and active leaders in school form the keystone of the education system in Singapore. High-quality teachers do not just happen – they are created as an outcome of thoughtful policy and processes starting from selecting teachers, and then training and grooming them. Singapore created a system to select, train, compensate and develop teachers and principals.

Singapore understands that high-quality performance from its schools and students requires effective leaders. The key is not just the training program, but the systemic approach to identifying and developing talented teachers and principals. For selection, the Ministry of Education selects potential teachers from the top one-third of secondary (high) school graduates. The selectees receive training from the National Institute of Education (NIE), which works very closely with schools where the master teachers in the institute mentor the new teachers for a few years. Teachers are assessed periodically to decide their potential career paths: school leader, master teacher, or specialist in curriculum or research. Then each one of these career paths has its process of development. For example, potential school leaders undergo training tasks to demonstrate leadership. After gaining experience and being assessed, the potential principals are nominated for interview. If they pass, they go to leadership situational exercises, and if they pass these, they go to a leadership training course with the NIE.

To be successful in the profession, commitment is required, especially in the education system since it strongly affects human resources, particularly in a small country like Singapore. Therefore, to attract talented teachers and principals and guarantee their commitment, the Ministry of Education makes sure that the compensation is competitive with other comparable occupations. The ministry surveys a range of occupational compensations and adjusts it for principals and teachers to ensure the attractiveness of the role compared to other professions.

Did skills development support Singapore in its economic diversification and development?

The main achievement of Singapore's government was the transformation of a workforce from unskilled to skilled and knowledgeable labor, which gave workers the ability to work in the high-tech, value-added and production industries, and to move between industries. Government initiatives for skill development led to raising the average skill level of workers. It contributed to technological advancements in the nation, due to automation, computerization and mechanization. For example, the implementation of advanced technology and value-added skills resulted in an increase in manufacturing output per employee from S$18,400 in 1980 to S$207,200 in 2019 according to the Singapore Department of Statistics.

An effective education and training system produces high-quality workers that can raise the quality and efficiency of the product and can transfer to another sector fairly easily. The availability of skilled labor and their transferability from one industry to another supports the diversification of the economy.

Singapore's economic development over the past five decades shows how the availability of skilled labor supports the nation's movement from low-skill industries in the 1970s to value-added and advanced industries in the 1980s (e.g., with electronics and computers), to high-skill industries in the 1990s (e.g., biotechnologies). Now Singapore's goal is to remain a leading knowledge-based economy. During all of these stages, the different entities involved in education and training were aligned and worked together to provide readily available and skilled individuals.

These individuals have been willing to move to new industries looking for new opportunities for financial or cultural reasons. Added to this, Singapore introduced many incentives to encourage workers to upgrade their skills, including offering grants to workers who completed post-secondary education, and payments to enable workers to gain qualifications in areas of market demand. Grants were also given to students in the polytechnic institutes to study for graduate-level qualifications. As well, the different institutes and agencies responsible for training and upgrading skills kept pushing the workers to develop their skills and provide training, coordinating with the EDB and different agencies in the market for the required skills.

Human development is not only education and training, but housing and health as well!

Housing and health do not contribute directly to economic diversification and development in measurable terms, however, as discussed earlier, a better standard of living and health leads to increased productivity among workers. The Singaporean government realized the importance of housing and health to the development of the economy and, accordingly, worked to transfer its people from the slums to adequate housing and to create a health system to take care of the people. In line with the strategy to upskill the population, as the people moved to a higher standard of living, the government simultaneously raised the level of requirements in education and skills. This resulted in more people taking advantage of higher education and becoming engineers, scientists, researchers and PhD holders.

Housing

The government of Singapore created the Housing Development Board (HDB) in 1960 to plan and provide affordable houses to the people. Through the instrument of the HDB, the government was determined to provide housing for all the people. Between 1960 and 2015 more than one million flats in twenty-three towns were built. The HDB has provided homes for 80% of Singaporeans. The state encouraged ownership of houses because owners would pay for the program, and as part of "nation-building" where citizens have a "stake in Singapore".

Housing's contribution to economic diversification is the development of the construction sector, where the input to house building was one of the major construction activities in the 1970s and 1980s.

Healthcare

The healthcare system in Singapore is a unique combination of government control and free-market principles. Singapore managed to achieve a high-quality healthcare system while controlling the cost of healthcare. According to the World Bank, the government healthcare expenditure is the lowest globally among the high-income nations reaching 2.1% of the GDP in 2018. The healthcare system impacted Singapore significantly. In 1960, Singapore's infant mortality rate was 35.5 per 1,000 live births, decreasing to 1.8 per 1,000 by 2020. Also, the average life expectancy of Singaporeans was 65.6 years in 1960, which subsequently increased to 83.9 years by 2020.

The government embarked on comprehensive reform in the 1980s for the healthcare system, including building new medical centers and restructuring the existing public hospitals. The state gave the hospitals autonomy to function more like private hospitals. Most of the hospitals were privatized in the 1990s. The goal was to gain high-quality services at competitive prices through competition with the public hospitals. This action helped stabilize prices throughout the system. The reform succeeded in providing more choices in healthcare to the consumers and assisted in reduced costs. The reform also increased the share of the private sectors in the expenditure and reduced the government expenditure from 51% in 1965 to 37% in 2020. It encouraged the private sector to be part of the system by providing healthcare services to the public.

In the 1980s, the Healthcare Manpower Development Programme (HMDP) was launched giving specialists opportunities to work and train at internationally known institutes. The HMDP actions supported a new generation of highly skilled specialists and set the stage for developing Singapore's current world-class capability in highly specialized, advanced medicine. Over the years, Singapore has continued to forge strategic partnerships with healthcare organizations all around the world and continues to send doctors for training to world-class medical facilities. In 2019, about 3,000 doctors practicing in Singapore were foreign-trained.

How does healthcare contribute to economic diversification?

According to the World Health Organization (WHO), Singapore's healthcare system is the sixth-best globally, while the nation has the fourth-best healthcare infrastructure worldwide. The healthcare system is the medical hub for the region and is considered Asia's best. Healthcare has developed into an industry, which provides services to patients locally and internationally. As an economic sector, the Medical Tourism Index placed Singapore second worldwide in the medical tourism rankings for 2020. Each year between 500,000–700,000 international patients travel to Singapore for treatment. Medical tourism has not only led to the development of the healthcare sector but also facilitates economic diversification by allowing the growth of secondary sectors related to tourism e.g., hotels and hospitality, transportation, etc.

Leadership development is the hidden factor

Even though leadership does not contribute directly to economic development and diversification, leaders play a major role in the efficiency and quality of the entities under them. For fifty years, Singapore has been successful in building itself as a nation, in developing and diversifying the economy, in recovering after each economic catastrophe, and continuing this success with different generations. The elites of Singapore understand that for their nation to prosper, they must have competent leaders in different entities. Since the government and public sector play major roles, the public service must have the capabilities to succeed, prosper and add value to the organizations they lead.

Therefore, a strong public service leadership pipeline is critical for Singapore to be successful. Public service leaders work with politicians to structure and execute policies. The high competencies of public service leaders in Singapore have resulted in greater efficiency in the public entities, statutory boards and SOEs. High efficiencies in government entities have led to the success of their role as part of the nation's holistic strategy. This, in turn, has led to high-quality outputs of these entities that have contributed towards the success of the economic diversification and development of Singapore.

All governments experience levels of bureaucracy that hold back the prosperity of the nation. But bureaucracy in Singapore was successful because it managed the development of teamwork at one end while rewarding individual achievements at the other end. The leaders go through a process of development and experience-building until they become heads of organizations. There is no shortcut to leading an entity. The experience of the leaders of the different organizations contributes significantly to the cohesion of the nation's goals. Most leaders have rotated between several policy positions in different entities and institutions. For example, Dr. Beh Swan Gin, chairman of the EDB since 2014, had previously served as the permanent secretary for the Ministry of Law, as a Director of the Ministry of Trade & Industry's Energy Planning Division, and as an Executive Director of the Biomedical Research Council. He also served as a Managing Director of the EDB between 2008 and 2012.

Job rotation between leaders builds the commonality of purpose between entities. Strong communication and connections across different agencies are key factors to the success of Singapore. It is significant to note that these practices show a prior design and intention to build those leaders. This can be seen in the job rotation, the structural links and processes that facilitate mutual decision-making, the teamwork mode across all agencies, and the culture of support among the other agencies to succeed, instead of trying to control everything and undermine the work of others.

The Management Associates Programme (MAP) is one of the pipelines for the administrative service. It is a program where Management Associates (MAs) receive strong foundational training on policy development and management and are given wide exposure to different areas of government to broaden their views on public policies and grow their leadership capabilities. After the program, Mas get appointed to the administrative service.

As part of their career progress, Administrative Officers (AOs) and Mas are posted across different sectors: social, economic and public administration. In addition, they can be seconded to the private sector, international organizations, and statutory boards. The deployment exposes them to different aspects of governance to build up a holistic perspective as they progress and take on more senior positions.

How does a good outcome from the human development factor impact economic development and diversification?

Table 4.1. Impact of human development strategies/policies on diversification

Strategies/ policies	Outcome	Impact on economic diversification
EDB involvement	• Connects skill development to the requirements of foreign investors. • Creates local institutions in cooperation with international partners.	• Provides high-skilled workers to different sectors. • Provides trustworthy workers to investors in different economic sectors.
Creation of different training institutions	• Training covers different industries and at all levels.	• Provides a specialized workforce • Ability to transfer workers from one industry to another with specialized training.
Education reform	• Enhances creativity and entrepreneurial behavior.	• Increases innovation, entrepreneurs and new startups in different industries.
Leadership development	• Creates skilled government officials with a private sector mentality. • High level of communication and alignment between different entities.	• When a new sector is established, different entities know their role and do their part which completes the role of the others and the new sector becomes a success.
Healthcare system	• Enhances the productivity of workers • Supports existing and creates new industries such as medical tourism, pharmaceutical and biomedical industries	• Creates new industries • Increases the attractiveness of the country

Abu Dhabi human development

Abu Dhabi has paid attention to human development since its early years: schools were established across the emirate, housing was constructed and distributed to the public for free, and hospitals and remote clinics were established to provide health services across the emirate. The 2019 UAE Human Development Index value of 0.890 placed the nation in the category of "high" human development, ranking it 31st out of 189 countries in the world.

Improvements in the standard of living, health services and public education have led to a decreasing death rate from 7.3 per 1,000 people in 1970 to 1.6 per 1,000 people in 2020. The infant mortality rate has dropped dramatically from 66.7 to 6.4 per 1,000 between 1970 and 2019 and life expectancy rose from 64.8 years on average to 77.81 years in the same period. Similarly, the literacy rate in 2015 was 93.8%.

As presented in Vision 2030, Abu Dhabi would adopt reforms that supported the enhancement of education and training outcomes. The objective of the economic vision was to reduce the risk of fluctuating oil prices and the uncertainty of the global petroleum market to develop a non-oil and knowledge-based economy, and to ensure sustainable development over time.

To benefit from the capabilities of advanced countries, Abu Dhabi hosts a number of global universities, such as Paris-Sorbonne University, INSEAD business school, and New York University and Massachusetts Institute of Technology campuses. To date, Abu Dhabi has invested heavily in the development of its education and training system, with a large number of Emiratis attending universities. However, even though the universities have advanced curricula, the graduates do not meet the requirement of the economic development and diversification strategies.

An Ernst & Young (2015) report into education in GCC coun-tries titled *How Will the GCC Close the Skills Gap?*, found that only 29% of employers think that students are equipped with the right skills for the job. Abu Dhabi Vision 2030 highlighted a set of sectors for the economy in the future. The Abu Dhabi Education Council (ADEC) built its strategy in relation to Vision 2030 by conducting industry surveys to determine which skills are required for what industry, and thus what training needs to be provided. For example, universities are not producing enough graduates in STEM (Science, Technology, Engineering and Mathematics), and produce more graduates in the humanities and business subjects, which means initiatives to encourage STEM must be used, such as scholarship programs.

From the Ernst & Young (2015) report, it is clear that unless local educational content is directly in line with what GCC employers need, young nationals cannot be adequately prepared for employ-ment in the private sector. The government of Abu Dhabi should survey and analyze the skills required for industries and ensure the availability of appropriate training courses and supervise the per-formance and monitor their outcomes.

A strategy to increase the number of engineers, scientists, and researchers

For a nation to become a knowledge-based economy, it needs its higher education system to produce high-quality researchers, engineers, and scientists. Abu Dhabi has invested in the higher education sector and many international universities have opened campuses in the emirate. There are currently twenty-four higher education institutions in Abu Dhabi, with four federal universities (UAE University, Higher College of Technology, Zayed University, and Khalifa University for Science, Technology and Research) providing free undergraduate programs. The remainder are international institutions such as Paris-Sorbonne University and New York University or local public or private universities such as Al Ain University and Abu Dhabi University.

In a survey and analysis before launching its strategic plan in 2012, the ADEC observed that the shortcomings of higher education in Abu Dhabi are due to challenges in the higher education system, which holds it back from meeting the objectives of Vision 2030. Universities in Abu Dhabi, and the UAE in general, are placed low on international rankings, mainly because of deficiencies in the research infrastructure, the poor preparation of students, not retaining talent, and most importantly, the lack of strategic planning. The ADEC 2012 strategic plan was aimed to transform the higher education sector in Abu Dhabi within ten years and address all the different issues that affected improving the standard of higher education. However, after five years of the strategy's implementation, those issues remain and are negatively affecting the education outcomes. There is no connection between what skills the industries need and the outcomes of the education system and there is no link with Vision 2030 in anticipating new skills required for the new sectors. So, the government of Abu Dhabi has decided to change the role of the ADEC and shift the role of planning and monitoring the education system to the Ministry of Education at the federal level.

Attempts to create a skilled workforce for industries

Abu Dhabi has made limited progress in developing vocational training since 2008. The emirate's ambitious plans to develop economic sectors were highlighted in Vision 2030, however, they were not supported with human development plans to attain the skills required by those sectors. According to a 2014 Statistics Center Abu Dhabi (SCAD) report, less than 2% of local students are in vocational education, whereas the global average is 10%.

The Abu Dhabi Centre for Technical and Vocational Education and Training (ACTVET) was established in 2010 to regulate Technical and Vocational Training (TVET), with the goal of increasing Emirati enrolment in TVET programs. ACTVET supervises the Abu Dhabi Vocational Education and Training Institute (ADVETI), established in 2007. TVET has programs at the secondary and tertiary levels and has campuses across the nation. It manages seven vocational institutes, which cover fields such as IT networking and multimedia, human resource management, accounting, and process automation. ACTVET also supervises the Institute of Applied Technology (IAT), which provides technical education through its affiliates: Abu Dhabi Polytechnic, Applied Technology High School and Fatima College of Health Sciences. All of which are supposed to support industrial development and economic diversification.

Even though the government is providing incentives for Emiratis to join vocational education and has opened training institutes across Abu Dhabi, only 3% of secondary school graduates join vocational training. This is believed to be the result of the stigma attached to vocational jobs and training, which are often viewed as substitutes for those who could not gain admission to a university or higher college of learning. To overcome this issue, the system allows students to transfer from a vocational school to a university, and thus encourages more students to join a vocational institute, since they can pursue a university degree at a later stage. Another issue is the high standards for admission to universities, which is directing the less academically successful Emiratis towards vocational training, and this affects the quality of the outcome.

Two-tier leadership competency

Abu Dhabi is undertaking substantial efforts in building human capability, however, these efforts are concentrated on the youth and are mainly on the technical side. There is no program for building capable leadership to manage and steer the different entities. The top leadership (H.H. Shaikh Mohammad Bin Zayed and his brothers) are extremely capable because they have been through leadership training and capability building in the military and as with Shaikh Zayed, they are more than worthy. However, people who are heading the entities have been appointed mainly based on relationships and family ties and not on inherent capabilities.[11] These people could improve their performance and add value to their entities if they were properly trained, and their leadership and management competencies were developed.

Abu Dhabi needs to have an entity responsible for the evaluation, training and selection process for managers and leaders. This process could apply to those in any entity in Abu Dhabi (government departments or SOEs) and when they reach the manager level, they are evaluated and a training plan is put in place and executed to prepare them for the next position. The evaluation and training would need to be an ongoing process whilst the person holds a position in government entities, and the process should include board members as well.

For capability development among its leaders, Abu Dhabi needs to establish:

1. A high-level academic course (i.e., a master's program) to develop leaders capable of running the implementation of complex

---

11   Hertog, S. (2010), *Benchmarking SME Policies in the GCC*. Brussels: The EU-GCC Chamber Forum, European Commission.

policies and programs. A similar program has operated in Singapore for more than twenty years and in Australia for more than twelve years.[12]

2. A senior officers course for existing managers to provide them with the core competencies necessary to manage complex programs. A similar course operates in the United Kingdom and Australia and was used in Malaysia to implement the 9th and 10th Malaysian Plans.[13]

3. A project management competency framework and certification process to match international standards, and a requirement that project managers in both the government and private contracts have the appropriate level of project management certification.

4. Officials, from the management level upwards, should go through a rotation cycle of positions between different entities, so that before a senior officer takes on a leadership position they serve in different entities and understand their work.

5. KPIs and targeted goals for each position so that when a leader assumes such a position, they know exactly if they are capable and can be nominated for a higher position, or if they need more training to overcome some weaknesses.

---

12 Dombkins, D. (2009), *Human Capital for Development in Organizing for a Complex World: Developing Tomorrow's Defence and Net-Centric Systems*. Washington DC: Center for Strategic and International Studies.

13 Ibid

Linking training to economic sectors

Abu Dhabi has training programs that target industries with the potential to provide workers with the required skills. The education and training system in Abu Dhabi has been providing graduates with different skills supposedly aligned with the skills required by the market. There has been improvement in the last few years with some specialized institutes providing the skilled workers required for that specific industry.

According to their website, ACTVET's technical institutes have several partnerships with different entities (private or public), which sometimes sponsor students to study and/or provide employment for them after completion. Such companies include the Abu Dhabi National Oil Company, Emirates Steel, Emirates Nuclear Energy Corporation (ENEC) and Etihad Airways.

The impact of the human development factor on economic diversification

Abu Dhabi, which only began serious efforts to develop and diversify the economy during the last decade, has made significant achievements. But similar to the rest of the UAE, although the higher education system has made it possible for Emiratis to graduate with college degrees, the education system has not been responding well to the market demands of skills and could not equip the workforce with the skills required by industries as it stands.

While there have been increased efforts by institutes and universities recently to redress these issues, the results are not yet clear. In comparing the differences between Singapore's approach to human development and Abu Dhabi's, the following points stand out:

- *Strategic planning, future prediction, and implementation*: Singapore is competent in predicting and anticipating global economic trends and preparing the requirements and a skilled workforce to take advantage of the opportunities. In Abu Dhabi, there was Vision 2030 and many other sound strategies, however, Abu Dhabi is ineffective at implementing and executing these strategies. The systems supporting the individual factors lack both resilience and robustness. Because of weaknesses in the individual factors, Abu Dhabi effectively lacks the capacity for foresight, prediction, and the ability to implement and execute strategies. In addition, it lacks an effective system of systems to bring the factors together to gain the impact of synergy. This weakness manifests itself in how Abu Dhabi responds to changes in the economic environment. By way of overview, Abu Dhabi during the good times has relied on the significant income from oil and gas. It expends this wealth inefficiently through SOEs and avoids deeper transformation. During the bad times, Abu Dhabi dramatically cuts back on programs and looks for quick fixes, similar to other GCC countries, again avoiding any deep transformational change. Abu Dhabi needs to create a predictive and strategic planning unit to support better planning and not rely on consultancy firms. Johann Hari (2010), in his study "The Management Consultancy Scam", indicates that big-name consultancies develop strategies, however, they do not develop realistic execution plans, in what he calls a "consultancy scam".
- *Connections between the skills required and training courses*: in Singapore, the Ministry of Education overviews the education and training system to make sure that all players (institutes, universities, and boards) are coordinating and working in synergy. There are two entities that coordinate to ensure the availability of skills for different industries: the EDB for international investors, and the CPTE for skills in general

required for the economy, and for current and future needs. These two entities work with each other and with other entities to provide the right skilled personnel at the right time. In Abu Dhabi, there is no such coordination because there is no entity overlooking the activities for providing skilled workers to industries. ACTVET, ADEC and the universities presumably coordinate together, however, there are no indications of real cooperation. Abu Dhabi's DED is not taking the leading role in identifying the skills requirements for industry as this does not fit their remit or responsibilities. As the entity responsible for economic development, the DED needs to undertake analysis and provide recommendations on the skills needed for different sectors, similar to the role of the EDB in Singapore.

- *Loss of focus*: entities in Abu Dhabi tend to lose focus and direction with time, and shift from the original purpose/remit. For example, higher colleges of technology were established to provide the required skills to the workforce as per the market requirements, however, over time, they have shifted to become just like other universities in the UAE.

- *Higher education outcome*: Singapore, on its path to becoming a knowledge-based economy, forced the higher education institutes to produce high-caliber researchers, scientists, and engineers. Abu Dhabi should also develop researchers and scientists. So, like Singapore, it needs to attract foreign high-caliber researchers and talented faculty in its institutes. Also, Abu Dhabi and the UAE should have a roadmap for new local graduates in science and engineering, to groom them and enhance their capabilities and not abandon them, as is done now, to hunt for any job and mostly end up working in administration jobs.

- *Provide training at all stages and levels and for specific needs*: under the umbrella of the Ministry of Education, in Singapore, there are many bodies that monitor and coordinate the training in their focus area. For example, the PSB is mainly responsible for increasing productivity and efficiency in local firms, while supporting companies to analyse their weaknesses and find the proper training to increase the productivity of workers. However, there is no such entity in Abu Dhabi to assist and support companies in providing the right training for their workers.

- *Leadership development*: Singapore created a system and process to develop and groom leaders to manage and control the different entities. An individual undertakes training, evaluation, monitoring and mentoring throughout their career, moving to different positions to build their capabilities. In Abu Dhabi, although an individual might take a course on leadership, there is no system or process in place to develop and groom leaders. Another issue is that heads of entities in Abu Dhabi are stretched out over many positions and bodies and have too many areas to cover. They are unable to focus on one task, which leads to a lack of performance among the entities they lead. This rings true of the Arabic saying "A person with two minds is a liar", which means that a person cannot perform well on more than one task at a time.

- *Teachers*: Singapore organized the selection of teachers and groomed them to become competent teachers to guarantee high-quality results within the education system. Abu Dhabi, on the other hand, does not have such a system in place, which means that the system does not guarantee to produce high-quality teachers.

There is a need for accountability when executing the strategies and plans for education and training. The DED needs to play a greater role in deciding what skills are required for the market, for both the present and future. In addition, there must be strong cooperation and coordination among agencies – i.e., ADEC, ACTVET and DED – and each needs to fully understand and know their role precisely, without overlapping with other entities, for the strategy to be successful.

Human development in the GCC

GCC states were ranked highly in the Human Development Index for 2019, ranging from 0.806 for Kuwait to 0.890 for the UAE. This placed the GCC states at the higher end of human development efforts. For example, an average 25-year increase in life expectancy at birth for GCC countries can be observed from the 1960s to the present (see Table 4.2).

Table 4.2. International ranking and economic indicators for GCC states

		Bahrain	Kuwait	Oman	Qatar	KSA	UAE
GDP 2019 (US$ billion)		41	144	84	196	781	450
GDP/Capita 2019 (US$)		23,551	32,373	15,343	62,276	23,139	42,701
Corruption Index Rank 2021		42	42	54	63	53	71
Control of Corruption 2020 (highest is 2.5)		-0.07	-0.06	0.23	0.78	0.27	1.11
Rule of Law 2015 (highest is 2.5)		0.425	0.001	0.377	0.770	0.118	0.641
Human Development Index (2020)		0.852	0.806	0.813	0.848	0.854	0.890
Life Expectancy at Birth	1960	52	60.5	42.7	61.2	45.7	52.2
	2019	77	75	78	80	75	78
Global Innovation Index (GII) 2021		78	72	76	68	66	33
WEF Infrastructure Ranking 2019		31	66	28	24	34	12

data sources: international organizations such as CI, GCI, GII, HDI, and WB

On average, the literacy rate in the GCC is 94%. Of those working in the private sector, the percentage of nationals is very low. For example in Qatar and the UAE, only 1% of the private sector workforce are nationals, and in Saudi Arabia, it reaches only 18%.

The GCC governments have supported the vocational training and enhancement of technical skills among their national workforces. They have created initiatives to support their technical capabilities and created many technology-focused institutes and entities, such as the King Abdullah University of Science and Technology in Saudi Arabia, the Education City of Qatar Foundation, and the Masdar Institute of Science and Technology in Abu Dhabi. In addition, GCC states are hosting international institutions to absorb knowledge and technology locally in order to create a high-quality education system.

But these efforts are not producing the skilled workforce required in the labor market as highlighted in the Ernst & Young (2015) report *How Will the GCC Close the Skills Gap?*.

Regardless of the substantial investments in training and education, the outcome of these efforts and education performance are still lagging. For example, in the 2018 Program for International Student Assessment (PISA), the performance of the UAE and Qatar was less than the average of the OECD.

Table 4.3. PISA performance of the UAE, Qatar and OECD in 2018

	UAE	Qatar	OECD
Science	434	419	489
Mathematics	435	414	489
Reading	432	407	487

source: PISA

One of the issues that negatively affect the education system in GCC states is the shortage of skilled educators. The teaching method is rote learning, which deters creativity and imagination, and has had a negative effect on the creation of skilled and knowledgeable employees who can contribute to establishing a diversified and sustainable economy.

GCC governments do not pay attention to teacher development. Even though the governments have drawn on school systems from the West and East, unfortunately, they have failed to build the capabilities of the teachers. As occurs in Singapore, the teachers are developed from the time they graduate from high school. Selection involves the high-end students then going through a development process to become teachers, and the system keeps monitoring and mentoring them across their career to make sure they are competent because they are responsible for educating new rounds of students. By contrast, the GCC governments are concentrating on textbooks and curriculum and not on the messengers who deliver the information and shape the personalities of these children.

In the GCC countries, similar to Abu Dhabi, most of the education is in the humanities and low-level technical areas. There is a lack of effort invested in the development of competent leaders. Many of the people in high positions do not have the required skills or competence levels. They obtain their positions through social ties and the small number of competent people are stretched over many executive positions, which reduces their effectiveness within the entities they lead.

Given the low number of nationals working in the UAE and Qatari private sectors, to drive innovation these countries will need to import PhD holders from other countries. By contrast, the Kingdom of Saudi Arabia has a current problem with nationals who graduate from university, many of whom have masters and PhDs but are unable to find work. This problem will increase because of the young population and the high number of students entering university and higher education institutes. There are not enough suitable jobs for these graduates. The GCC governments set policies to replace foreign workers with nationals, which never met expectations and were misused by entities and individuals.

The GCC governments should create systems to groom competent individuals – this includes selection, training, and evaluation processes – for leadership in science, engineering, research and technology. This system has to develop competent people from high school or even elementary school, similar to the process used in Singapore. In his 2004 book, *Managers Not MBAs,* Henry Mintzberg proposed a new definition of management as a blend of craft (experience), art (insight), and science (analysis). This reflects the approaches taken in Singapore, Australia, and the UK. The GCC states should consider adapting the Australian or Singaporean process of developing leaders to increase the competency level of leaders in the public and private sectors and use scholarship schemes to move the focus of postgraduate studies from the humanities to science and technology.

In their report on the academic background of the world's most powerful CEOs, StudyEU found that such individuals are well-educated professionals. In its 2017 international survey, StudyEU found that 97% of CEOs hold at least a bachelor's degree, 64% have a master's degree or equivalent, and 10% have a doctoral degree. For GCC countries to effectively reach their goals, socially and economically, and enhance the outcome of the factors of the wheel of economic development and diversification, they need to develop suitably qualified graduates and postgraduates in sufficient numbers to become senior managers and cohorts of future leaders.

Along with education and leadership, productivity growth is a key issue in GCC countries that is restricting economic growth. The 2016 report by the Competitiveness Office of Abu Dhabi (COAD) on the emirate's competitiveness showed very mixed results in productivity outcomes during the period from 2005 to 2014. The COAD report found productivity drops in mining, education, utilities, transport, financial services, construction, and manufacturing. The issues with education and the poor performance of SOEs could easily be viewed as the primary causes for the poor performance in productivity. In light of this, the GCC countries need to establish formal systems to drive productivity improvement, as Singapore did.

Conclusion

Human development needs to focus on building competencies in areas of technology and in managing complex adaptive systems. Since human development improvements are a precondition for economic diversification and growth, government policy and public funding and support is, therefore, necessary to raise the quality of the output of human development systems. However, the high-quality outcome of education cannot be gained until there is a comprehensive strategy and policy that is implemented correctly and sufficiently flexible to adopt the necessary changes that arise during implementation. To be successful, the process should be treated as a complex and adaptive system of systems.

The government, also, should have a strategy and policy for national skill development. The government should emphasize technological enhancement, capability building, and knowledge sharing. The strategy should cover school education, new worker training, worker development (upskilling) during the job, and transition training to a different industry. This strategy should consider international trends and demand. The outcome of the human development system should be linked to the industries, have competency-based outcomes, and emphasize entrepreneurship, innovation, competition, and discipline.

The human development factor has had a very high impact on Singapore's economic diversification and development. Singapore has proactively developed its leaders and systemically developed the competencies that the country needs to deliver efficiently in current markets and to prepare for future market changes. The skilled, high-quality workforce was one of the attractions that the EDB worked to prepare for international investors to come to Singapore.

The human development factor has had a low impact on Abu Dhabi's economic diversification and development. In Abu Dhabi and the UAE, the government needs to have an overall strategy to increase the capabilities of the workforce and prepare researchers, engineers and scientists to contribute to the efforts in building a knowledge-based economy. This strategy should be applicable and have a robust execution plan. To ensure the right execution of the plan, the people involved in developing the strategy should be responsible and accountable for its implementation.

The human development factor has had less impact on economic diversification and development in GCC countries as it should. These countries have not developed competencies in the workforce required by industry, nor have they developed leaders with the competencies required to develop and implement complex policies and programs, and they have failed to attract and retain competent expatriates.

CHAPTER 5

Governance, Institutions, and Policies

Ensure protection, quality, fairness, and ease of business

"Global governance cannot be limited to the crafting of instruments related to the promotion of democracy. A key component must be the creation of fair and equitable rules to enhance the development prospects of developing countries."

— KAMLA PERSAD-BISSESSAR, TRINIDADIAN AND TOBAGONIAN
POLITICIAN (1952–PRESENT)

The government of any nation is the body that has the power to manage, coordinate and force things to happen in a certain way. In the economy, for example, the government has a major role in managing the movement of money and funds, setting the laws and governance to force fair play for everyone, and providing the incentives to develop and create new industries.

History has shown us that some form of government intervention is necessary for the social and economic development of the nation. In every nation, there is a relationship between government and business, which differs depending on the maturity of the economy, in general, and the specific sector in focus. The 2008 financial crisis showed that even in the free-market economy of the Western world, governments had to step in to manage the crisis and save their economies. The United States, for example, injected more than US$800 billion into its economy as a stimulus package to support the country in facing the crisis. Governments use policies and institutions to manage and organize the relationship between different partners and stakeholders in the nation.

The economy in small states is usually very thin and has deficiencies in institutional capacity such that economic difficulties are probably more noticeable than among larger states. The market is very small for competition and relies on foreign markets more, which means needing to create globally competitive products and services. As a result, the role of government is more interventionist in small states. The government should support the economy by establishing policies and the environment to enhance productivity and efficiency in firms and business entities, encourage export since the local market is very small, develop the private sector, support innovation and entrepreneurship, and manage public companies in an efficient and commercial manner to make sure there is value for investment purposes.

There is a strong systemic relationship between the three parts discussed in this section (governance, policies, and institutions). All countries have the three parts and use them but what differs between the developed nations and developing nations is the quality of those three parts. In developed nations, the quality is good and the roles are managed effectively. In most developing nations, the three parts are weak and the quality of their outcomes is poor. In developing nations, the policy is good most of the time, but governance and the institutions are still not strong enough. Policies are good because it is easy to review policies used elsewhere and to choose the best. However, implementing these policies is difficult, leading to weak governance and institutions.

All states develop some kind of governance but good governance is not easy to achieve. Good governance covers many aspects, some of which include accountability, transparency, broad participation, rule of law, fairness and effectiveness. All these elements are very important for the development of a nation in general, and for economic advancement.

Governance supports the economy with laws that manage and support economic activity and transactions through property rights protection, enforcing contractual agreements, and enforcing transparency and rule of law. Through governance, the state has the ability to create an attractive environment for development. The state needs the support of the organizations and institutions of civil society to monitor and facilitate the governance regulations. Governance is focused on organizing and monitoring the process of social and economic development, for both the private and public sectors. It includes the institutions and rules that form the framework for private and public firms to work within.

Governance in this book would mean the methods, regulations, policies, rule of law, anti-corruption, transparency, etc., that systemically integrate the elements within a nation for the prosperity of the nation and its people.

Many organizations, such as the World Bank and United Nations Development Programme, have presented fundamentals of good governance and their effects on development. These elements are similar in principle but are framed differently. The UNDP's *Governance for Sustainable Human Development* (1997) report recognizes eight elements of good governance: rule of law, transparency, accountability, participation, equity, consensus orientation, responsiveness, and effectiveness and efficiency.

Good governance and perfect policies and laws cannot be effective unless there are institutions to monitor and enforce compliance. The quality of the outcome of governance and policies depends on the quality of the institutions. Institutions complement governance and some studies have presented this connection. For example, Campos and Nugent (1999), in their article "Development Performance and the Institutions of Governance: Evidence from East Asia and Latin America", claim that governance demonstrates five institutional elements including civil society, the executive branch of government, rule of law, bureaucracy, and the character of the policy-making process.

Government's supporting role in economic development and diversification

There are many studies in the body of literature verifying the relationship between institutions and economic development and growth. In sum, established political and economic institutions affect the level of investments in human development, infrastructure and technology, as well as creating processes and legal frameworks in nations for stakeholders to operate in a fair and just manner, and the capacity and quality of goods and services produced in a particular nation. The business environment in which firms operate is an essential driver for the development of the private sector and entrepreneurship. The ability for a company to invest and to grow and expand depends on the characteristics of the business environment. Some of the elements of this environment are the ease and costs of doing business, the risks of doing business, and many other elements controlled by the government.

Governments have the responsibility to ensure economic and social stability, to achieve good employment levels, to create confidence in the country and economy, to create the tools for economic development and diversification, to create strategic plans and drive the whole nation to implement them, and in general to guide the nation to success.

The government's role not only creates a favorable investment climate for domestic players, but also attracts foreign investors. FDI is a powerful tool for enhancing economic development and diversification as well as creating competitive enterprises and improving their productivity through the transfer of technology and know-how. It is also an important driver to support and enhance innovation. The government's role is to create a trustworthy environment through contract enforcement, intellectual and property rights, and antitrust regulations among many other regulations.

The private sector is usually hesitant to enter new economic sectors because of the high risk and uncertainties accompanying the developments in the new sectors. For this reason, in most cases, governments step in and take the risk of investing to pave the way for private investors and to reduce the uncertainty related to that sector.

The government, also, should enforce the partnering between public and private sectors, because both are responsible for creating and implementing the national economic initiatives. The government should force public entities to engage with and support the private sector, to build the trust and cooperation needed to grow the economy and achieve the national goals of development and the diversification of the economy. In the post-COVID era, private and public cooperation is more essential because of the financial stresses faced by governments as a result of the health and stimulus bills to mitigate the pandemic problems.

Does government intervention affect economic diversification?

The intervention of governments to develop and diversify the economy is an attractive idea. Many countries have done it all over the world, the most successful of which are the East Asian nations. In these countries, the government has involved itself in planning and implementing the strategies for all aspects of the nation's social and economic development. Even though there are many critics of this approach, especially in terms of the democratic aspects, it did help these nations rescue their people from poverty, while some have even become competitive with the West. This is not acceptable to the West, as the West tries all the time to undermine the success of these nations and hold them down.

In his 2006 study "Industrial Development: Stylized Facts and Policies", Dani Rodrik highlighted the role of policy in defining the "patterns" of the economy. He gave examples of China, Singapore, Taiwan, and South Korea, highlighting their ability to sustain economic growth because they could "diversify into more sophisticated, technically-demanding activities". In his analysis, Rodrik explained that the growth of the economy is correlated with growth in the productivity of a competing sector and the non-traditional export sector, which he called the modern sectors of the economy. According to the analysis, without the intervention of the government to set the right policies for both modern sectors to grow, the output would not be satisfactory and would affect the economy negatively.

The state needs tools and means to drive all the players in the country toward the success and development of the nation. Bob Jessop, in his 1990 book *State Theory*, describes how the government possesses effectiveness through a set of policies and institutional structures, as well as social practices that give it authority and the power to make the necessary changes to reach its national goals.

When the government of South Korea decided to walk the path of economic development and diversification, it started to invest in new economic sectors and supported the private sector in entering new industries such as shipbuilding, car manufacturing, the electronic industry and many others, which had not existed in South Korea. The private sector did not get involved until the government took the risk and invested heavily in the new sectors. For example, when President Chung Hee Park ordered the construction of the Seoul-Pusan highway he was criticized because there was no economic benefit at that time compared to the high cost. But with time, this highway has played a critical role in the logistical movement and creation of industrial sectors in different regions of the country.

Mixing power and wealth leads to corruption

After the death of the Prophet Mohammad (Peace be upon him), Abu Baker became the Calipha. He was a trader. A few days after he became the Calipha, Omar Ibin Al Khattab met him going to the market to conduct his trading business. Omar asked Abu Baker where is he going? Abu Baker said that he is going to trade to earn money to feed his family. Omar replied, that cannot be, and both went to Abu Obaidah, who was responsible for Beit Elmal (the treasury), and all agreed to give the Calipha a salary so that he would not get involved in trading.

Another story involves Omar when he became the Calipha. Omar saw very well-fed camels in the market and wanted to learn who these camels belonged to? When he was told that the camels belonged to his son "Abdullah Ibin Omar", he ordered his son to sell the camels with no gain. Omar told his son, these camels were very well fed because you are the son of the Calipha, when your camels are in the pasture, everybody says let these camels eat because they belong to the son of the Calipha and that is not fair.

In both stories, Omar Ibin Al Khattab viewed the relationship between power and trade as an unbalanced relationship. Power will always influence business in favor of the one in power. You cannot be in a position of power and be a businessperson at the same time; this will lead to corruption. Even if it is not intentional, as observed in the above two cases, the firewalls against corruption should be there. It does not matter how good and transparent the person is. Throughout history, corruption almost always exists if the same individual engages in both activities. It is human nature that aspires to build wealth, and if an individual has the power to manipulate circumstances to gain wealth, most likely he/she will do it, irrespective of whether he is a prince or a commoner.

Corruption is the abuse of public power for private benefit. It is a phenomenon that, if it spreads, affects almost all aspects of economic and social life. Corruption can be committed by different activities besides bribery, such as embezzlement of funds, patronage and nepotism, sale of government property by public officials, and grafting. The World Bank estimates US$2.6 trillion, or 5% of the world's annual GDP, is lost due to corruption. The African Union estimates that 25% of Africa's annual GDP is lost due to corruption.[14]

Some believe that politicians work for the public interest and for the good of the country and that they consider their personal gains to be less important. However, in a study on public choice theory, Buchanan and Tollison (1984) suggest that such an assumption is unrealistic. They stress that people perform to maximize their personal gain in both the public dimension and personal lives.

---

14   UN Meetings Coverage and Press Releases (2018), "Security Council 8346th meeting (am), SC/13493", 10 Sept 2018.

They gave a good example of political corruption in reference to Lyndon B. Johnson (the 36th American President) who, as a member of Congress during the 1940s and 1950s, used his connections with the Federal Communication Commission to obtain licenses for his radio and television stations and to block competitors from entering the market.

If this is the case in the United States, where corruption is regarded as low compared to most of the other countries in the world, the question arises as to what would be the case in Asia, Africa and Latin America. Many of the politicians in these continents, where rule of law is weak, take advantage of their political position to gain personal wealth.

Corruption has negative effects on the economy, since corrupt government officials are motivated to select projects that increase the opportunities for bribery and maximizing their personal gain, rather than projects that serve the public. Corruption escalates into unemployment, reductions in tax revenue, a decline in business operations and the collapse of the economy. Corruption also has negative effects on the flow of FDI and the contribution of FDI to the development of the country.

How successful are East Asian governments?

How the government can play a pivotal role in diversifying and developing the economy is provided by the examples of the East Asian countries. The governments in these nations were managing all aspects of the country: social, political and economic. As the World Bank's (1991) report explained, "the miracle of East Asia" is a result of the governments' abilities in planning for and providing elements such as the legal framework, macroeconomic environment, domestic and international competitiveness, and human development. In these countries, the government interventions ranged from planning and setting the direction of the economy, to education and skills development, private sector support, a robust financial system, and so on.

In these countries, government intervention is clear and occurs on multiple levels to support economic diversification and development, and sometimes a certain industry is targeted for creation or enhancement. This intervention comes in different forms such as the protection of domestic products, financial regulations to ease the burden of sustaining business, encouraging export, public investment in new technologies, and encouraging the transfer of technology. Many Asian countries have used policies to support specific industries. One of the best examples is Japan, which created policies including import protections and financial subsidies to enhance the development of heavy industry.

Most Asian countries passed through an import-substitution phase to protect the local industries and encourage growth. They then changed to an export-orientation approach in order to expand into bigger markets and to be more efficient and competitive on a global scale. The import substitution and export promotion led to the diversification of the economy by prompting the development of new economic sectors.

Export strategies differed from one nation to another. Some, such as Singapore and Hong Kong, created a free-trade system to be connected with and expanded to the global market since the domestic market was small. Both created incentive systems to promote export. On the other hand, policies in Japan, South Korea, and Taiwan were a mix of both import substitute and export encouragement. These countries were strongly committed to protecting and promoting export for the local manufacturing industries. So, the governments used policies to protect specific industries from international competitors and promoted export for other industries. For example, South Korea used export targets for firms as an incentive policy.

The export policies were very effective in the East Asian countries. Economic growth in East Asia has been underpinned by rapid expansion in manufacturing exports. On average, exports as a portion of East Asia's GDP have grown from about 20% in the 1980s to about 45% in 2005. East Asia's share of global trade has increased from 16% in 1980 to 30% in 2019 according to United Nations Conference on Trade and Development (UNCTAD) export data. Also, trade liberalization and investment policy reforms have greatly reduced barriers to trade and investment (outward and inward), which attracted MNCs to create manufacturing capabilities in the region.

Singapore's governance, institutions, and policies

Singapore is the second-most "free economy" in the world, according to the Index of Economic Freedom issued by the Heritage Foundation in 2021. Singapore is regarded as having a low level of corruption and in 2020 it was ranked the fourth-least corrupt nation and first in Asia by Transparency International. However, Singapore has had the same political party controlling the government since independence, which has been involved in planning and executing the national agenda of development and diversification.

When Singapore gained independence, the elite decided to develop their country to be one of the leading Asian nations and to raise the standard of living locally. Even though Singapore is a free-market economy, the role of the government has been crucial for the social and economic development of the nation. Government intervention has had a significant effect on the welfare of Singaporeans.

Besides job creation, the government has elevated the standard of living of its people by providing housing, education, health, and public transportation.

To support economic development and diversification, Singapore established strong services and manufacturing sectors. Since the domestic market was small, the government adopted an export-orientation approach attracting international companies for support and to become involved in the diversification of the economy. The government in Singapore set the policies to create new industries to respond to the needs of the global market and to increase employment.

For a newborn state, the economy was weak and lacked manufacturing capabilities, while local firms were weak in providing good services and did not yet have the courage to move to new industries. To address these problems, the government decided to attract foreign investors to establish manufacturing in the country and to be part of the economic development and diversification.

Upon independence, Singapore, like all other newly established states, had many problems such as high unemployment, lack of infrastructure, poor living conditions, and corruption. Today, Singapore is an advanced nation and global business hub. This transformation was not by chance, but achieved through good governance, policies and institutions. Government is the major player in the economy: it created SOEs to drive diversification; created institutions, policies and mechanisms to drive the economy; and created and managed human and infrastructure development. For Singapore, economic success comes not only from government intervention or control, but its ability to sustain a stable political atmosphere. This draws foreign investors and increases the sense of trust among the people in the government, all of which contributes to economic growth and diversification.

How Singapore manages policies

Governments use policies to align different stakeholders to common goals, to ensure everyone works in supporting the nation. As with many nations, in Singapore policies were used to direct all stakeholders to do their part on the path to economic development and diversification. For example, during the 1970s, the government introduced a policy called "forward-looking empowerment" to enable citizens to obtain capabilities (skills, suitable regulations, access to finance) to create businesses and compete regionally and internationally. The policy was designed to encourage cooperation between local and international partners, which would lead to the transfer of technology and increase output quality and efficiency in the country.

The policies were designed to serve the economy and create wealth for Singapore and its people. In the 1960s and 1970s, for example, the policies were targeted to support labor-intensive industries and reduce unemployment and diversify the manufacturing base. The policy aim was to attract foreign investment and accumulate funds to support local production. By the end of the 1970s and 1980s, the policies were modified to enhance technology transfer and increase the technology-intensive industries and manufacturing, such as pharmaceutical, computers, electronics, and machinery.

One of the main issues the government had to deal with was the multiracial society. In a region where fights between different races occur all the time – a result of which was the breakaway from Malaysia – the state had to create a national identity and social unity. Policy development in many areas supported these goals. For example, the education system supported the development of national identity and built unity through fair competition and presenting the different cultures as the main players in society.

Specialized zones were created to attract foreign investors, who wanted to have complete ownership of their businesses, which would be integrated into the holding company's supply chain, production, and marketing plans. Creating a free-trade regime was to provide incentives to international investors to open their businesses in Singapore and support the country in reaching its goal of technological advancement and diversification of the economy. Those policies and many others helped the nation to transfer from a developing to a developed nation in four decades.

How successful are institutions in Singapore?

The success of Singapore is clearly connected to how the state and its domestic institutions are able to adapt and respond to changes in global economic trends. In order for Singapore to diversify and develop the economy, the creation of institutions specific to certain tasks was necessary. Singapore used the concept of the statutory board to manage and take responsibility for sector or task. Each statutory board's role is to manage specific portions of ministries' roles and coordinate the development of a sector or industry. The statutory boards act partially autonomously and have the flexibility to work as a private sector and avoid the ministerial bureaucracy.

It is hard for governments to segregate policies from institutions. In the case of Singapore, statutory boards were added to enhance the government's efficiency. Each ministry manages a number of statutory boards for different activities in the field of that ministry. Statutory boards were established to manage specific parts of the government's role (such as economic sectors) and coordinate sectoral development and growth. There are around sixty-six statutory boards in Singapore, such as the Economic Development Board, Housing Development Board, and Infocomm Development Authority (IDA).

Singapore created statutory boards which allow them to act autonomously to avoid the constraints that regular government entities face. Statutory boards can have long-term planning, independent budgets, and stable staff (unlike public servants who rotate systematically) who can raise funds, invest and create companies, and design their own salary and compensation programs. In fact, they are meant to operate more like enterprises than traditional government institutions.

The government keeps control of the statutory boards through one of the ministries, which monitor and ensure compliance to the stated boundaries. The relationship between the ministry and the board is a cooperative relationship without competition.

Statutory boards allow the government the flexibility to plan and execute strategies (social and economic) along with responding to global demands and economic crises. Boards that operate in similar areas are assigned to the same ministry to ensure synergy and the avoidance of overlapping responsibilities. For example, the Ministry of Trade and Industry has ten statutory boards under it which work in supporting industries, such as the Economic Development Board (EDB), Jurong Town Corporation (JTC), Agency for Science, Technology and Research (A*STAR), Standards, Productivity and Innovation Board (SPRING) and other statutory boards.

An example of an effective statutory board is the EDB, formed in 1961 to be responsible for economic development. The aim was to attract international firms to set up manufacturing facilities in the country for export. The role of the EDB was to facilitate and remove any obstacles to reach that goal, such as reducing tax and tariffs, provision of incentives, and ensuring the availability of skilled labor and sufficient infrastructure. To be successful, the EDB had to cooperate with other boards to facilitate the incentives for international companies such as training, education, infrastructure, and innovation.

Governance and rule of law in Singapore

Singapore is regarded to be one of the least corrupt nations and was rated the fourth-least corrupt country on the Corruption Perception Index issued by Transparency International in 2021. It has also been named the least corrupt country by the Political Economic & Risk Consultancy (PERC) for the past fifteen years. Singapore did not reach this level of indexation easily and has faced many internal challenges and obstacles during the past fifty years.

As with all countries emerging from a colonial past, corruption was common, and bribery was used as a way of getting things done. Singapore had the Prevention of Corruption Ordinance, however, this body was weak. Therefore, the government of Singapore identified corruption control as one of the top priorities of the government.

As Singapore's economic development was dependent on international investors, a trustworthy system an environment of fairness needed to be in place. This created assurance in the government to perform its duty without favoritism. It was critical for Singapore to eliminate corruption for national survival.

The government took bold steps to fight corruption. The law was reviewed and reinforced to the point that no one was considered above the law, and punishment was severe. The anti-corruption bureau was strengthened. In addition, the government administration was improved and became more efficient, and the salaries of public servants were increased significantly. These measures provided the tools to transform Singapore from a corruption-infested state to a corrupt-free state.

Singapore's economic success is founded on the solidity of its legal rules. International enterprises could safely bring people and capital to the country under the strong protection of Singaporean law. One of Singapore's attractions for international firms was freedom from corruption and the protection of property rights and contract enforcement.

Foresight and getting ready for the future

For the past forty years, Singapore has maintained the ability to anticipate global trends and certain crises. This ability gave it the leverage to plan for new directions and prepare the environment in Singapore for new trends, and to be ready for crises when they occurred. The Singaporean government has managed to maintain its growth and development through both the bad and good times.

The challenge for the policy-makers is how to make plans and policies that are robust and remain valid for a long time, since assumptions, conditions and technologies are changing. This becomes more challenging because of the unknown interruptions, such as black swans (strategic surprises) and game-changers, which are low-probability but high-impact events. These disruptive shifts can occur in technology, geopolitics and in society generally as indicated by the Centre for Strategic Futures (CSF) in Singapore. The last two decades have seen some large shocks, such as the 1997 Asian financial crisis, the al-Qaeda attacks of September 11, 2001, and the global economic and financial crisis in 2008. Each event has created new dynamics and new challenges.

Anticipation and planning have been essential for Singapore to ready itself for different events. It was fundamental to Singapore's efforts to understand and plan for the future. The genesis of Singapore's foresight enterprise is similar to various think tanks and foresight agencies, with its origins in the military domain. Singapore is a tiny country between relatively big countries and armies. It has to foresee the changes in the neighboring armies such as military growth in capabilities, expected threats, doctrinal changes and changes in technology. Because of the military mind-set of strategic planning, the Ministry of Defense (MINDEF) has to predict and plan for future activities. In addition, there has been a need to plan for large projects sustained over long periods of time, and to anticipate technology trends. The capability of future planning in the Ministry of Defense has been growing strong.

As a result of its success in military planning, the Scenario Planning Office (SPO) was set up in the Prime Minister's Office during the 1980s. The idea was to expand the planning technique for different departments and government entities. Today, this technique is part of the national strategic planning process and part of the annual budget cycle.

However, scenario planning has its limitations – i.e., it cannot anticipate black swans. To address this, the government added foresight tools such as 'back casting', 'causal-layered analysis' and 'horizon scanning', which are collectively called Scenario Planning Plus (SP+).

In 2004, Singapore developed Risk Assessment and Horizon Scanning (RAHS), a software tool relating to big data systems that can perform data analytics for future thinking and planning and can explore evolving strategic threats and opportunities.

Despite Singapore's best endeavors, it cannot eliminate all the risks and uncertainty in the real world and there will always be threats. However, the government needs to respond to crises in a manner that demonstrates confidence in its actions, which can be achieved with the pre-analysis of crises and risk mitigation plans, as shown previously.

The Singapore government was able to respond effectively to the 2008 crisis when it drew from the national reserves to support the economy with a funding package of S$20.5 billion. This package was used to support companies to enhance competitiveness and preserve jobs through retraining and part-time employment arrangements. This was not just a case of injecting money into companies; this action supported Singaporean enterprises to respond quickly and benefit from the recovery of the global economy.

Immigration

Since Singapore is a small country in need of diversifying its economic base and increasing its talent pool for advanced technologies, migration policy has been essential to the workforce plan. Singapore has one of the most attractive immigration policies in the world. The government formed the migration-based talent policy in the 1970s and has been committed to it ever since. Foreign talent is central to Singapore's vision of a "dynamic, global city", because it supports the nation in advancing its technology and innovation.

In the beginning, the government considered using the emigrant workforce as a short-term necessity for certain jobs. However, with time the government realized the importance of foreign talent for the nation's development, particularly with advanced technology. Singapore continues to view skilled migrants as a crucial factor in the development of the nation.

How did this factor impact economic development and diversification?

Singapore created an environment of business fairness for everybody, foreign or local. The anti-corruption regulation inspired Singapore to be one of the least corrupt nations worldwide. The rule of law was applied to everyone without favoritism, which attracted the MNCs to operate in Singapore in a favorable environment for business.

Table 5.1. Impact of governance, institutions, and policies on diversification

Strategies	Outcome	Impact on economic diversification
EDB	• Enforces the modification of policies and regulations to support economic development • Creates incentives to attract FDI and MNCs in different sectors	• Creates new economic sectors • FDIs directed to invest in certain industries at different times
Setting up and working of statutory boards	• Independence to provide focus on economic-sector development • Flexibility in managing economic sectors	• Development of new industries • Strengthens the economic sectors and supports the spin-off of new sectors
Establish rule of law	• Corruption-free nation	• International investors came to open or create business • Local private sector and new startups invested in new industries with no constraints or fear of injustice
Creating Scenario Planning Office	• Foresight planning and future thinking • Future (potential) risk assessment	• Pre-analysis of crises and risk mitigation plans • The ability to minimize the negative effects of many crises

Abu Dhabi: governance, institutions, and policies

The rapid growth of the Abu Dhabi economy in the last fifty years, and its transformation from a tribal system to a central government system, was not an easy journey. In the past, the region was disunified and free of an overarching government, so when the new states were established, it had to work by using a trial and error system for a while. It then used the experience of other nations to set up laws, processes and systems, which necessitated the establishment of a new system. In the first three decades, Shaikh Zayed bin Sultan Al Nahyan laid the foundations of a global city in Abu Dhabi and worked to transform the desert emirate into one of the world's modern states. Many policies and institutions were established to enforce the rule of law and the sovereignty of the state.

Economic policy, planning and regulation are critical for economic diversification. For example, reducing the barriers to FDIs would allow different industries to move into the emirate. The creation of special investment zones such as Industrial Cities of Abu Dhabi (ICAD) and Khalifa Port Free Trade Zone (KPFTZ) was to serve this purpose.

Abu Dhabi Economic Vision 2030 was created in 2008 to transform the economy from a petroleum independent economy to a diversified economy through the creation of new economic sectors and to become a knowledge-based economy. Many policies and regulations emerged to serve this vision. Laws and decrees were publicized to facilitate economic restructuring and strengthen the coordination between government entities.

Policies

In 2007 Abu Dhabi initiated an agenda to change and modify policies and regulations to support Vision 2030. The Policy Agenda 2007–08 highlighted the main initiatives of the government to develop the economic environment and enhance the contributions of the different public and private entities towards the vision, as declared by the Executive Council in 2007.

The policies were outlined for individual sectors such as tourism, hydrocarbon and different industrial sectors. In pursuing the economic vision, the government did not leave out the environmental policies. Environmental and infrastructure policies were part of the overall development agenda of Abu Dhabi.

Institutions

The institutions that serve the diversification initiative require the capabilities to execute their roles properly and the power to enforce their agenda to support the development and diversification of the economy. In Abu Dhabi, the institutions that play a major role in the economy are all public institutions, such as the Department of Economic Development and the Industrial Development Bureau.

Department of Economic Development

The Abu Dhabi Department of Economic Development is the main player in the economy. It is the entity whose sole purpose is to develop and diversify the economy. The DED is responsible for the economic development of Abu Dhabi and for looking after the realization of Vision 2030 through proposing, formalizing and implementing policies. Its mission, as was declared in the *Abu Dhabi Competitiveness Report* (2012), is to "… lead Abu Dhabi's economic agenda towards a balanced, diversified and sustainable knowledge-based economy that enhances the competitiveness of Abu Dhabi in the global economy and ensures prosperity for its people". The DED is also responsible for strengthening the efficiency, productivity, competitiveness, innovativeness and growth of different industries in Abu Dhabi. In summary, the DED holds the planning, regulation and execution roles in the economic system.

The DED is the main driver of Vision 2030 for Abu Dhabi, whose ambition is to create an environment for business characterized by transparency and sound governance. To build a diversified and strong economy, the DED announced its priorities as:

- Adopting liberal economic policies and reducing regulatory requirements;
- Asserting Abu Dhabi as the preferred destination for FDIs, and;
- Diversifying the economy by increasing manufacturing and industrial sectors.

The DED has two strategic offices to support economic development and diversification: the Competitiveness Office of Abu Dhabi and the Industrial Development Bureau. The former was established in 2011 to encourage competitiveness, efficiency and productivity. COAD's aim is "to enhance the competitiveness thinking and commitment of Abu Dhabi's people and enterprises (…) and to create a business environment conducive to innovation and productivity" (Abu Dhabi Competitiveness Report, 2012).

Industrial Development Bureau

While the Abu Dhabi Economic Vision 2030 addresses the entire economy, the approach to industry has been fine-tuned through outcomes in industrial strategy and the establishment of a dedicated entity, the Industrial Development Bureau (IDB). The key role of the IDB is supporting the industrial sectors, to create an environment for the establishment and growth of industries.

Established in late 2013, the IDB is tasked with developing the industrial sector via a mandate that falls under three pillars. The first of these is industrial strategy and policy which encompasses the development of a strategy for the entire sector such as the industrial zones, policies and regulations, industrial performance management, and industrial information and intelligence. The second pillar is sector development, which establishes the body as the chief source of sector planning and coordination, and promotes the sector to all potential participants. Third, the IDB is tasked with overseeing investor services including support and regulatory services for industrial business, such as licensing, health and safety, and the environment.

In 2014, the IDB identified several targets for future development such as building materials, petrochemicals, metals engineering, iron and steel, plastics, aluminum, food industries, renewable energy, oil and gas, packaging, aviation, and transportation equipment. The forward aim is that there will be increasing localization of manufacturing supply chains, a dramatic increase in competition to attract FDI, innovation in material sciences due to the scarcity of resources and intensified public policies to enable the manufacturing supply chains. According to the IDB, Abu Dhabi grew its non-oil industrial manufacturing sector by 9% in 2014, more than double the average GDP growth in Abu Dhabi and over three times more than global growth indices. Industrial manufacturing is becoming increasingly important as the UAE is looking to diversify its GDP into sustainable industries.

With the establishment of the IDB, the government of Abu Dhabi has shown its commitment to broadening the emirate's industrial base. Moreover, its Vision 2030 plans for the manufacturing sector, which include the ongoing development of the emirate's burgeoning aerospace and defense industries, and high-tech, knowledge-based industries in life and material sciences, testify to Abu Dhabi's determination in best positioning itself for long-term, sustainable economic diversification.

Abu Dhabi's Quality and Conformity Council

Since Abu Dhabi is developing industrial sectors and pursuing the high-end part of industries, efficiency and quality are becoming essential. Recognizing the importance of this matter, Abu Dhabi established a regulatory body responsible for quality and conformity infrastructure. The aim was to develop and improve standards for competitiveness for industries in Abu Dhabi so that it can compete in the global market.

Established in 2009 by the government, the Abu Dhabi Quality and Conformity Council (QCC) is mandated with improving the quality of the emirate's traded goods, exports and services, ensuring that the quality of testing infrastructure is on par with the best international standards, and creating a globally recognized national brand. The function of the QCC is key to facilitating Abu Dhabi's transition towards a more diversified, knowledge-based economy. The QCC activities cover different areas, such as infrastructure, testing infrastructure, standards, conformity schemes and certification, consumer safety, metrology and legal metrology. The QCC also supervises the regime standards in services and products to ensure international and national requirements are met.

Governance and rule of law

The restructuring of Abu Dhabi's government and policies occurred in 2008, and since then policies for different sectors (economic and social) have been aimed at increasing transparency and accountability to the government within the emirate.

The success of modernizing the legislative and judicial process as well as the regulations such as intellectual property, contractual enforcement, etc., have been essential to the successful restructuring of the Abu Dhabi government, and ultimately contribute to an enhanced global reputation. This provides assurance to both foreign and domestic investors that they may establish their business in a safe and lawful environment.

Corruption

The UAE has been named the least corrupt country in the Middle East, according to Transparency International's 2020 Corruption Perceptions Index (CPI). The UAE was ranked 21st globally out of 180 countries covered in the index. The UAE was ahead of most EU member states, including France and Spain.

Bribery is punishable according to the Federal Penal Code (Law No. 3 of 1987) and the Federal Human Resources Law (Law No. 11 of 2008). Both the Federal Penal Code and the Federal Human Resources Law contain anti-bribery provisions. In particular, the penal code criminalizes active and passive bribery, embezzlement, and abuses of functions. Also, Article No. 234 of Law No. 3 of 1987 and its amendments state that those who give or take bribes will be punishable for jail terms up to a maximum of 10 years.

However, the 2017 report *Economic Crimes in UAE* by PricewaterhouseCoopers (PwC) found that 47% of respondents reported economic crimes within their organization. Asset misappropriation is the most commonly reported crime at 49%, followed by procurement fraud at 16%, bribery and corruption at 15%, and cybercrime at 12%. The report shows that the level of economic crimes in the UAE is higher than the regional and global levels and Abu Dhabi and the UAE need to reduce it.

To eliminate or at least reduce corruption, anti-corruption entities need to address corruption in both private and public companies. The sources of corruption, especially in public entities and SOEs, should be addressed with a special emphasis on procurement and hiring practices. Furthermore, SOE boards and executives should be accountable for addressing and mitigating corruption issues in their firms.

Impact of governance, institutions, and policies

Since 2008, the Abu Dhabi government has improved the legislation and set policies for different sectors to develop them and improve the outcomes. Vision 2030 emphasizes strong policies to achieve its goals.

Abu Dhabi has developed many processes to ease and speed the activities for people and investors. However, challenges still exist for industrial investors in the emirate, and improving coordination between entities (such as municipalities and the DED) and reducing organizational procedures, will facilitate more efficient services.

In comparing the ways that Abu Dhabi and Singapore deal and manage their governance, institutions and policies, it is noticeable that two very different mentalities are at work in creating, managing and executing this factor. In referring to the discussion on this factor, the following can be concluded:

- Singapore is an attractive environment with an open and commercially driven attitude taking advantage of any opportunity that arises. On the other hand, in Abu Dhabi, regardless of the efforts of the Crown Prince, the attitude is hesitant, non-commercial, too protective, and risk-free. This attitude has led to the buildup of a bureaucratic system that is harming the efforts of the emirate for diversification and developing its economy. The avoidance of risk is shown by the extensive use of brand-name consultants, where blame cannot be placed on the individual. Abu Dhabi is being held back through not being attractive to international investors, especially in a region where there are other strong competitors operating, such as Saudi Arabia and Qatar.

- Singapore, in its approach to developing the economy, created entities to play roles on the pathway to development, an element that is missing in Abu Dhabi. In Singapore, there is a statutory board for each economic and social sector. The idea is to have sector-focused entities where the main role and responsibility for each is to develop their sector without losing focus in coordinating with other entities, while having the flexibility to adapt to global trends and to be accountable. If the board does not meet these goals, it is replaced. However, Abu Dhabi is lacking that which has led to a loss of focus and the loss of accountability. One such example is Vision 2030, which does not have a body to ensure its implementation. Even though the economic sectors were identified in the vision, sector-focused entities were not in place, thus it was left for everyone to do their part, which was unfocused and lacked accountability.

This was particularly evident in the first few years, with many entities and SOEs jumping from one project to another, in order to publicly demonstrate their contributions to the vision. Yet, there were delays, over-budget spending and sometimes no success in implementing many of the individual projects. The DED is responsible for the economic development of Abu Dhabi but is a government body with a bureaucratic system slowing it down. Abu Dhabi needs to create entities for each economic sector, similar to the statutory boards of Singapore, that report directly to the Executive Council of Abu Dhabi, which is the local ministerial council, and not to another body. This will assign the responsibility for each sector to a particular entity to develop it and be held accountable for it. Also, people in charge of these boards should be fully committed and not involved in another board or entity, because partial commitment leads to a decline in performance among many entities in Abu Dhabi.

- Historically, the traditional approach to corruption in most Middle Eastern countries has been to turn a blind eye. However, by enforcing corruption laws, Abu Dhabi believes the quality of its business environment will be strengthened. The authorities are forcefully broaching the problem; the emirate is committed to a transparent and level playing field to help strengthen its reputation as a regional business hub operating to global best standards. Despite the government's efforts, a blind eye is sometimes applied if the case involves a high-ranking figure, to avoid negative publicity. Abu Dhabi needs to follow Singapore's lead in enforcing anti-corruption laws to establish a corruption-free nation, to attract foreign investors, to engender trust in the rule of law and fairness in regulations, and to prohibit anyone from gaining an unlawful advantage through personal relationships.

- As with Singapore, Abu Dhabi needs to have a law and procedures for the recovery of illegally obtained funds and to impose severe penalties on any person convicted of improperly obtaining funds or benefitting from illegal actions.

• In Abu Dhabi, public entities and SOEs are often hampered in their aims to be more efficient and profitable because of poor leadership. The heads of these entities have been nominated and appointed, not for their capabilities or merit, rather on their personal relationships with those close to the leaders. When the head of an entity is perceived as weak, the people around them can work that to their advantage and corruption can occur. Changing the entity heads periodically could assist in the faster development of these entities, as when an incumbent remains in the same position for ten years or more the entity stops developing through a lack of new ideas and having no pressure to change.

To meet the goals of Vision 2030, Abu Dhabi needs to have a set of capabilities that support governance and institutions. Abu Dhabi needs to be more demanding in areas of accountability and responsibility. Employees and entities need to be held to account and judged accordingly. It is useful to keep in mind the old Arabic saying, "The one who is guaranteed no punishment, misbehaves".

GCC governance, institutes, and policies

Policies have been developed and implemented to enhance the business climate in each of the GCC countries. Reforms have been used to reorganize the regulatory and legal environment in many areas, including licensing procedures, competition policies, investor and consumer rights, and bankruptcy.

The institutions and administrations in the GCC were established without fiscal discipline or systemic architecture, because of the high revenues from oil and gas. Similar to other resource-rich countries, these administrations have become inefficient. Since there is no accountability, the quality of the output of these institutions is low and seems to be getting worse over time.

Since the 1990s, every time the oil price falls, the GCC countries embark on structural reform aimed at enhancing the efficiency of the public and private sectors, encouraging the private sector to become more involved, attracting international investors, and creating plans to diversify the economy. However, if one is to judge those reforms by their outcomes, one must conclude that the record of these countries after more than four decades in governance, institutions and policies is appropriate in structure, but modest in the quality of the outcomes and the effectiveness of these reforms.

It is broadly acknowledged that there are significant weaknesses in the public entities in the GCC states and the governments realize that to develop and diversify the economy, these entities must be strengthened. For example, the Qatar National Vision 2030 acknowledges that efficiency, transparency and accountability need improvement to achieve economic growth.

It is time for the GCC states to transform from an ad hoc and tribal system of governance, to institutionalized and twenty-first-century governments. The institutions need to be given a clear mandate to implement policies and programs. Rule of law must be applied to everybody and to every organization. The rule of law and anti-corruption oversight are not strong in all GCC states, even though some of them (the UAE and Qatar) are ranked higher than the others. The GCC states need to stop corruption at all levels and in all its forms. The rule of law will build trust in the government and its regulation among the people and within the international community.

In GCC states there is a lack of law and regulation to reduce inefficiency and corruption. Even in countries where corruption has been reduced to very low levels, inefficiency in services and production is still very high.

Conclusion

Governance, policies and institutions form the means and ways to connect all the different elements of the nation to service its success in economic, social and political areas. The three elements must all be strong to produce a quality outcome. A lack in any element might result in corruption, injustice, weak institutions, and weak policies, which will lead to the weak economic and social development of the nation.

The intervention of governments at all levels of the country has resulted in transforming the Asian nations from a state of poverty to wealth. For a nation to be successful in its strategy for diversifying the economy, the government needs to be more involved in setting the goals and creating the system to support firms to reach such goals in manufacturing and export with high quality and efficient results.

Governments are the main player in planning and implementing strategies to reach national strategic goals. In a region like the GCC, the involvement of the government is very important because of the lack of maturity in many industries, so there is a need for mixed policies of protection for local firms and free trade to attract foreign technologies. In addition, the lack of skilled manpower forces the governments to train and develop the local workforce.

The governance, institutions, and policy factor has had a major impact on Singapore's economic diversification and development. The Singaporean government has played a vital and positive role in the nation's development and success of the economy. Singapore's government and administration are one of the most effective and non-corrupt worldwide and its policies play a strong role in support-ing the nation's approach to its economy, in creating new industries and ensuring the success of these industries.

The governance, institutions, and policies factor has had mini-mal impact on the UAE's economic diversification and development. Abu Dhabi is lacking in competent leaders in its institutions and has not been effective in enforcing policies. The weakness in this factor has even had a negative impact on diversification efforts – for example, the lack of real corporate governance for the SOEs has led to these entities making investments that are not always governed by economic logic.

The governance, institutions, and policies factor has had a minor positive impact on economic diversification and development in the GCC countries. In some instances, this factor has had a nega-tive impact on the development of the nation. While governments have developed vision statements, they have failed to develop and implement robust programs of delivery. In a similar way, govern-ments have initiated laws but have failed to have them effectively enforced.

CHAPTER 6

Infrastructure

How does infrastructure affect economic diversification and development?

"In developing countries, lack of infrastructure is a far more serious barrier to trade than tariffs."

— JOSEPH STIGLITZ, US ECONOMIST (1943–PRESENT)

Infrastructure development is a key factor for a country's path to economic diversification, development and growth. Good infrastructure enhances both a country's and a firm's efficiency and productivity, encouraging firms to be more competitive and enter the global market. Infrastructure provides incentives to public and private investors and the quality of infrastructure determines the attractiveness of a nation to foreign investments.

As discussed earlier, human capital plays a vital part in economic diversification. The health of the workforce and the life quality of the population, depends on the quality of infrastructure systems, which support the lifestyle of the people. According to the United Nations' *World Water Development Report* (2021), two in every five people worldwide has insufficient access to water, due mostly to a lack of infrastructure. In India for example, the annual cost of treating diseases resulting from the use of unclean water is $600 million, with 73 million days of lost labor, according to the World Bank's 2017 report *Waterlife: Improving Access to Safe Drinking Water in India*.

Enhancing infrastructure quality is one of the major tools to reduce and eliminate poverty. The availability of good infrastructure is crucial to enhancing the opportunities for economic equality and a greater selection of future directions for individuals. For example, in the developing countries, the availability of schools, hospitals and an adequate transportation system would give the poor a better chance to make good choices for their future and to lift themselves from poverty, as argued in the UNDP's 2020 Human Development Report *The Next Frontier*.

Infrastructure investment forms a key driver to economic growth. A sufficient infrastructure network will attract FDI, inspire the private sector to expand and invest, and enhance efficiency, productivity and competitiveness. Infrastructure assists in expanding and enlarging the market for local firms. Infrastructure has a major effect on economic development and diversification. The efficiency of manufacturing in a country is not only dependent on the production facilities of the firm but expands also to the availability and efficiency of the infrastructure, in areas such as IT, transportation networks and energy.

A strong connection exists between economic diversification and the quality of infrastructure. In their 2011 article "Broadband Infrastructure and Economic Growth", Czernich and colleagues stressed that in nations with poor infrastructure, the economy depends on one prime sector and per capita income is low. If a nation can develop good quality infrastructure, the economy diversifies, and the per capita income is higher. It is easy for local and foreign investors to move from one sector to another when supported by the infrastructure through the availability of sound roads, IT systems, power, water, etc.

There is no unified definition for infrastructure. Different definitions offered by different researchers depend on their field of study, be it social, economic, environmental, governmental, etc. The basic definition of infrastructure is a set of facilities and systems that provide services to the people and entities of the nation. It provides input to other economic activities and thusly forms a major factor in economic development and growth. Infrastructure refers to transportation (including roads, bridges, railway lines, ports, etc.), IT and communication, the education and training system along with the health system (including clinics, pharmacies, health insurance, etc.), the energy and power system, and many other systems that are necessary for the nation and the economy to operate.

How important is infrastructure?

Infrastructure is a critical component when it comes to economic development. A high-quality infrastructure assists the nation in building a robust economy by enhancing its capabilities for efficiency and productivity, as well as acquiring new technologies and creating new economic sectors and industries. High-quality and accessible infrastructure will enhance the competitive advantage of the nation and provide incentives for businesses to expand and prosper. An advanced infrastructure is what kept the West ahead of everyone during the entire twentieth century and gave East Asia the edge to catch up over the last 30 years.

The Global Competitiveness Reports highlight the critical effect of the infrastructure on the nation as a whole and the economy in particular. These reports placed infrastructure as the second pillar to show the competitiveness of a nation and its capabilities to pursue economic development.

The availability of infrastructure facilities to continuously provide quality outcomes are necessary conditions for economic development and diversification. Infrastructure, like power and telecommunication networks, and transportation systems, is vital to economic diversification and development as well as the modernization of the nation. Infrastructure facilities also need to be maintained to continue providing quality outcomes to the nation and the economy.

Infrastructure impacts the economy in different ways. Accessible and affordable infrastructure services are critical for firms to be more efficient and allows them to enhance their productivity and expand; it affects the operations directly by reducing cost production. It also provides firms with tools to pursue new industries and reduce the hurdles for entrepreneurs to create new businesses and sectors.

In addition, infrastructure has indirect effects through supporting education and training for human capital and providing a health system to have healthy workers, which supports national economic diversification and development.

The economic miracle of the Asian economies was accompanied by the extensive development of the infrastructure. The Asian economies, including China's, made huge advances in economic development and diversification, attracted investment, enhanced exports, and created employment, all because of the massive investment in infrastructure.

There is a strong correlation between the quality of infrastructure and economic growth, and it affects the output from different areas of the economy and different sectors significantly. In the 2006 study by Fedderke et al., "Infrastructural Investment in Long-run

Economic Growth: South Africa 1875–2001", the authors showed that an increase of 1% in the stock of infrastructure increased a nation's GDP by 1%.

How does infrastructure contribute to economic diversification?

The contribution of infrastructure to economic diversification can be seen in many ways. Infrastructure contributes to enhancing productivity by linking the supply chain to manufacturers and smoothing the transfer of products to markets (local and international). This allows firms to diversify into new markets through exports.

Infrastructure also contributes to economic development and diversification by making it easy to expand and/or create new industries. Infrastructure provides services to explore new business arrangements through global connectivity (i.e., through communication, finance, transport), which supports human capital development, enhances the ability for innovators and entrepreneurs to start businesses easily, supports product competition by providing access to high-quality and low-price resources, and assists firms in responding to new trends and market demands.

The type of infrastructure put in place also determines the performance of the different sectors of the economy. For example, the availability of good telecommunication supports banks in boosting the financial sector and online business to grow, and the availability of good roads and ports enhances the logistics sector and manufacturing, as well as trade.

Does investment in infrastructure have a positive impact on nations?

The strong relationship between good infrastructure and economic growth has not been overlooked by the world's most populous countries, China and India. The experience of the two nations in economic growth shows the effects of infrastructure development.

India is a good example of how a nation with great economic potential was held down because of poor infrastructure. On the other hand, China has invested heavily in developing its infrastructure, especially since the 1980s, which has led to enormous economic development. Both nations have similar capabilities deriving from their land, and human and natural resources, but China created infrastructure systems that cover the whole nation and connect it with the world through advanced infrastructure, which has supported it in becoming the second-largest economy in the world. By contrast, India did not invest as much in infrastructure and a good portion of its infrastructure is old and needs upgrading. This kind of infrastructure impedes India from progressing at the same pace as China. Although India has advanced information technology services, its insufficient and outdated infrastructure has slowed the manufacturing sector and other industrial sectors. The manufacturing sector in India is suffering because of inefficient infrastructure, such as roads, railways, ports, and power. The inadequate infrastructure not only discourages foreign investors by creating hurdles for their business, it also has negative effects on domestic business. For example, 40% of vegetables and fruits are spoiled before reaching the market because of a lack of refrigeration, as highlighted in the research by Mishra et al. (2013), "Growth and Infrastructure Investment in India: Achievements, Challenges, and Opportunities".

China's expenditure on infrastructure is more than that of India because the investment was part of China's economic growth, where fiscal injection into the economy was designed to keep the growth wheel rolling. This spending supported the growth of China's economy at a faster pace than in India, which also led to raising the standard of living at a faster pace. Data presented by the World Bank indicates that before the 1990s, India was ahead of China in GDP per capita. Since then, China's economy has grown at a very fast pace, comparable to India's slower economic growth. By 2020, China's GDP per capita was US$10,500, whereas India's GDP per capita was US$1,900.

How did Singapore successfully use infrastructure to support economic diversification?

As a new and independent nation, Singapore faced issues in many areas, some of which involved the lack of proper infrastructure and the excessive limitation of land. The government's major mission was to develop the economy and create jobs. As there was no single solution to the challenges facing Singapore, the government created entities to be responsible for tackling each of the issues: examples include the Urban Redevelopment Department (URD), the EDB and the Housing Development Board (HDB). From the start, Singapore understood that for economic development to proceed, it needed to manufacture goods, and for that, it needed to attract foreign investors which meant it created an attractive investment environment. A major attraction was to have a high-quality infrastructure, which Singapore has kept updated and well maintained since.

In 1974, the URD became an independent statutory board renaming itself the Urban Redevelopment Authority (URA). The URA is the main entity responsible for the use of land and facilitating the physical development of the nation. To manage the complexity of problems in infrastructure development, conflicting demands and preparedness to adopt future trends, a system of systems approach was used from the beginning. The reality is that Singapore is a very small country with limited land, so the planning for infrastructure development needed to be flexible and adaptive to present and future demands. The constraint was to develop an infrastructure to meet the needs of social and economic development, while using minimal area and allowing for potential change and maneuvering within the plans.

Singapore applied a system of systems approach to most of its infrastructure projects, such as housing, transportation, port development and facilitation, the Jurong Island project, power systems and the ICT systems. Such an approach allows for continuous evaluation and the flexibility to make changes when required.

One of the major components of the infrastructure was social development, where projects related to housing, education and health were used to move people living in the slums to new and clean organized areas with health and education facilities. It was also used to build harmony between the different races of the population, where everybody was treated equally and there were no areas segregated for one race only. The Housing and Development Board was responsible for providing houses for Singaporeans in areas where all facilities needed for the people were available, such as schools, medical clinics, transportation, and shopping centers. Planning for housing faced the key issues of land scarcity and housing affordability within the population. To provide sufficient housing to the people at affordable prices, the HDB came up with the idea of high-rise buildings. The government gave assurances to the people it was looking after them socially. In return, the people worked to develop their skills and levels of education and training to meet the challenges and contribute to the efforts towards economic development and diversification.

Since attracting foreign investors was the main target to boost the economy, Singapore needed to provide incentives to draw people to the country and needed to create and improve the environment for investors. One of the major steps was to develop the infrastructure to attract investors by reducing the set-up time for their businesses in Singapore by providing ready to use facilities. The EDB created the Jurong Town Corporation (JTC) as the place where investors would go and find all the facilities they required and to make the life of the workers easier. The JTC was not only a collective of industrial facilities, but included residential areas, parks, schools, clinics and shopping centers.

In pursuing diversification, Singapore established industrial zones for different sectors and industries. These sites established ready to use facilities for investors and startups. Some of these parks covered specific industries, for example, Tuas Biomedical Park, Seletar Aerospace Park, Jurong Island (Petrochemical), CleanTech Park, and One-north (Biomedical, ICT and Media), and some of them accommodate multiple industries, for example, Changi Business Park, International Business Park, and Airport Logistic Park.

Creating a transportation hub

Infrastructure has supported Singapore's diversification programme in transportation through creating an integrated global logistic hub and a system coordinating land, sea, and air movement. When a shipment arrives at one of the seaports or airports, it is transported by land to another port to be sent out via air or sea.

When the Singapore government set the goal of becoming a global logistic hub, it established sufficient infrastructure and transportation systems across land, sea, and air. The airport was transferred to a new open area to allow expansion when needed.

The government established clusters to support the trans-shipment, and infrastructure such as roads and ICT are always kept up to date to support the transportation hub.

The transportation and logistics hub also serve local economic sectors and a range of services was created to support the management of cargo, which covers the whole value chain of logistics and maritime transport, such as financing, insurance, arbitration, brokerage, shipbuilding and maintenance. Singapore's ports have become an organizer of global logistics networks.

To become an efficient global transportation hub, Singapore needed to create facilities to receive and maneuver products. So, it created the Port of Singapore Authority and Changi Airport.

Port of Singapore Authority

When the British controlled Singapore, they made it the crossing point for all ships travelling to East Asia. By the time the British decided to leave Singapore, there was a mature industry related to entrepot activities, such as maintenance and logistics and some associated small manufacturing. The Singapore government built on that base and started to develop the port to become one of the busiest ports worldwide. The Port of Singapore Authority (PSA) was created in 1964 to control all activities relating to the port area. This included not only the movement of ships, but extended to the creation of industries in the port area, such as logistics, maintenance, insurance and finance.

The government of Singapore in its forward-thinking, tasked the PSA with planning and executing building facilities ahead of demand. New berths were always rolled out just before the demand, so it was never caught short. As noted on their website, in 2020 the PSA operated 58 berths with a capacity of 36.6 million twenty-foot equivalent units (TEUs) per year, regardless of the effects of COVID-19 on the global economy and the transportation of goods. The PSA established different locations for container terminals such as Keppel, Brani, Tanjong Pagar, and Pasir Panjang.

According to the PSA's annual reports, more than 50% of the world's crude oil supply and one-fifth of containers shipped worldwide pass through its facilities. Singapore was ranked the second-busiest port in total tonnage shipping in 2018.

Over the years, the PSA has established good relations and an excellent network of more than 200 shipping lines connecting with 600 ports around the globe. The logistics and maritime industry contributes about 8% to Singapore's GDP and employs about 90,000 people.

Changi Airport

In its pursuit to become the hub for transportation and sea and air logistics, a new airport was built in Changi and opened in 1981 to become the heart of the air transport hub in Singapore. Since then, the airport has been expanded and redeveloped many times to cope with the demand. The budget terminal was opened in 2006 and Terminal 3 was opened in 2008, as well as business parks surrounding the airport, such as Airport Logistics Park and Changi Business Park.

Changi Airport is one of the busiest airports in the world. In 2019, an estimated 68.3 million passengers passed through the terminals which serviced 100 airlines connecting to more than 320 cities in 80 countries. In addition, 2019 saw some 2.01 million tons handled as airfreight in the airport.

The infrastructure development for Changi Airport and the facilities around it is an example of how Singapore could plan ahead and take advantage of the regional boom in tourism, aviation and logistics. The Airport Logistics Park was opened in 2003 for air cargo and trade.

What is the role of infrastructure in creating a knowledge-based economy?

After the economic crisis in Singapore during the mid-1980s, the Economic Strategies Committee in 1986 recommended that the economy should be transformed into a knowledge-based economy. However, the nation's infrastructure was not adequate to make the leap to a knowledge-based economy at the time. To bridge this gap, the government introduced plans to establish advanced technology systems to tap and utilize the latest developments and discoveries in technology and advanced industries. In 1981, Singapore established the National Computer Board (NCB) to encourage computer education and to support the different industries with suitable employees. In 1991, the NCB launched its 'IT2000' plan to transfer Singapore's ICT sector into the twenty-first century and connect the different industries to the world, and keep business in Singapore ahead of the game compared to other countries. In support of this plan, an infrastructure plan called 'Singapore One' was developed to provide high-speed telecommunications to connect computers and information gadgets across the nation.

The infrastructure was not only the ICT and it also embraced other infrastructure including the National Science and Technology Board (NSTB), which was established to encourage R&D and was to become the Agency for Science, Technology and Research (A*STAR) in 1991. A*STAR established nineteen research institutes and centers to support and coordinate R&D activities in Singapore with many entities in this field, both foreign and local.

Development of industrial zones

Industrial zones have played a major role in the economic advancement of Singapore, where they are used to create the infrastructure to encourage investors to start their businesses. The major local player in this field is the Jurong Estates, which includes many industrial zones covering many industries.

In 1968, the Jurong Town Corporation (JTC) was established to create appropriate infrastructure to attract foreign investors to the new nation. The JTC provided the infrastructure to investors, including the choice between ready to use factories or land with the necessary infrastructure for investors to build their own facilities. The JTC created zones for new economic sectors and industries such as transport, engineering, precision engineering, chemical engineering, biomedical technology, electronics, and information and communication.

The JTC manages 43 zones with 3.2 million square meters of built space accommodating 5,100 tenants. Some of the industrial zones are the Chemical Hub, Research and Development Park, Singapore Science Park, Tuas Biomedical Park, and One North, along with business and industrial parks such as the Airport Logistics Park, International and Changi Business Parks, and Seletar Aerospace Park. These zones were designed as urban centers to provide all the facilities required by the people including recreational parks, shopping centers, schools, restaurants, etc. The JTC also manage the Jurong Industrial Port, which provides a service to tenants in JTC zones to export and import their equipment and products.

One of the recent mega-infrastructure projects for JTC is the merging of seven islands to form a petrochemical hub with first-class infrastructure and facilities. The idea is to cluster the value chain of the petrochemical products into one area. The hub is hosting plants from large, international players in petrochemical, such as ExxonMobil, Infineum, Afton Chemical, Huntsman, and many others.

Was tourism part of the infrastructure plan?

The tourism industry is an example of the Singapore government's creation and development of the economic sector. Unlike other Asian nations, Singapore did not have historic or natural sites to attract tourists. The government decided to take the opportunity to tap the growing tourism market and create and develop an industry out of it.

The Singapore Tourism Board (STB) decided to take advantage of the middle-class growth in Asia, especially in China and Indonesia. As many of these tourists did not speak English, Singapore facilitated tourist attractions in the nation with multi-language sign systems, building different tourist attractions to cover the multiple tastes of tourists, such as resorts, shopping areas and theme parks. Table 6.1 shows the increasing numbers of international tourists to Singapore as a result of the expenditure on construction in the tourism industry.

To attract tourists, Singapore created resorts that integrated many activities and can be used for business, entertainment and leisure. An example is the development of Sentosa Island, which has parks, lagoons, museums, beaches, gardens, trails, and golf courses.

Table 6.1 Number of international visitors 2000–2019

Year	Number of international visitors (million)
2019	19.11
2015	15.23
2010	11.6
2005	8.9
2000	7.0

sources: Singapore Tourism Board annual reports

How does the infrastructure factor impact diversification?

Table 6.2. Impact of infrastructure strategies/policies on diversification

Strategies/ policies	Outcome	Impact on economic diversification
Creation of Urban Redevelopment Authority	• Efficient use of the nation's limited land size	• Prepares infrastructure to serve existing and new sectors • Accommodates the requirements of new economic sectors
Creation of Port of Singapore Authority	• Manages and develops the transportation industry	• Creates transport connections to facilitate export of different economic sectors • Facilitates different industries to become part of the global supply chain • Supports creating industries and services related to transportation within close proximity to ports
Creation of Jurong Town Corporation	• Creates infrastructure attraction to investors	• Creates many industries • Creates clusters for different industries
Creation of Industrial Zones	• Different zones for different industries • R&D capabilities	• Imports technology • Creates genuine technology • Markets products to global customers • Creates partnerships between local and international companies

Strategies/ policies	Outcome	Impact on economic diversification
Creation of National Computer Board	• IT2000 plan to spread IT infrastructure to all countries to have interconnecting computers everywhere (home or office) • Transforms Singapore into intelligent island	• Connects different industries to the world and facilitates transactions • Facilitates access to foreign markets • Enhances business productivity • Develops export-oriented IT industry
Creation of Singapore Tourism Board	• Invests in tourism infrastructure • Creates tourist attractions	• Creates tourism industry • Supports enhancement of other industries such as food and beverages

Has Abu Dhabi been successful in creating a sound infrastructure?

Over the course of five decades, Abu Dhabi has developed from having no roads, no infrastructure, and few buildings, to one of the most modern cities in the world. Through the establishment of infrastructure, Abu Dhabi has transformed itself into a first-class city of the region. The diversification and development of the economy rely on the extent of appropriate infrastructure. The Abu Dhabi Economic Vision 2030 highlighted the importance of this factor. The establishment of infrastructure such as transportation, energy systems, industrial zones and ICT are important for economic diversification as they collectively enhance the efficiency of production and the supply chain and facilitate their expansion to wider markets.

To achieve the Abu Dhabi Economic Vision 2030, the government of Abu Dhabi highlighted large-scale infrastructure projects to invest in, such as Khalifa Port as part of the Khalifa Industrial Zone Abu Dhabi (KIZAD), and Masdar City and Industrial Cities of

Abu Dhabi (ICAD). In addition, as a result of the growing demand for electricity, the government is creating alternative energy sources in renewable and nuclear energies. For renewable energy, Abu Dhabi is developing the Shams solar power plant near Madinat Zayed. Abu Dhabi is building four nuclear power plants at a cost of US$20 billion. These will supply about one-quarter of the energy needs of the entire UAE.

In its efforts to diversify the economy away from oil, and to support the different economic sectors and industries, Abu Dhabi's government invested in mega-infrastructure and constructions projects. For example, to support service sectors, it built the Louvre Museum on Saadiyat Island for tourism purposes, and the Cleveland Clinic on Al Maryah Island for the healthcare sector. As for manufacturing, it established Strata Manufacturing as an aerospace manufacturing facility, and many other investments in aluminum, steel, copper and petrochemicals.

Transportation in Abu Dhabi: from no roads to highways, jets, and railways

Transportation forms a fundamental feature of infrastructure for both social and economic development and diversification, and Abu Dhabi has developed many projects to facilitate transportation and connect different parts of the emirate with the world. These include roads, airports, ports, and railways.

Abu Dhabi's extensive road network connects the different regions in Abu Dhabi with the rest of the UAE. The road network also links the UAE with neighboring Oman and Saudi Arabia, further facilitating trade and enhancing economic activities.

Aviation is one of the major drivers of non-oil economic growth in Abu Dhabi, and there are two international airports located in Abu Dhabi and Al Ain. Abu Dhabi is home to Etihad Airways, one of the leading and fastest-growing international airlines. In an effort to enhance its position as a services destination, Abu Dhabi is modifying its airport with new terminals to boost capacity to 40 million passengers annually when complete. In addition, a special zone for aviation economic activities has been created next to Al Ain International Airport called Nebras, which will host aviation service providers such as Horizon (a training institute for pilots and other aviation professions), as well as manufacturers such as Strata Manufacturing.

The Abu Dhabi Ports Company (ADPC) manages all the ports in the emirate including Musafah Port, Zayed and Khalifa ports. ADPC established a strong well-equipped port to support the diversification of Vision 2030. Khalifa Port is the largest port and the ADPC centerpiece, being directly linked to the KIZAD industrial zone. This facilitates both the movement of raw materials and finished goods. Through phased development, the port is designed to reach a total capacity of 15 million TEU and 35 million tons of general cargo upon completion.

The Etihad Rail project is set to bring rail transport to the entire country and connect it to the wider GCC through Saudi Arabia and Oman. Etihad Rail will cover a network of approximately 1,200 km of track and is expected to cost US$11 billion to construct. Phase 1 of the project will be in the western region of Abu Dhabi, connecting Shah field with the industrial port of Ruwais. Phase 2 will extend the network throughout the rest of the emirate and create links to the rail networks of Saudi Arabia and Oman as part of the GCC network. Phase 3 of the project will extend the railway to the northern emirates.

Information and communication technology

Abu Dhabi has invested significantly in ICT systems to provide services to citizens and businesses and has established itself as one of the leaders in advanced ICT infrastructure. All government authorities have transferred to e-government to provide improved services. Abu Dhabi created sufficient ICT infrastructure to attract high-tech companies and 85% of the people in Abu Dhabi have access to at least one type of connection. In the Network Readiness Index issued by the World Economic Forum (WEF) 2020, the UAE ranked 30th and first in the region.

The ICT infrastructure is so good that it allowed much employment and education to be performed remotely during the restrictions and lockdowns of the COVID-19 pandemic. Government and companies found it easy to perform office jobs remotely, and the Ministry of Education allowed remote teaching from schools with only minor changes.

But has Abu Dhabi created the infrastructure for economic diversification?

Similarly to all nations, Abu Dhabi wants to attract foreign direct investment. For that, the government created specialized zones to host such investments. Abu Dhabi created ZonesCorp to manage most of these zones.

ZonesCorp

In its efforts to support the diversification of the economy and boost industrial sectors, the government of Abu Dhabi established specialized zones with the aim of attracting local, regional, and global investors.

The Higher Corporation for Specialized Economic Zones (ZonesCorp) was created in 2004 to build infrastructure for manufacturing in the emirate, and to create and manage industrial zones. ZonesCorp is responsible for enabling different economic sectors to grow and expand, and for developing new industries. For that, ZonesCorp created and manages the Industrial City of Abu Dhabi (ICAD) – the total area of the combined ICAD 1, ICAD 2 and ICAD 3 will be 60 sq. km when completed. The three ICADs are fitted with different requirement facilities, such as shopping centers, medical centers, banks and recreational facilities. These areas are supposed to host many industries such as equipment suppliers, plastic and chemical producers, oil and gas facilities, and construction materials.

Khalifa Industrial Zone Abu Dhabi

One of the major infrastructure programs that the government is developing to boost economic development and diversification and realize Vision 2030 is Khalifa Industrial Zone Abu Dhabi (KIZAD). Abu Dhabi Ports opened KIZAD in 2010 next to Khalifa port and it will be connected to the railway, which will give it the advantage of being part of the logistic services across whole of UAE and GCC region.

KIZAD is using a cluster model to attract investors and is targeting many industries such as engineered metal products, aluminum, pharmaceuticals, packaging, food processing, automotive spare parts and logistics.

How is Abu Dhabi planning to boost tourism?

The government of Abu Dhabi is taking deliberate action to create assets and high-quality attractions to draw tourists and develop the tourism industry in the emirate. The Tourism Development and Investment Company (TDIC) was established to develop and manage most of these assets. As the leading developer for the major tourism projects, TDIC cooperates with the private sector to encourage involvement to a larger extent.

One of the major tourism projects in Abu Dhabi is the development of Saadiyat Island as a cultural attraction for regional and international tourists. It will host museums, such as Shaikh Zayed National Museum, a modern art museum, a Biennale Park, and a performing arts center. Saadiyat also hosts two international museums, the Guggenheim Abu Dhabi and the Louvre Abu Dhabi, which opened in November 2017.

Was Abu Dhabi successful in its strategy to diversify the economy through infrastructure?

Similar to Singapore, Abu Dhabi built infrastructure to support the development of existing sectors and the creation of new sectors. As with the Jurong Town Corporation in Singapore, ZonesCorp and KIZAD were established to attract investors and create manufacturing capabilities in the emirate. However, in contrast to JTC, they do not have the mandate to create R&D facilities or support R&D with investors, and they do not facilitate new technology, innovation and entrepreneurship, or the transfer of technology to local partners.

There has been a large investment in Abu Dhabi's infrastructure over the past five decades, which has transformed the emirate into one of the most advanced GCC states. However, it is noted that some of the infrastructure projects were not planned properly and have cost more than was anticipated, as indicated in a 2015 dissertation by Ghias Rehman titled *Cause of Delay in Construction Projects in Abu Dhabi*. Singapore, on the other hand, planned and managed its infrastructure project efficiently. Following the analysis of this factor, a comparison between the two states can be presented as follows:

- Both states used SOEs to manage many of their projects and assets, but in Singapore, they were more efficient because the SOEs were managed as a profitable entity and on a commercial basis, unlike those in Abu Dhabi.
- In the 1990s, Abu Dhabi privatized utilities and infrastructure into SOEs to achieve more efficiency and productivity. The idea was for these entities to act as efficiently as the private sector in the West, with greater efficacy and less cost. Unfortunately, the Abu Dhabi SOEs did not meet the expectations and retained the bad habits of government entities. In addition, since the SOEs were connected to the government, they were given the role of developing infrastructure in different fields, such as utilities, construction, tourism, manufacturing, etc.
- Abu Dhabi and Singapore created entities responsible for urban development: the Department of Urban Planning and Municipalities (DPM) in Abu Dhabi and the Urban Redevelopment Authority in Singapore. The URA plans the use of Singapore's limited size efficiently to serve the diversification efforts of the nation, whereas in Abu Dhabi, the DPM created a great urban plan "Abu Dhabi 2030" to "transform Abu Dhabi for the next generation". This plan was never executed because it was not realistic and too costly.

- Singapore used a system of systems (SoS) approach to manage its infrastructure projects to serve existing requirements and be able to adapt to future requirements without wasting a lot of money and time. On the other hand, in Abu Dhabi, there is not much flexibility and projects cost more than planned because of the continuous changes. There is a need in Abu Dhabi to create a gateway approval process for planning and executing the projects to ensure their success with minimal cost.
- Singapore created different kinds of industrial zones to serve different purposes, such as the Export Processing Zones (EPZ), industrial clustering, and R&D parks. All of these serve the diversification efforts through importing and coordinating technology for local companies to benefit. In Abu Dhabi, all the zones are working as real estate, renting out land without creating the environment for transferring the technology to local companies.

Essentially, Abu Dhabi needs to have a master infrastructure plan that is executable and connected with the economic targets of diversification. It needs to monitor the execution of the infrastructure projects very closely to manage the costs, schedules and outcomes. Also, it should be flexible to incorporate changes needed for new trends. Financial support for SOEs should not be based on the quality and efficiency of the infrastructure projects, but on the outcomes delivered. SOEs need to be commercially viable and able to survive in a competitive market without constant protection.

GCC infrastructure

The GCC countries have been implementing policies and activities to support economic diversification for many years. One of the focus points has been investing in infrastructure. The GCC countries already invest massively in infrastructure, viewing it from a policy perspective as an important precondition for economic development and diversification. According to the WEF infrastructure ranking for 2019, the GCC states rank highly. The UAE, for example, ranks 12th and Qatar is 24th; the lowest of the GCC states is Kuwait, ranking 66th out of 141 nations.

Over the past few decades, the GCC countries have transformed from desert habitats into twenty-first-century states. The investment in infrastructure has been massive and has covered all areas – from stowage, electricity, water, and ICT, to hospital, high-rise construction, transportation, and so forth.

One of the areas that the GCC countries invest heavily to support economic development and diversification is transportation and logistics infrastructure. The GCC railway network is currently under construction and will be completed in the next few years. The railway network, which will be approximately 2,000 kilometers long, will offer passenger and freight services. The railway will run from Kuwait, through Saudi Arabia, the UAE, and Oman, with branches linking Qatar and Bahrain.

Overall, the transport systems are well developed in the GCC countries, with good road networks and modern facilities for air, sea, and land transport. The GCC states coordinate infrastructure development in some areas where it is needed, such as power and railway.

Commercial ports and business hubs have been developed in different GCC states to handle and store tens of millions of containers annually, such as Jabel Ali in Dubai, Khalifa Port in Abu

Dhabi, Salalah Port in Oman, and Hamad Port in Qatar. Billions of US dollars have been spent on these ports to enhance the trade and transport services to support the economic visions.

The air transport industry in the GCC grew rapidly during the past two decades. Airline companies in the GCC, such as Emirates, Qatar, and Etihad Airways, have become major players worldwide, capturing a large share of the global air market between the Western and Eastern hemispheres. These airlines connect the gulf region to the rest of the world directly without going through Europe.

Industrial and business clusters are other areas that the GCC countries are invested in to establish infrastructure as these support the diversification of the economy and its focus on attracting domestic, regional and international investors. Despite the availability of physical infrastructure, as shown in Lara Lynn Golden's 2008 study "200 Industrial Clusters in GCC", the industrial clusters in the GCC face a set of difficulties such as unskilled workers, an absence of suitable financing mechanisms, poor connectivity between different stakeholders, and the absence of institutional frameworks for these kinds of projects.

The tourism sector has a large share of the infrastructure projects, with huge projects in tourism being initiated, such as Ferrari World in Abu Dhabi, Formula One (in Abu Dhabi and Bahrain), Atlantis, Burj Khalifa and many other projects in Dubai, the World Cup 2022 in Qatar, and many mega-projects in the GCC and Saudi Arabia, especially since Prince Mohammad bin Salman became Crown Prince. The GCC countries host millions of tourists every year and the number of visitors is increasing. International tourism rose from 8.6 million visitors in 1995 to about 43.8 million in 2019.

The GCC governments have spent heavily on infrastructure to boost the diversification and development of the economy as well as for social purposes. The dilemma facing the GCC states is that the cost of infrastructure projects is usually very high and improper handling, inefficiency and corruption, further increases the cost. According to a 2012 report by the Qatar Financial Centre Authority (QFCA), the size of infrastructure development activities could create efficiencies that save about 15–20% of costs, which could be worth billions of dollars since the planned investment in infrastructure is approximately US$2 trillion. The impact of the current inefficiency is so significant that it has to be tackled or eliminated.

To reduce the pressure on the budgets and to reduce costs, a public–private partnership (PPP) method should be considered to execute infrastructure projects, but without involving the SOEs, which have issues with their governance and efficiency, and to avoid a conflict of interest in competing with the private sector.

David Dombkins, in his 2018 paper "Sharakah: Shaping the Future of Public–Private Partnerships", stated "Many countries seeking economic growth are looking to Public–Private Partnerships (PPP) to fund and finance infrastructure projects. Three key issues have however limited the ability of countries to use PPP: lack of PPP readiness; lack of capacity/willingness in the community to pay user charges; and impact of government borrowing on credit rating. The outcome has been that many developing countries are not able to take advantage of PPP".

The GCC states recognize the significance of PPPs to reach their goals of developing infrastructure and, in the meantime, reducing costs, enhancing efficiencies, and encouraging private sector involvement in infrastructure projects. Over the past decade, the Saudi and Qatari governments have considered establishing a PPP Centre of Excellence in conjunction with the United Nations PPP Centre of Excellence in Geneva. However, they have decided not to pursue PPP centers. It is only with the drop in oil prices and loss of discretionary spending for infrastructure that GCC countries are starting to use PPPs.

Like the rest of the world, GCC governments are under financial pressure because of the COVID-19 effects (recession, stimulus packages, drop in trade, health spending, etc.) and the drop in oil prices. This means many of the infrastructure projects will need funding from entities other than the governments, which means the private sector will be invited to participate in PPP projects. The PPP concept will play a critical role in the economy post-COVID-19.

In the past, some of the GCC governments have applied PPPs without having laws or regulatory frameworks in place, but because they find PPPs useful to support megaprojects, they have developed regulations to support these types of projects. Kuwait and Dubai were ahead of the others to issue PPP laws in 2008 and 2015, respectively. In the last two years Abu Dhabi, Oman, Qatar, and Saudi Arabia have issued PPP laws. Before issuing the law, Qatar applied PPPs to projects in support of the World Cup 2022 and Qatar 2030 Vision.

The major challenges are the low level of PPP readiness and the resultant high risk of doing business in GCC countries. The United Nations Economic Commission for Europe's (UNECE) International PPP Centre of Excellence in Geneva uses PPP readiness to assess the level of capability required within a country for PPPs to be effective. The GCC states have a very low level of PPP readiness in all areas except finance[15]. As a consequence, equity investors, financiers, contractors, and operators are generally unwilling to participate in PPP projects in the GCC. For PPPs to be effective, the GCC countries will need to fast-track the development of core PPP readiness areas and develop a local version of PPPs that the international community is willing to trust and invest in.

---

15   Dombkins, D. (2018), *Sharakah: Shaping the Future of Public–Private Partnerships. UAE Public Policy Forum*. Dubai: Mohammed Bin Rashid School of Government.

Conclusion

Infrastructure is key to economic development and diversification as well as raising the quality of life for the population. Efficient infrastructure will enhance productivity and reduce the cost of operations and thus enhance the competitiveness of the nation. For many countries that succeeded in developing their economy, one of the major factors is the competency of their infrastructure. China and Southeast Asia are very good examples.

It is significant for national development to invest wisely in the infrastructure and to keep upgrading it. When planning for infrastructure, this should occur in consideration of economic and social trends, both locally and globally.

Abu Dhabi and the GCC states have some of the most advanced infrastructures in the world. From roads to airports to telecommunications, the GCC states are home to world-class facilities that can support economic growth and enable the development and diversification of the economy. But Abu Dhabi and the GCC governments need to develop plans and processes for using their infrastructure to diversify the economy and create indigenous technologies through R&D and spillover technology from partnering with international companies.

The revenues from oil and gas safeguard the GCC governments when facing financial issues, but as a result of COVID-19 costs and pressure on their budgets, GCC states need to use the PPP model to execute many infrastructure projects. While these are estimated to be around US$2 trillion, the states need to find the right framework to achieve a successful outcome.

The infrastructure factor has had a major impact on Singapore's economic diversification and development. Infrastructure played a vital role in Singapore's development and an even stronger role in its economic diversification. Infrastructure was used as a way to attract foreign companies to invest in certain sectors and provided incentives to local companies to expand into different sectors. The government established technology parks, cluster zones and technology institutes covering different economic sectors to ensure the development and growth of these sectors, which resulted directly in diversifying the economy. The government established education and training facilities to provide well educated and skilled workers for different industries.

The infrastructure factor has had a significant impact on the economic diversification and development of Abu Dhabi. The emirate's infrastructure is capable of supporting the efforts to grow and diversify the economy. The existing projects and future projects for infrastructure all support the development of Abu Dhabi, socially and economically. For example, Saadiyat and Yas Islands were developed as tourist attractions, and the huge investment in infrastructure at Khalifa Port will make it one of the main logistic centers globally.

The infrastructure factor has had a significant impact on economic diversification and development in the GCC countries. Most GCC countries have used funds from oil exports to develop a very advanced infrastructure that supports diversification strategies.

CHAPTER 7

Export Orientation

How can export enhance economic growth and diversification?

"Achievements in successful export industries, which need highly skilled people, can create an area as flourishing as South Korea and Singapore. Germany and South Korea were able to lower unemployment through success in export industries."

— STEF WERTHEIMER, ISRAELI INDUSTRIALIST (1926–PRESENT)

*I*n the late 1970s and 1980s, many developing nations shifted from import-substituting strategies to export-oriented strategies, most notably in East Asia. The main goals were to have bigger markets for products, to raise the quality of manufacturing capabilities, to attract international companies already active in the global market, and to create more employment opportunities for citizens.

The export-oriented strategy started in the 1950s with Japan and Germany who had just come out of the war with strong industrial bases, and the need to develop their economies. During the late 1970s and early 1980s, East Asian countries (namely Taiwan, South

Korea and Hong Kong) used Japan as a model to follow and shifted from import substitution to export orientation. Mexico took advantage of the considerable wage difference with the United States to attract American companies to produce goods and export them back to the United States.

The export-oriented strategy was not only for the less populated nations with small domestic markets. The most successful nation in this strategy was the most populated, China. In 2009, China became the largest exporter in the world. The nation differed from other emerging economies with large domestic markets (such as India, Indonesia and Brazil), which had implemented import-substitution strategies to protect and support their local industries.

Export-led or export-oriented strategy is an economic strategy used by some nations to enhance their economic capabilities, open foreign markets for their products, increase their manufacturing base and create more jobs for their people. This strategy concentrates on foreign markets to capture the economic and technological benefits, and to gain exposure to best practices in operations and quality control, as well as exposure to competition.

The aim of the export-oriented strategy is to inspire manufacturing and economic growth by developing and enhancing certain sectors for export. It has been suggested that to develop and support specific niches for export, governments should develop incentives such as protection within domestic markets and supporting sales to the international markets. Export-oriented policies should include different incentive schemes to support selling products abroad. These policies should manage the allocation of resources to enhance the comparative advantage, improve technology, and enhance efficiency and economies of scale.

Export-oriented strategies aim to increase manufacturing and the export of products from different sectors, thus pushing the diversification process of a nation, enhancing economic development and growth. Export-oriented manufacturing has been successfully adopted by East Asian countries to develop their national economies and catch up with the West.

Is export orientation appropriate as a development strategy?

Export-led growth is a strategy to encourage and support the production of exports. The justification is that trade is the main activity for an economy to advance, so a nation needs to produce goods for other countries to acquire. To have the advantage, a nation needs to be more efficient in using its resources and capabilities and be competitive in the global market.

Early analysis of the connection between economic growth and export-led policies was undertaken by Balassa (1978) in his study "Exports and Economic Growth". He analyzed the results of applying industrial policies in eleven nations from 1960 to 1973 and found a strong correlation between export growth and GDP, where a 1% increase in export raised GDP by 0.8–0.9%. Balassa anticipated that export-orientation policies positively affect export growth, which accounted for a 37% increase of GDP in South Korea and a 25% increase of GDP in Singapore.

Feder (1983) analyzed the effect of concentrating on export sectors on the growth of GDP in his study "On Exports and Economic Growth". His research focused on the effect of moving capital and labor from a low-productivity sector (not for export) to a high-productivity sector (for export). Feder found that productivity increases because of the growth of exports, which accounts for a 2.2% increase in GDP in semi-industrialized countries.

In his article "Openness and Growth", Baldwin (2004) points out that economic openness and export orientation has a more positive effect on economic growth than an "inward-looking economic approach". In addition, he highlights other important elements for an export-orientation strategy to be successful, such as the need for practical monetary and fiscal policies and corruption-free government.

Export orientation leads to export diversification by increasing the number of export sectors. Export diversification contributes to the development of the economy in three ways. Firstly, by creating new products or modifying existing products, which enhances productivity through knowledge adaptation. Secondly, by enhancing the output of different industries by creating a supply chain to ensure competitive products for export. Thirdly, diversifying exports decreases the volatility of export revenues, which supports the growth of the economy.

The increase in high-tech exports positively affects economic growth. Exports from the high-tech sector have a more significant effect on economic growth than other sectors. For developing countries, exports with advanced technology are important for long-term economic growth.

The East Asian nations achieved high economic growth and national development through export-orientation strategies. These strategies led to economic diversification as well, since the goal was to develop different products in different sectors. Another advantage of export orientation is exposure to the latest technologies and supporting the innovation capabilities in the country, since there is a need for better quality and efficiency. Since countries need to finance social and economic development, revenues can be improved by enhancing exports through increasing production and economies of scale. Also, countries with natural resources generate revenues by exporting resources (e.g., oil, diamond, gold, copper, etc.) to finance social and economic strategies.

The positive impact of export orientation can be seen in the comparison between the economic progress of East Asia (export-led strategies) over Latin America (import-substitute strategies). East Asian countries switched from an import-substitute to an export-led approach for the economy to produce and compete globally, which led to economic development and diversification, alongside substantial national development. The Latin American countries stayed with an import-substitute approach to protect local industries. Although this approach did not fulfil the goals of economic development or the protection of local industries, governments still could not break out totally from the import-substitute strategy and protectionism mentality.

The experience of East Asia with an export-led strategy and its role in the development of the region provided a convincing argument for the benefits of using such an economic approach. Over the past few decades in East Asia, export-led strategies have produced high economic growth rates, diversified the economy, reduced poverty, increased employment, developed the manufacturing capabilities, attracted FDI for technology and capital, increased revenues through export, and improved the wealth of the people and stability of the individual nations.

Some highlights of the importance and effectiveness of the export-led strategy include:

- the enhancement of competitive economies-of-scale production;
- an increase in government revenue;
- improvements in employment rates;
- competitive advantages that power economic development if production is directed into the international markets;
- enhanced importation achieved through material imports for manufacturing (in this regard, it is important to emphasize the

openness to importation because global competition requires cheaper and higher quality inputs, which if not extant in the local market should then be imported);

- benefits from technology transfer and efficient operational and managerial systems;
- attracting FDI, which brings new technologies since international companies keep investing in new technologies, and;
- the chance of survival for companies to mitigate declining domestic demand.

Export-led strategy success depends on the access to outside markets, so there is a need for free trade agreements as the basis of international or regional frameworks and bilateral agreements.

How export orientation leads to the diversification of the economy

There are two main reasons for an export-led approach. Firstly, it provides revenue from exports, supporting countries in balancing their financial accounts. Secondly, export growth can lead to the creation of new products and new economic sectors that enhance diversification and stabilize the economy.

An export-led approach can contribute to the diversification of the economy and the effects of the strategy can be seen in various ways. The following points are examples of how an export-led approach can support the diversification of the economy:

1. An export-led approach incentivizes manufacturing in sectors that could not operationalize to the necessary economies of scale when the market was only domestic. Only through interaction with foreign consumers would a domestic manufacturer know

the existence of foreign demand on their existing products or new products. Through exporting, foreign customers become knowledgeable of the products and manufacturing capabilities, which can trigger greater foreign demand for different products.

2. Export orientation opens the door for new ideas and inspires entrepreneurs to tackle opportunities. Introducing new products and new production systems increases the possibility of new sectors developing as human capital is exposed to new industries and technologies, through which new ideas and opportunities arise.

3. Diversification exists because of the ability to develop, produce and expand the range of goods. The knowledge gained from export orientation provides opportunities to create new products and services or develop the existing ones.

In summary, the export-orientation strategy plays a major role in diversifying the economy for many reasons: it provides revenues and funding for other activities; it enhances the technical capability of the nation; it provides a larger market for local products, which supports the economies of scale for local firms and provides the opportunity for local businesses to diversify their range of products; it exposes local companies to international competition, which assists in enhancing the quality and efficiency of the local firms, and; it generates knowledge and technology spillover that assists in pursuing new industries.

South Korea: a nation transformed by applying an export-led strategy

The economic history of South Korea shows strong economic growth since the 1960s. From the early days, the government understood the importance of exporting for the economy and provided different incentives to support the practice. The results of the government's export-orientation strategy can be seen clearly in the value of exports, which rose from US$87 million in 1963 to be US$17.5 billion in 1980, and then to US$363.5 billion in 2009. In 2020, exports had reached US$601.6 billion, as reported in the World Bank data.

The South Korean government established entities to support and promote export. The government introduced financial incentives as well as tax relief. The export policies provided different subsidies including taxes and credit. South Korea had a mixed system with an export approach and import-substitute policies. It developed low trade barriers to protect certain industries and products, and high incentives for local manufacturing to export.

To be successful in its export-led policies, and to integrate into the global economy, the South Korean government ensured discipline within all elements of the economy, such as capital and labor. There was a consensus between big business and the government that determined the investment environment. The export-oriented strategy, which started in the 1960s under the military regime, was a form of controlled integration into the global economy, and the government understood the importance of being part of the global economy.

The success of the South Korean economy comes not only from the export policies, but many other policies such as those involving competition, labor, trade, and the industrial and financial markets. The result of the government's intervention in the economy and creating a favorable environment for economic development was evident in 2019, with South Korea being the fourth-largest economy in Asia and tenth-largest in the world, as cited by the World Bank.

South Korea adopted an export-oriented economic strategy in the 1960s to develop and grow its economy, and by 2019 was the sixth-largest exporter and ninth-largest importer worldwide. The diversification of exports since the 1960s is shown in Table 7.1.

Table 7.1. Diversification of South Korean industries for export

	1960s	1970s	1980s	Since 1990
Industries	Cement, textiles, electrical machinery, small appliances industry, automotive parts	Steel, shipbuilding, machinery, electronics, non-steel metal, petroleum, chemicals heavy industries	Semiconductors, automotive (full supply chain), metalworking, small-sized aircrafts	IT industry, biotechnology, environmental technology cultural technology, nano-technology, space technology

source: Hong (2010)[16]

Singapore export orientation

As with many newly independent states, Singapore adopted an import-substitution approach to support industrialization. The merger with Malaysia was expected to serve this approach by creating a bigger market. The change from import-substitute to export-led approach occurred after independence from Malaysia in 1965. The aim of both approaches was to solve the unemployment issue. In order to tackle this issue, the government had to build strategies and

---

16 Hong, Y. S. (2010) *Private-Public Alliances for Export Development: The Korean Case*. (CE-PAL, serie Comercio internacional No 102), Santiago: United Nation Publications.

plans to diversify the economy away from its reliance on entrepot economic activities. In 1961, the government of Singapore assessed the entrepot trade and came to the conclusion that it had very limited possibilities for expansion and needed to create more jobs. Since then, the government has built its strategies to diversify the economy.

Singapore has faced challenges in pursuing the diversification of its economy away from re-exports only to manufacturing and an export economy. There were four main issues that hindered the diversification approach.

- First, most of the businesses in Singapore were related to entrepot services and not manufacturing.
- Second, there was a severe lack of private sector and industrial entrepreneurship.
- Third, Singapore did not have the financial funds to support its strategies and the domestic savings were very low.
- Fourth, the regional markets more than likely would be closed to Singapore's products because many countries had recently achieved independence from colonialism and sought to protect their industries by imposing trade barriers.

These factors meant that Singapore had to be creative in establishing new industries, generating the funds, and looking beyond the regional market.

Establishing manufacturing for export was not an easy task for the government of Singapore. The private sector was concentrating on trade and services and there were no incentives for local investors to establish factories. The local investors were hesitant and did not have the experience to embark on industrial investment and support economic growth. Therefore, the government decided to use foreign investors to support its strategies of development and diversification of the economy through an export-led approach.

The Economic Development Board was established to attract foreign companies to establish their manufacturing in Singapore and export to the international market. Singapore created export-based industries using foreign capital to finance them.

The foreign firms brought manufacturing processes and capabilities to Singapore along with the technology, finance, and essentially the market for their products. To attract international investors, the government provided financial incentives such as tax breaks, a skilled workforce, infrastructure, and an attractive lifestyle for foreigners.

One of the steps for attracting foreign investment was establishing the Export Processing Zones as a duty-free zone for products destined for export. In 1976, export incentives were introduced, where the exporter could get up to 90% tax exemption for five fifteen-year terms. The EPZ covered different industries such as energy, food processing, textiles, chemicals, timbers, metals, mechanics, auto industries, and electronics components.

As a result of the government's efforts, and according to World Bank data, exports increased from US$1.15 billion in 1965 to about US$600 billion by 2020. In 1960, manufacturing generated 7.2% of GDP and by 2020 it had reached 47% of GDP. Manufactured exports, as a percentage of merchandise exports, accounted for only 24.3% in 1960, reaching a high of 85.6% in 2000 and dropping to 78% by 2020. Singapore's export manufacturing includes many products such as textiles, electronic goods, refined petroleum and semiconductors. Table 7.2 shows the growth in merchandise exports since adopting the export-led strategy, which resulted in creating new industries and enhancing others.

Over the past five decades, there has been growth and decline among different sectors due to the export orientation. From 1965 to 1985, the manufacturing sector grew to reach its peak in 1980, contributing 36% of GDP and the services declined to 58% in the same year. However, after the government's strategic economic review of

1985, one of the recommendations was to support export services. The service sector started to pick up, and by 2020 its contribution to GDP had increased to 71%, while the contribution of manufacturing had decreased to 21.5%.

Table 7.2. Singapore's growth in merchandise exports since adapting to export orientation.

Year	Merchandise export (Current) S$ billion	Manufacturing as % of Merchandise export
1965	0.981	30.3
1970	1.55	27.53
1975	5.38	41.52
1980	19.38	46.70
1985	22.81	51.21
1990	52.73	71.57
1995	118.27	83.91
2000	137.80	85.64
2005	229.65	81.14
2010	351.87	73.13
2015	351.5	68
2020	362.5	78

source: UNCTAD and SingStat

Re-export

The British established Singapore as a hub for exchanging materials and products between Southeast Asia and Europe. In 1960, re-export formed the main economic sector, accounting for 94% of total exports and generating one and a half times the GDP (see Table 7.3). Singapore's decision in 1965 to emphasize export-led industrial development and the growing success of the strategy over time, resulted in a significant change in the structure of the economy.

As shown in Table 7.3, the proportion of re-exports decreased to about 50% of total exports in 1990, decreasing further to 40% by 2010. Though the value of re-exports has ballooned over the five decades from US$1.08 billion in 1960 to US$176.9 billion in 2010, the share of re-exports among the total export (40%) in 2010 was a marked decrease from 94% in 1960. The country has advanced from a re-export economy to a diversified economy with more services and manufacturing sectors, as shown in Table 7.3.

Table 7.3. Singapore export indicators

Singapore	1960	1970	1980	1990	2000	2010	2020
Gross Domestic Product (billion US$)	0.704	1.92	11.86	36.1	95.9	217.2	337.9
Export (billion US$)	1.15	2.42	24.0	64.0	184.5	442.2	599.2
Re-export (billion US$)	1.08	2.2	13.9	32.5	88.0	176.9	208.6
Re-export (% of total export)	94	91	58	50	47	40	35
Export (% of GDP)	162.9	126.1	202.6	177.4	192.3	203.6	176
Manufacturing value (billion US$)		0.38	3.14	8.64	24	44.32	72.6
Manufacturing (% of GDP)		19.6	27.46	25.1	23.24	21.63	21.5
Manufacturing % of merchandise export	24.3	27.5	46.7	71.6	85.6	73.1	78
Service value (billion US$)	0.378	1.08	7.1	23.3	58.4	148.5	240
Service (% of GDP)	53.7	56.3	59.8	64.5	61.2	68.4	71
Service (% of total export)	33.9	44.6	56.2	48.1	32.9	24.7	31.3

sources: World Bank and UNCTAD

How did Singapore's government support export orientation?

Over the past six decades, and since adopting the export-oriented approach, the government of Singapore has controlled all elements of the economy such as the workforce, policies, incentives, SOEs, and SMEs. To enforce its directions and reach its strategic goals, the government created many statutory boards, the main one being the Economic Development Board, which led to the economic diversification and development of Singapore.

The EDB was established in 1961 to create the economic environment and attract international companies to set up their factories in Singapore to export to the international market. The EDB was the main player in successfully switching from an import-substitute to an export-oriented strategy. The EDB was not the only entity working to advance the economy, it was part of a whole government system for economic development. The EDB was tasked to consolidate the efforts of the different entities in Singapore in order to support economic development. The EDB was involved in many activities such as education and training, policy formation, taxation, and infrastructure.

Manufacturing for export was the backbone of the economic diversification and development of Singapore. In the 1970s, the government pushed for industrial advancement based on middle-level technology and low-cost labor that could be exported. In order to encourage exports, the government liberalized trade and opened the market by removing tariffs on exports and imports. The government eliminated tariffs on imports to lower the cost of production, so that the products could compete globally.

In the 1980s, Singapore faced competition from low-skill manufacturing in other Asian countries (mainly China and Vietnam). In response, the government took the initiative to move to higher-skilled industries and attract international companies in sectors such as computers and electronics. In addition, Singapore used regional cooperation to support its industry by using cheaper products from neighboring countries. Regionalization was used to relocate low-skilled and labor-intensive processes to other Asian countries.

To support the export and diversification of the economy, Singapore enhanced external ties by joining the WTO and signing many free trade agreements (FTA) besides the regional co-opera-tion. Singapore has around thirty FTAs with countries including Australia, Japan, China, New Zealand, Korea, Peru, and the United States, in addition to FTAs with regional economic blocks such as European Free Trade Association and Gulf Cooperation Council.

International Enterprise Singapore (IE Singapore) was estab-lished in 2002 to support trade and the local companies to expand globally. Its role was to motivate local companies to invest abroad to penetrate closed markets. Singaporean companies invested in many countries such as Vietnam, Cambodia, and China. Mexico was also targeted because of its proximity to the United States, as well as Eastern Europe.

Export and economic diversification

Trade has been Singapore's lifeblood since its founding in the nine-teenth century. Singapore is one of the few countries where total international trade (exports plus imports) is greater than the total GDP of the nation. According to the World Development Indicators (WDI), in 2020 international trade for Singapore was 3.24 times the GDP. In Singapore, trade and manufacturing are tied to each other and enhance each other. Most of the production is for export. The international firms in Singapore are not only manufacturing companies but also MNCs that have established technical support facilities as well as several thousand international firms in services, finance, and trading. The government supported the international-ization of the economy and external trade to support the diversifi-cation and development of the economy and to protect it from the trade fluctuations of different economic sectors.

Singapore has grown significantly and diversified the range of products for exports to reach 4,257 products in 2019 as cited in the WDI. In the 1960s, exported manufactured products were few, such as wigs and toys, as well as some food processing goods (corn oil and soy sauce). In the 1970s, machinery and transportation equipment were added, as well as integrated circuits, data processing, telecom-munications equipment, radio receivers, and plastics.

In the 1980s, the oil sector grew to almost 50% of exports. Still, some low value-added products, such as food, beverages, furniture, and garments, remained. Electronics grew to reach about 30% of exports, with production concentrated on consumer electronics. Disk drives were the largest non-oil item exported in the 1980s from Singapore.

In the 1990s, the share of electronics in exports increased with the growth in the production of personal computers and disk drives. Because of growing competition among Asian countries over low-skilled manufacturing, from the late 1990s Singapore started to move to high value-added production. Plants for semiconductors were opened and efforts were started to establish biomedical and petrochemical sectors.

How did export orientation impact economic diversification and development?

All the economic activities in Singapore were feeding into export. The attraction for the MNCs was to build manufacturing in Singapore and sell globally. Creating clusters was designed to facilitate economies of scale and be cheap to sell abroad.

Table 7.4. Impact of export strategies/policies on diversification

Strategies/ activities	Outcome	Impact on economic diversification
Export-led approach	• Local manufacturing for global market • Produces competitive products globally • Increases the technology level of the manufacturing	• Creates new industries to serve global market • Joins the supply chain of industries worldwide
Creation of EDB	• Attracts FDI • Forces the creation of incentives for foreign investors	• Use foreign investors to develop different economic sectors • Facilitates the cooperation between foreign and local companies to create new business • Supports technology transfer
Creating Export Processing Zones (EPZ)	• Hosts the production of international companies • Creates specialized zones	• Imports manufacturing technology • Creates clusters for different industries
GLCs (SOEs)	• Creates strong companies that can manufacture competitive products • Creates cooperation with international companies for transfer of technology	• Paves the way for newcomers to the emerging sectors • Imports new manufacturing technologies in different economic sectors

Export orientation in Abu Dhabi

Vision 2030 views exports as a major goal in the growth of targeted industries. In the Strategic Plan 2011–15 issued by the Department of Economic Development (DED), the focus was to develop the export capacity of Abu Dhabi's industrial sectors, mainly for aluminum and steel, refining and downstream petrochemicals, aerospace, defense, food and beverages, and clean-energy technologies.

There is an understanding in the Abu Dhabi government that exporting is essential for economic diversification and development. Foreign markets are very important since the local market has small demands, and companies cannot produce efficiently for only the local market. Many of the government investments in manufacturing are directed for export, such as petrochemical and aluminum. As stated in Vision 2030, industries targeted under the plan are notably capital-intensive and export-oriented sectors, where the emirate can gain a competitive advantage.

Abu Dhabi's economy is dominated by hydrocarbons generating activities. Oil and gas remain the main player in the emirate's economic development. However, economic diversification away from oil and gas has been the main desire for years. Expanding the industrial base is a cornerstone of this process. The government has created a number of anchor industries and expects the private sector to take a bigger role in the downstream opportunities that have resulted from the heavy industry. The economic strategic plan issued by the DED in 2010 encourages and supports the private sector to be more involved in export activities.

Abu Dhabi's initiatives to support export

In its *Abu Dhabi Competitiveness Report* (2013), the DED supports local exports through three activities: support for companies to build their capabilities in skilled workers, information and communications; developing exports through increasing value-added features and the creation of quality employment, and empowering companies to explore new markets.

The Industrial Development Bureau was created to support and facilitate export-oriented industries. Its role is to minimize and eliminate obstacles facing exports and to encourage the private sector to enter new markets. This is intended to help diversification as it will boost industrial activities and create products that can compete in the international market.

Export manufacturing

Abu Dhabi is aiming to take advantage of its large natural resources, which provide a good level of feedstock supply for petrochemicals manufacturing, and establish a petrochemicals and plastics manufacturing sector, which accounts for about 50% of the manufacturing production. According to the SCAD, in 2018 petrochemical production reached 6.8m tons. The value of the exported portion was 6.5m tons, and these products include urea fertilizer, polyethylene, ammonia, and polypropylene. The petrochemical industry is becoming a strong player in Abu Dhabi's manufacturing sector, however, the government needs to take a long-term strategic view of making this sector competitive globally without the subsidy of raw material or energy.

Another important manufacturing area for export is basic metal, which in 2017 accounted for 11% of production among the manufacturing industries, 0.9% of the GDP, and 47.6% of total non-oil exports. Aluminum became a valuable product for export, increasing significantly from 1.9% of total exports in 2013 to 12.2% in 2017.

Non-oil exports in Abu Dhabi

Annual reports published by the Abu Dhabi Statistics Center (SCAD) indicate that non-oil exports grew in value from AED 919 million in 2001 to AED 11.61 billion in 2010, and to AED 64.4 billion in 2018. Re-exports also increased in value from AED 900 million in 2001 to 11 billion in 2010. In 2018, re-exports had risen to AED 48.1 billion and accounted for about 14.5% of total exports. The range of export products has broadened from being only those related to petrochemicals to include transport equipment, machinery, food and chemicals. Re-export activities in the UAE doubled over a decade, contributing to the UAE's reputation as the region's leader in re-export activities, and as the third-largest re-exporter in the world sitting just behind Hong Kong and Singapore. From Table 7.5 it is observable that jewelry forms the main re-export product followed by plastics, cars, phones, food, and fiberglass. The rapid growth of the non-oil exports and re-exports has been facilitated by the FTZ, which provides administrative and logistical advantages for companies. The growth in exports has also been supported by the enhancement of seaport and airport infrastructure and services.

Table 7.5. Abu Dhabi's non-oil export by sector 1995–2015 (AED million)

Item	1995	2000	2005	2010	2015
Live animals and products thereof	2	3	49	112	805
Vegetable products	9	14	34	60	68
Animal or vegetable fats, oils and waxes	1	52	126	154	166
Foodstuffs, beverages, spirits and tobacco	95	97	48	181	588
Mineral products	35	44	68	36	189
Products of the chemical or allied industries	19	21	142	509	425
Plastics, rubber and articles thereof	23	79	1,875	2,148	6,042
Articles of leather and animal gut; travel goods	3	1	9	1	3
Pulp of wood, waste, scrap and articles of paper	6	12	115	184	320
Textiles and textile articles	10	16	39	70	252
Articles of stone, mica; ceramic products and glass	2	6	76	399	304
Base metals and articles of base metals	50	165	229	1,414	7,193
Machinery, sound recorders, reproducers and parts	27	276	261	553	644
Vehicles of transport	51	172	40	5,699	641
Photographic, medical, musical instruments and parts	0	1	11	8	6
Works of art, collector pieces and antiques			0.3	2	8
Articles of wood, cork; basket ware and wickerwork			40	11	13
Pearls, stones, precious metals and articles thereof			4	12	13,080
Footwear, umbrella, articles of feather and hair			0.4	9	-
Miscellaneous manufactured articles	0	2	21	10	53

source: SCAD annual reports

The World Trade Organization ranked the UAE as the nineteenth-largest exporter of merchandise in 2016. According to the WTO, the UAE exported US$266 billion (AED 980 billion) of merchandise in 2016 or around 1.67% of global exports. According to SCAD reports, Abu Dhabi counted for about 20% of UAE exports with a value of AED 192 billion. In 2013, when the oil price was high, the UAE contributed 2% to global exports, with a value of US$379 billion (AED 1,395 billion), while Abu Dhabi was 37.5% with a value of AED 523 billion.

By reviewing the SCAD annual reports, the export value of goods from Abu Dhabi dropped by about 50% between 2013 and 2016 when the oil price fell, which shows the significant contribution of oil and gas to the emirate's export range. On the other hand, non-oil exports and re-exports grew regardless of changes in the oil price, which reinforces the efforts undertaken in these areas.

Comparison between Abu Dhabi and Singapore on using export orientation for economic diversification and development

The way Singapore and Abu Dhabi view this factor creates differences in how each plan and execute economic diversification and development. For Singapore, export orientation is the driver for economic development and diversification, and all the regulations and policies serve this approach. Abu Dhabi, on the other hand, views export orientation as one of the initiatives to support economic development and diversification but not the main driver. So, from the previous analysis of this factor, the differences between Singapore and Abu Dhabi are as follows:

- Abu Dhabi has taken some action to support exports, for example, by not applying export taxes or tariffs. The government established free-trade zones to encourage export. The FTZs allow the production of goods and provide services, and permit 100% foreign ownership of the firms. Additionally, firms in the FTZs can import goods with a duty-free tax or no tax. Singapore not only created these incentives but also clusters to reduce the cost of production and create local suppliers.
- Singapore attracted and encouraged MNCs to establish manufacturing facilities to export to international markets, whereas Abu Dhabi does not take this approach.
- Singapore forced its GLCs (Government-Linked Companies) to operate on a commercial basis to compete and sell products globally. GLCs worked as the first entrant to new industries and sometimes as a vessel to receive new technologies. In Abu Dhabi, SOEs are concentrated only on the domestic market and do not pursue foreign markets, except for some of those in the GCC arena.

Abu Dhabi's non-oil exports are increasing, which is a positive sign for the economy. However, part of the product still relates to petroleum, such as base metals, plastics and chemicals. Abu Dhabi needs to enhance its services export sector, which at the present, is very small.

The DED should be the agency made responsible to support, encourage and provide incentives for local companies to export their products. The role of incentives is important, especially with the introduction of taxes on companies, and can be used to incentivize by exempting companies from taxes if a certain level of exports is reached or by refunding customs payment for the materials used in the production of export items. A variety of ways exist to incentivize companies to export, however, these need to be carefully structured so that companies cannot manipulate the system and fall within the WTO limits for incentives that countries can provide.

Since many SOEs work in manufacturing, exports need to be in their mandate. Unsurprisingly, these enterprises like to work within their comfort zone and unless they are forced to export they will not willingly embrace an export-oriented mindset. The performance measurement for SOEs needs to include the level of exports achieved.

Singapore used the export-orientation strategy to enhance its manufacturing capabilities and the quality of production. It also attracted international companies to support certain new economic sectors over time. In all activities, the spillover of technology was a cornerstone in its strategy to create technological capabilities in local companies, which they used later to support the strategy for innovation.

By contrast, Abu Dhabi's export growth is irregular, with no strategic implementation plan on how to support the economy through these activities. There are no steps to enhance the manufacturing capabilities locally and there is no plan to attract high-tech companies and connect them with local companies to enhance the capability of the local firms.

Export orientation in the GCC

Export orientation is significant to economic diversification and development as it improves the quality and competitiveness of products, provides income, and provides local employment. Exports require using economies of scale and facilitating the transfer of technology. The GCC states enforce increasing non-oil exports to ensure the protection of the economies from fluctuating oil prices. According to the WTO, in 2013 the trade value for GCC exceeded US$1 trillion, which is about 5.7% of world exports. When the oil price dropped in 2016, the trade value dropped to reach US$625 billion. It should be noted that most exports are oil-related exports or re-exports.

The trade surpluses that the GCC states have enjoyed are from the export of oil and gas. It should be noted that the major non-oil export products are petroleum-based, such as petrochemicals, or energy-intensive products.

Some GCC countries began developing enablers to support export-oriented sectors. These enablers include renewable energy and solar power for metals. The GCC countries have also led the establishment of new sectors in high-tech manufacturing in the fields of biotechnology and pharmaceuticals. In addition, the services sectors have contributed through tourism, trade, transport and logistics. Government support is essential to develop and sustain these sectors, however, there are serious concerns about the level of competitiveness of manufacturing in the GCC arena, especially when government support exists.

International Monetary Fund (IMF) reports shows that non-oil exports have improved in the GCC countries. Between 2000 and 2017 the percentage of non-oil exports (goods and services) increased from 13% to 32% of the non-oil GDP, respectively. In the same period, non-oil products for exports increased from 8% to 24% of non-oil GDP, which explains the increase in the total non-oil exports of goods for the period.

According to the IMF reports, and with the exception of the UAE and Oman, the overall diversification in GCC exports has not shown any significant improvement since 1990. Diversification in products for export has shown a marked level of improvement only in the UAE and Oman, and has been very limited in other GCC states.

From the analysis of horizontal diversification and comparing the UAE to other resource-rich countries, it does not appear that achieving an increase in horizontal diversification by itself has increased GDP greater than what was achieved by other resource-rich countries that have not increased their horizontal diversification. An explanation of why this has occurred is that the UAE has subsidized the establishment and development of export industries and that these exports possibly are not profitable.

One of the expectations was that exports would lead to improved quality. However, the continuous export of manufactured goods to global markets did not improve quality. In the GCC states, the quality of exports had not improved significantly since 2000 and remains low compared to other regions. This is a result of inefficiencies among the entities producing these goods since there is no system or agency to monitor the quality and efficiency of production, and since there is guaranteed government support regardless of the outcome.

The GCC governments need to create export-orientation policies and development strategies to support this approach. The GCC states should create incentives and motivation to inspire and encourage firms to develop products that can compete in the global market. In addition, the GCC states should create an innovation and entrepreneur ecosystem across all Arab countries to benefit from the many talents that exist locally. Also, they need to create incentives to attract and retain international talent.

Conclusion

A small nation in the current global environment most probably would not be able to build its economic strategy if it is not based on export orientation. If small nations want to catch up and advance, they need to integrate with international players and attract international capital and technology. Small nations need to have a comprehensible and long-term, export-oriented strategy. Small nations should not use an import substitute approach because they do not have an adequate market size, and as economic history has shown, only nations who adopt an export-oriented strategy can move up the advancement ladder.

There are many factors that have contributed to the success of an export-led strategy. It needs a long-term industrial policy that is comprehensive and connected with the controlled liberalization of the domestic market, government intervention, human development, innovation, technology transfer and its competent absorption, and capable of attracting international firms.

For an export-orientation approach to succeed, a competing product has to be manufactured by efficient firms that ensure quality products that are within the reach of customers. That case will not happen without a baseline of technical and manufacturing capabilities that can be established in cooperation with international firms and institutes. Also needed is a good legal framework to protect the rights of all stakeholders without prejudice and create the right environment for innovation and entrepreneurship.

This leads us to the next factor in the wheel of economic diversification and development: innovation. This forms the spine of sustainability. Innovation is what keeps the nation advancing and at the top of the ladder. The United States did not feel threatened by China until 2019 when China became the biggest source of applications for international patents in the world, pushing the United States out of the top spot held since the global system was set up more than 40 years ago.

The next chapter will discuss innovation, how governments can use it to support economic diversification and development, how Singapore built its capability in this field, and how it manages its innovation activities.

The export orientation factor has had a major impact on Singapore's economic diversification and development. Export orientation drove Singapore into its economic diversification and development. This factor was the reason for Singapore being what it is today. Because of this factor, Singapore's products have become competitive globally.

The export orientation factor has had a minor impact on Abu Dhabi's economic diversification and development. While Abu Dhabi is trying to have an open trade regime, some limitations and conditions still exist, such as the foreign investment ownership maximum of 49% and the need to have local agents to conduct business. Abu Dhabi needs to establish a system of incentives to encourage companies to produce locally and export. Within the UAE, Abu Dhabi has enhanced market access to its products through regional and bilateral trade agreements, but needs to encourage local manufacturing.

The export orientation factor has had a minor impact on the economic diversification and development among GCC countries. While many GCC countries export oil they have failed to establish manufacturing sectors that can compete on the international market and that contribute to GDP growth. The GCC countries are not fully exploiting their export potential to enhance the competitiveness of local products and support economic diversification.

CHAPTER 8

Innovation

The bloodline for advancement and civilization

*"The calculus of innovation is really quite simple:
Knowledge drives innovation, innovation drives productivity,
productivity drives economic growth"*

— WILLIAM BRODY, US ACADEMIC ADMINISTRATOR
(1944–PRESENT)

There is stiff competition between the United States and China in advanced technology and innovation. The US Senate approved US$120 billion over five years for activities at the National Science Foundation to research and development priorities in key areas like artificial intelligence and quantum science. China, on the other hand, surpassed the US as the biggest IP producer spending US$378 billion in 2020, which accounted for 2.4% of the national GDP.

Innovation is very important for the development of the economy. There is a general belief that where innovation exists, the creation of new products and services exist. In fact, technological advancement is a driver for economic development. So, if the aim of the government is to focus on technology development, it means the government wants to enhance its manufacturing and production capabilities.

Innovation is a strong factor in economic development and diversification efforts. It opens new opportunities for the economy to expand into new economic sectors and creates new products for manufacturing and services. All the developed nations support innovation and investment in R&D activities because it is vital to their advancement and competition in the global market.

But what is innovation? Many definitions exist for the term and these definitions are related to the aims of the research in which they appear. But put simply, innovation is the ability to translate an idea into a product (goods or services) that creates value. For an idea to become innovative, it must be reproduced and economically viable and must satisfy certain demands. Innovation is the intentional implementation of imagination and information to create or enhance value from initial resources.

Innovation is a new idea that leads to a more effective process or device. It is the application of new solutions that meet the requirements of the market. This can be accomplished through products, processes, or services. Innovation is something more effective and newer, which breaks into the market or society. Innovation is the result of a process that enables ideas to have an impact on society.

One of the main requirements for economic diversification is innovation because it can create new products and industries. Innovation is the ability to create change which leads to new performance, especially in the national economy. This means the ability to absorb, apply and use innovation effectively in the industrial sectors to enhance competitiveness and create added value.

Innovation in Singapore

Innovation is not only about technology or technical progress but is a driver for economic diversification and growth. Innovation is influenced by a wide range of drivers from policies, infrastructure, human development and natural resources. Knowledge capital is similar to other capital (human, infrastructure, and funds), and to be effective it needs to be managed smartly. Innovation systems and industrial policies create knowledge and provide the means to use it. Innovation contributes to the diversification and development of an economy by creating new economic sectors and new businesses.

The Global Startup Ecosystem Report 2018 listed Singapore as one of the world's ecosystems to watch for artificial intelligence (AI), blockchain, advanced manufacturing and robotics, and health and life sciences, as well as for its renowned fintech sector.

In the 1960s and 1970s, Singapore's economic strategy focused on applying foreign technology through manufacturing by international investors. This strategy did not support technology transfer to local firms and did not plan for innovation and creation activities.

The government of Singapore did not view innovation as a driver of the economy until after the Economic Strategic Committee review in the mid-1980s. As a result of the recession in 1985, the committee set new directions for Singapore's economy. It recommended moving away from low-tech manufacturing to high-tech clusters and services. So, Singapore started to work on the advancement of technology manufacturing and attracting new high technology industries.

Singapore evaluated its capabilities and assessed whether it could support the potential innovation system. The result was that a pool of talent should be created alongside the infrastructure and labs. However, creating talent was not an easy task, so the decision was made to attract international talent to support the innovation efforts and train local talent.

In the 1990s, the aim of the government was to develop Singapore as an innovation hub. The government took action to enhance the innovation system by, for example, creating different research institutes for different technologies and sectors (IT, microelectronics, and biosciences). It also created different funding schemes to serve different levels of innovation. These actions encouraged international technology firms to move R&D activities to the country. The National Science and Technology Board, later known as A*STAR, was established in 1991. It developed the first National Technology Plan for five years (1991–1995).

The strong commitment from the state for innovation and R&D was the driver of the success of the innovation strategies and the development of an innovation ecosystem in Singapore. This includes research institutes, universities, funding entities, incubators and industries.

National Technology Plans

In 1991, A*STAR developed the National Technology Plan (1991–1995). In this plan, S$2 billion was dedicated to establishing and developing technological capabilities, including research institutes, technology parks and workforce development, and to supporting private-sector R&D through funding and secondment of scientists and engineers from national research institutes.

A*STAR has implemented seven plans, each one covering a period of five years. These plans were implemented to position Singapore as an innovation-driven, knowledge-based economy. Each one of these plans had short-term objectives and targets to achieve, however, the main and long-term objectives of the plans can be grouped into five streams:

- Fund R&D activities and promote industry-driven R&D;
- Provide grants and financial incentives to encourage R&D by private firms;
- Support attracting, recruiting and developing an R&D workforce (including scientists, engineers, researchers, and technicians);
- Establish research institutes and fund associated activities, and;
- Assist in the industrialization and commercialization of R&D outcomes.

Table 8.1 shows the accomplishment of the technology plans (1991–2020). From this, it can be seen that the expenditure of the private sector grew from S$881 million in 1995 to almost S$5.8 billion in 2020. The expenditure of the private sector is 63% of the total expenditure on R&D, more than the government's expenditure. The number of researchers increased from 8,340 in 1995 to 52,989 in 2020.

Table 8.1. National Technology Plan accomplishments

	1st Plan	2nd Plan	3rd Plan	4th Plan	5th Plan	6th Plan
Period of Plan	1991–1995	1996–2000	2001–2005	2006–2010	2011–2015	2016–2020
Budget (S$ billion)	2	4	7	13.5	16	19
Achievements						
R&D intensity (% of GDP)	1.15	1.89	2.4	2.05	2.4	2.0
Government expenditure (S$ million)	485.2	1,143.5	1,550.9	2,541.4	3,710.8	3,399.4
Private sector expenditure (S$ million)	881.4	1,866.1	3,031.3	3,947.6	5,824.6	5,882.4
Private sector share of R&D (% total expenditure)	64.5	63	66	61	61.1	63.4
Researchers	8,340	14,483	21,338	28,296	43,178	52,989
PhD researchers	1,887	3,111	4,575	7,477	10,300	

sources: A*STAR reports and SingStat

The S$25 billion Research, Innovation and Enterprise 2025 Plan (RIE2025) was launched in December 2020. Of the budget, 29% or S$7.3 billion will go towards strengthening Singapore's core capabilities in universities and research institutes. RIE2025 will be organized across four domains:

1. Manufacturing, trade and connectivity (MTC)
2. Human health and potential (HHP)
3. Urban solutions and sustainability (USS)
4. Smart Nation and digital economy (SNDE)

Science and technology governance

The Ministry of Trade and Industry supervises Science and Technology (S&T) activities, and A*STAR coordinates these activities through four bodies. Those bodies support and manage the public and private sector research including basic and applied R&D.

- The Biomedical Research Council (BMRC): oversees seven research institutes, which focus on biomedical science, pharmaceuticals and other human life sciences.
- The Science & Engineering Research Council (SERC): oversees public research in the physical sciences and engineering and has seven research institutes.
- The A*STAR Graduate Academy (A*GA): administers science scholarships and fellowships and coordinates collaborative programmes with universities.
- Enterprise Division: manages the commercialization of intellectual property created by research institutes in Singapore and facilitates technology transfer to industry.

Singapore recognized the need for connection between its innovation efforts and industries to raise the country's technology level and to have successful R&D activities. In 1991, the first National Technology Plan laid the foundations to establish science and engineering research institutes. The main purpose of the institutes was to serve the manufacturing industries, such as engineering, electronics, chemicals, and biotechnology. In 2006, the Research, Innovation and Enterprise Council (RIEC) was created to strategize and coordinate innovation activities. The RIEC included local and international members and was chaired by the Prime Minister.

In 2010, Singapore formed an Economic Strategic Committee (ESC) to review the economic strategies after the global financial crisis and to set future strategies. The ESC recommended many things, some of which included the commercialization of R&D outcomes; strengthening the business aspects of innovation, and; creating platforms to enable integration of the capabilities of the R&D entities.

Singapore recognized that the capacity and needs to conduct and encourage R&D varied between companies (MNCs, local, SMEs and startups). Singapore created partnership frameworks and innovation platforms customized to meet the different needs and conditions. For example, SMEs have limited or no resources for R&D and are interested in readily available products to generate revenues quickly – the institutional efforts should support them to obtain licenses of the required technology or enhance their capabilities and to be in the supply chain of high-tech international producers.

The A*STAR supports the transfer of technologies and expertise from its research institutes to local companies. For example, the Growing Enterprises through Technology Upgrade (GET-Up) seeks to stimulate technology transfer from public and international partners to the local private sector in order to promote the R&D capabilities of small firms, and to seconder scientists to these firms to enhance capacity.

Infrastructure for innovation

To organize and control the activities in innovation and to attract international technological companies, infrastructure first needed to be in place. The Singapore Science Park (SSP) was established in 1980 to attract international technology firms and create new industries close to research institutions. The SSP was an incubator for high-tech industries.

In 2001, to fulfill the strategy and support the establishment of new industries for the high-tech industries, One-North was established. The aim was to place Singapore as a regional and global R&D hub, and the initiative hosts research institutes, startups, and multinational companies. It creates the atmosphere of a research community, with schools, public transport, shopping malls and other facilities. One-North was established for scientists, researchers, and technopreneurs to learn, live and work together. It is a high-tech cluster for industries such as biomedicine, ICT and media.

Science and technology workforce

Singapore recognized that its shortage of scientists and engineers would harm its efforts to become a technological hub of R&D and to compete in the international market. Being a small country, the local pool of engineers and scientists was not sufficient. Therefore, the government had to create a system to attract foreign talent and use them to enhance the technological capabilities of the nation.

The National Technology Plans were aimed at improving R&D and transforming the national universities into advanced research institutes. The Academic Research Council was established in 2006 under the Ministry of Education to oversee the funding and workforce policies for the academic entities. To support the two national universities, the National University of Singapore (NUS) and the Nanyang Technological University (NTU), five Research Centers of Excellence (RCEs) were established to attract foreign talent, train local talent and be the host for new knowledge in its specific field. As a result, the position of Singapore's universities in the international ranking progressed significantly. In the Times Higher Education global university rankings for 2016, NUS and NTU were ranked 26th and 55th respectively, up from 34th and 174th only five years earlier.

Singapore is building its R&D capabilities using international scientific talent to develop capabilities and guide young local scientists. Approximately 30% of Singapore's research pool is foreign, which keeps it tapping into a strong global network full of ideas and expertise. Through this process, Singapore has created an internationally diverse innovation ecosystem.

To enhance R&D capabilities, Singapore created partnerships with international R&D institutes such as MIT (Massachusetts Institute of Technology), ETH Zurich, Peking University (China), and Cambridge University. These partnerships support in creating a pipeline of talent, ideas, and research capabilities to develop the R&D in Singapore.

As a result of the different initiatives to enlarge the pool of talent, as shown in Table 8.1, the number of researchers has increased from 8,340 in 1995 to 52,989 in 2019. The number of foreign researchers increased significantly from 2,837 in 2003 to 11,224 in 2015 as cited in the A*STAR 2015 report.

How did Singapore fund innovation activities?

Singapore encouraged R&D in both the private and public sectors. Its successful transformation to a knowledge-based economy can be attributed to the intense efforts by the public and private sectors in science and technology activities.

In all innovation plans since 1991, increasing the involvement and funding of the private sector to R&D was always one of the main objectives. As a result, and as presented in Table 8.1, private sector spending on R&D increased from S$881 million in 1995 to almost S$5.8 billion in 2019. In the same period, government spending also increased from S$485 million to more than S$3.4 billion.

Table 8.2, from the Singapore Department of Statistics (SingStat.), shows the entities and organizations performing innovation activities. The number of entities executing R&D grew from 454 in 1995 to 1,134 in 2019, and 1,052 of these are private entities.

Table 8.2. Organizations performing R&D in Singapore 1995–2019

Organizations	1995	2000	2005	2010	2015	2019
Private	427	513	765	799	808	1,052
Higher education	6	6	9	11	17	15
Government	16	24	25	29	31	40
Public research Institutions	5	15	12	22	24	27
Total	454	558	811	864	880	1,134

sources: A*STAR reports and SingStat

Bridging the technology gap by attracting international high-tech companies

From the early years, the government was attracting MNCs for not only employment and capital but also because the government believed that MNCs would bring technology that would spill over to local companies and the transfer of technology would take place.

A*STAR and the EDB, as the two main agencies involved in innovation and economy, were coordinating their activities to develop and enhance different industries. They united their efforts to attract foreign companies who were willing to create high-tech manufacturing and R&D. For example, they organized and supported applied materials, a global leader in semiconductor equipment manufacturing, to transfer their R&D operations to the country.

Another example of Singapore's efforts to attract foreign players in technology is the development of the aerospace cluster. The A*STAR

Aerospace Research Consortium was created as a partnership among many organizations, international leaders in aerospace industries (e.g., Airbus, Boeing, Pratt & Whitney, and Rolls-Royce), local companies, and A*STAR institutes. The consortium played a strong role in building the R&D expertise in the aerospace industry for Singapore, which gave them a competitive advantage over the aerospace hubs in Asia.

Singapore's approach to absorbing technology and benefitting from R&D has been achieved through creating bridging institutions. The role of the institutes was to facilitate and manage the knowledge spillover to local firms. Singapore tailored the innovation policy to attract international firms with advanced technology and was willing to establish manufacturing and R&D activities to facilitate the partnership with local companies.

How can good innovation outputs support economic diversification?

Efforts to support innovation and create an environment for R&D has had a significant impact on Singapore. The number of entities and organizations that are conducting R&D activities rose to 1,134 in 2019. The number of scientists and researchers grew from around 10,200 in 1995 to more than 52,000 in 2019. The number of patents owned in Singapore reached 9,865 by 2019.

The level of patenting activities increased significantly since the first innovation plan in 1991. These plans created talented people for R&D in different fields and it created an environment where such talent could blossom. As presented in Table 8.3, the number of patents owned rose from 256 in 1995 to 8,575 in 2015 and the number of patents applied for increased to 2,090 in 2015. The revenues from royalties and licensing increased from S$111.4 million in 1995 to S$322.6 million in 2015. The government created entities such as

ETPL to commercialize the IP and R&D outcomes. As a result, revenues from the commercialization of R&D reached S$15.6 billion in 2000 and S$23.2 billion in 2015, as shown in Table 8.3.

The private sector plays a major role in patents, filing 60% of all patents in 2015, which accounted for 70% of the awarded patents. As of 2015, the private sector owned 82% of Singapore's patents. Most of these come from sectors engaged in technology development such as biomedicine, chemicals and electronics[17].

Table 8.3. Patents and revenue 1995–2019

Patents and Revenue	1995	2000	2005	2010	2015	2019
Patents owned	256	1,268	3,475	5,450	8,575	9,865
Patents applied for	242	774	1,594	1,762	2,090	2,592
Patents awarded	51	239	877	653	988	1,476
Revenue from royalties & Licensing (S$ million)	111.4	74.63	93.7	32.2	322.6	
Revenue from commercialized R&D (S$ million)	Na	15,577.8	13,509	10,900.3	23,227	

source: A*STAR reports

Innovation became the driver of diversification and development for Singapore since the country decided to build a knowledge-based economy. The government set its policies and planned for human development and infrastructure, and facilitated the growth in innovation and R&D, creating and expanding industries to diversify the export products.

Innovation activities led to the creation of new sectors and clusters in the economy as shown in Table 8.4. The number of sectors increased between 2000 and 2014 and new economic sectors (underlined and bolded in Table 8.4) were created because of the innovation

---

17   ASTAR. (2015) National R&D Survey of Singapore 2015. Research and Statistics Unit.

efforts, where some sectors became pillars for manufacturing in Singapore, such as biomedicine, chemicals, and electronics.

Table 8.4. Industry/sectors of science and technology

2000	2019
1. Agricultural & Food Sciences	1. Agricultural & Food Sciences
2. Biomedical & Related Sciences	2. Biomedical Sciences
3. Biomedical Engineering	3. **Basic Medicine**
4. Aeronautical Engineering	4. **Biological Sciences**
5. Civil & Architecture Engineering	5. **Clinical Medicine**
6. Electrical & Electronics Engineering	6. **Health Sciences**
7. Marine Engineering	7. **Pharmaceutical Sciences & Manufacturing**
8. Material Sciences & Chemical Engineering	8. **Engineering & Technology**
9. Metallurgy & Metal Engineering	9. Aeronautical Engineering
10. Mechanical engineering	10. Biomedical Engineering
11. Chemical Sciences	11. Civil & Architecture Engineering
12. Computer & Related Sciences	12. **Computer Engineering**
13. Earth & Related Environmental Sciences	13. Electrical & Electronics Engineering
14. Physical Sciences	14. **InfoCommunication & Media Technology**
	15. Marine Engineering
	16. Material Sciences & Chemical Engineering
	17. Mechanical Engineering
	18. Metallurgy & Metal Engineering
	19. **Natural Sciences (excluding Biological Sciences)**
	20. Chemical Sciences
	21. Computer & Related Sciences
	22. Earth & Related Environmental Sciences
	23. Physical Sciences & Mathematics
	24. **Energy**
	25. **AI**
	26. **Cyber Security**

source: A*STAR

The impact of innovation on Singapore's economic diversification

Table 8.5. Impact of innovation strategies/policies on diversification

Strategies / policies	Outcome	Impact on economic diversification
Creation of A*STAR	• Manages and coordinates the R&D activities • Creates research institutes in different sectors • Develops technology plan every 5 years since 1991 • Creates and supports the funding schemes for R&D • Supports private firms with local talents from research institutes as a secondment	• Creates new technologies • Attracted MNCs to create R&D entities in the country • Encourages and supports spillover of technology to local firms • Creates new products • Creates new industries • Enhances the R&D capabilities of private firms
Developing National Technology Plans	• Set achievable targets for each plan • Encourages private firms R&D • Supports attracting, recruiting and developing R&D workforce • Encourages industrialization and commercialization of R&D products	• Produces new products for indoctrination • Local innovation of products • Produces bigger and better R&D workforce • Creates more private entities performing R&D • Creates new economic sectors
Attracting international high-tech entities	• Performs R&D activities in the country • Uses the local research institute • Uses local R&D workforce • Spillover of R&D activities to local firms	• Creates startups in different economic sectors • Creates new products through technology spillover. • Research institutes created their own R&D products • Many innovative ideas are translated into local profitable business

Innovation in Abu Dhabi

In Vision 2030, Abu Dhabi declares its aim to transform into a knowledge-based economy and to diversify the economy so that it is not dependent upon petroleum. Its intention is to proceed through investment in the people, and to develop new industries and an R&D base to enhance the technical capabilities for industries.

Even though Abu Dhabi has attracted substantial international investment and attracted skilled labor, the private sector still depends on government funds and support. Or it acts as an agent for international companies to provide products and services to consumers locally. There is no pressure or motivation on establishing indigenous high-tech products, which is reflected in the lack of innovation and R&D activities. The share of high-tech exports among Abu Dhabi's total exports is very limited.

Abu Dhabi's innovation status

The Abu Dhabi Innovation Index (2014) was prepared by INSEAD, the Department of Economic Development, and the Abu Dhabi Statistics Center. It provides an evaluation of Abu Dhabi's innovation capabilities and performance, and compares the results with 22 nations, which are natural resource-dependent economies. The report includes the results of an innovation survey of 532 firms in Abu Dhabi in the period 2008–2011. These firms operated in finance and insurance, ICT, transport, construction, manufacturing, and technical products. The main findings of the report are summarized below.

• Abu Dhabi and its firms are capable of implementing new technology, products, and services; yet, if the emirate is to build a significant high-tech economy, it must develop and grow its capabilities in innovation and R&D.

- Most of the innovation was in processes (59.4%) followed by products (38.5%).
- The expenditure of firms was concentrated on the acquisition of machinery, equipment, and software, which accounted for 39% of the associated R&D costs.
- Around 36% of innovating firms have cooperated with other parties on areas of innovation; the common partners are suppliers and government or public research institutes.
- Public sector (government entities) demand is the driver for innovation.
- Government procurement, oil and gas, construction and public services are the main sectors demanding innovation.
- The majority of innovations (64%) are in firms oriented towards business-to-business (B2B) transactions, while customer-oriented firms accounted for 36% of innovations.
- Cost is a significant barrier for innovation, with 60% of firms indicating that there were no funds allocated for innovation activities.
- The dominance of larger firms in some sectors did not make it easy for smaller enterprises to innovate.

How is innovation funded in Abu Dhabi?

The Abu Dhabi government sensed the importance of innovation as part of pursuing its diversification and development of the economy, and has created many programs and schemes to support the innovation efforts. Abu Dhabi manages the following programs and funds:

- The Ghadan 21 program – a three-year initiative with an AED 50 billion (US$13.6 billion) budget from the government to enhance the competitiveness of Abu Dhabi in driving economic development and innovation.
- The Abu Dhabi Investment Office (ADIO) – an AED 2 billion ventures fund to support new and innovative ideas in Abu Dhabi.
- The Khalifa Fund and it's 'Level Up' project – helps entrepreneurs, SMEs and startups to seize new opportunities that will stabilize, strengthen and up-scale their business.
- The Takamul Program – a support program to assist individuals, universities, and enterprises in the UAE to patent and commercialize their innovations. The Takamul IP Program provides support to file the patent internationally.

The UAE innovation strategy

Local firms in Abu Dhabi can benefit from the innovation support offered by the federal government of the UAE, since innovation is a high priority, with the declaration of the Innovation Strategy in 2015.

The UAE Innovation Strategy, which was launched in 2015, aimed to transform the UAE into an innovative nation by 2021 by focusing on seven sectors: space, health, renewable energy, education, transport, technology, and water. The plan was proposed to be executed in phases with the first phase to include thirty initiatives to be accomplished in three years. Included were incubators, private-sector incentives, enhanced specialized skills, international research partnerships, and legislation. As part of the strategy, all government entities were required to allocate 1% of their budgets to innovation and research. The National Innovation Committee

(NIC) was established in 2014 to monitor and manage the execution of the strategy.

Assessment of innovation in Abu Dhabi

The Abu Dhabi government is not spending a lot on R&D. Only 0.5% of the local GDP is allocated to R&D, as cited in the 2016 OECD report *GLCship, SMEs and Local Development in Abu Dhabi.* . This amount is very low compared to EU countries, the average of which is 2.0% of the GDP, and 2.4% of the Singapore GDP for 2015. Abu Dhabi should consider increasing its R&D spending given its aims to build a knowledge-based economy. Abu Dhabi's investments in R&D will create new technologies, products, and industries.

The majority of innovations in Abu Dhabi are based on technologies developed elsewhere, as noted in *The Abu Dhabi Innovation Index* published by the DED, INSEAD and SCAD in 2014. The majority of innovations are not developed locally but are imported readymade technologies, and all new businesses are either low or no tech. According to the 2013 report *Entrepreneurship: An Emirati Perspective*, Emirati entrepreneurs are not investing in high-tech industries because of the high risk and high cost of technological innovation.

The legal framework for protecting intellectual property has been established on the federal level. The UAE became a member in many conventions on intellectual property such as the Patent Cooperation Treaty (PCT), the Madrid Convention, the WTO, the World Intellectual Property Organization (WIPO), the Trade-Related Aspects of Intellectual Property Rights (TRIPS) and the Paris Convention. Patents are protected under the Federal Industrial Property Law. Similar legal protections are also established for copyright under Law No. 7 of 2002.

Abu Dhabi has a small number of citizens and similarly to Singapore, it needs to use foreign talent in the innovation system. However, it suffers from a deficiency of commitment and innovative performance by foreign workers. In the IMD World Talent Report (2020), the UAE ranked 3rd worldwide for the presence of "foreign high-skilled people". Yet, when it comes to "attracting and retaining talent", the UAE ranks 24th worldwide. Abu Dhabi has low retention levels for foreign workers, which is connected to the incentives and opportunities for immigrants.

Part of the problem relates to the professional progress or development path of workers (locals or ex-pats). Career progression incentives for scientists or engineers are not as promising as those for business management and finance specialists, and this drives many scientists and engineers into administrative studies and roles to progress their profession, instead of increasing a depth of knowledge in their scientific field.

The Abu Dhabi Innovation Index (2014) noted that Abu Dhabi is not competitive globally in the high-tech fields. Of note also was the absence of an important tool in the innovation ecosystem, venture capital. In addition, Abu Dhabi nationals are mostly in well-paid public jobs, which affects negatively the culture of R&D and innovation.

The Abu Dhabi government created the Takamul Technology Transfer Program for the commercialization of patents. In 2013, fifty-eight inventions were reviewed, one startup was supported, two licenses were negotiated, and ten detailed commercialization projects were completed.[18]

---

18 *The National Newspaper* (2016), "Scientific studies 'need more funding'". accessed September 26, 2016, https://www.thenational.ae/uae/education.

Building R&D capability

Innovation in Abu Dhabi is advancing rapidly with the government enhancing the policy framework and capabilities. However, it will take years for Abu Dhabi to build a strong innovation ecosystem that benefits from R&D output. For Abu Dhabi to benefit from R&D and innovative activities, it needs to find a system for the commercialization of new inventions.

Considerable advancement has been made to strengthen the R&D in Abu Dhabi including the establishment of centers of technologies such as Masdar, the Petroleum Institute and Khalifa University. However, until recently there was no entity responsible for strengthening the innovation ecosystem. An entity can set goals to create and attract talent, create and manage labs and coordinate between industries, academia, and government.

The Advanced Technology Research Council (ATRC) was established in 2020, and forms the overarching advanced technology research body in Abu Dhabi. The council is responsible for consolidating funds for efficient investment and driving policy and regulation to support innovation activities in Abu Dhabi. ATRC has two main pillars:

1. ASPIRE: a programme management body that works in consultation with cross-sector industry stakeholders, universities, and research institutes to frame problem statements.
2. Technology Innovation Institute (TII): an institute dedicated to "applied research" and new-age technology capabilities. TII has seven (initial) research centers in quantum science, autonomous robotics, cryptography, advanced materials, digital security, directed energy, and secure systems.

If Abu Dhabi is seeking to advance in innovation and research then it should enable ATRC to act in a similar manner to A*STAR in Singapore by monitoring the development of the ecosystem, creating talent, supporting local companies to acquire technologies, setting priorities and decisions, as well as administering research funding. Research funding needs to be targeted at commercially viable opportunities and wherever possible aim to promote collaboration between industry and academia and create incubator centers close to universities, while supporting private sectors to invest in and develop research ideas. The council should monitor and support research training, particularly PhDs, to increase the number of Emirati scientists and engineers with high-level research training. ATRC needs to apply international best-practice standards in its operations, from managing grants, creating cooperation between national and international entities, promoting research partnerships between industry and academia, and planning the pathway to commercializing the results of the R&D.

One of the main issues facing Abu Dhabi in enhancing R&D capability is creating a pool of scientists and engineers. Regardless of the commitment of the government to encourage STEM subjects, humanities and economics remain the preferred subjects for students in university, as cited in the PwC report[19]. Even the limited number of local engineers are not utilized properly. Many engineers stay home after finishing their university studies and are pushed to enroll in any job, irrespective of whether it relates to their engineering preference. This sees the loss of opportunities to groom good engineers and scientists.

---

19   PricewaterhouseCoopers (2016) *Understanding the GCC Education Sector – A Country by Country Guide – Country Profile: UAE*, accessed at https://www.pwc.com/m1/en/industries/education/education-country-profile-united-arab-emirates.html

In a study by Sanaa Ashoor (2019) "Quality higher education is the foundation of a knowledge society: where does the UAE stand?" where she conclude as a result of job requirements in the public sector, students in UAE pursue non-STEM degree paths (social sciences, business, humanities).

As the R&D talent is mainly international, foreign talent is attracted by the expectation of personal gain and where the research infrastructure exists to pursue scientific and research activities effectively. This provides an opportunity for Abu Dhabi since it can offer personal rewards, but it needs to strengthen the research infrastructure. Abu Dhabi needs to enhance its capabilities to attract international talent to conduct innovative activities in Abu Dhabi. The existence of high-level talent will support establishing a local knowledge base. And with their connections, the new talent will attract younger researchers and create a network to link research in Abu Dhabi to international research institutes. In time, this will position Abu Dhabi as a global forerunner in advanced R&D. Abu Dhabi needs to create an ecosystem for innovation with less bureaucracy and one that connects labs, academia, industries, scientists, and funds. The process must also keep supporting the products of innovation after their commercialization for export.

Innovation impact on economic diversification

Innovation performance is a function of the joint efforts of many players and the level of capabilities they acquire, through which they are able to interact with and support other players. The innovation system includes government, industry, funders, and education and research entities, among others. In conclusion, for Abu Dhabi to build an innovative knowledge-based economy, it should increase the capabilities and effectiveness in each one of these areas.

- *R&D funding and expenditure*: spending on R&D in Abu Dhabi is low and associated activities are restricted to large firms. Abu Dhabi does not invest much in R&D, and most of what is funded goes towards the modification of existing products, with very limited funding earmarked for R&D proof of concept research. Singapore, on the other hand, spends about 2.186% of the GDP on R&D, as cited in World Bank data for 2015.

- *Attracting talent*: there is a shortage of talented scientists and engineers who can perform R&D. Abu Dhabi can learn from Singapore and other countries that addresses those weaknesses by approaching foreign players, firms and individuals. Singapore created a system to attract international talent and companies and used them to enhance the technology base of the nation, retaining those players and keeping the technologies (as discussed above). Abu Dhabi needs to create processes and capabilities to attract individual talent and foreign technology firms to support and perform R&D, train locals, support commercialization of patents, and export the products.

- *Retaining talent*: Abu Dhabi should keep in mind that the market for R&D talent is global. As many countries are competing to attract the top scientists and researchers, high wages are not enough and there is a need for high-quality research facilities, and high-quality social and cultural amenities. In addition, the feeling of belonging to a place and the security of professional status are also factors that can influence the attraction of leading scientists. Changing the emigration regulations in the UAE is a step in the right direction.

- *A centralized entity responsible for innovation*: Abu Dhabi lacks a focused strategy on R&D and innovation, and the main reason is the absence of an organization responsible for managing, monitoring, and coordinating the activities in this regard. The ATRC was established in 2020 to play this role. Singapore established A*STAR to create and manage its innovation strategy. The creation of a government entity is an important step in developing and enhancing R&D capabilities in Abu Dhabi. Similar to A*STAR, the ATRC needs to create a science and technology strategy and manage it by coordinating the activities of the different players for the success of this strategy. It needs to create a system to attract foreign firms to perform R&D in Abu Dhabi, establish specialized R&D institutes, manage the funding support, create linkages between local and international technology companies, and create processes to benefit from the spillover technologies.

• *Grooming and supporting local scientists*: in Abu Dhabi, the local engineers and scientists generally do not sustain their career path to develop specialist capabilities as it is not financially and professionally rewarding. For example, engineers or scientists who have devoted considerable time to becoming specialized and expert in their field are paid less compared to administrators who have higher positions in organizations, even though they mostly are less qualified than the engineers or scientists. Unfortunately, this leads many engineers and scientists to take on an administration position, which is seen as the right step in their career and offers the rewards they deserve. To address this flow of engineers and scientists to other sectors, Abu Dhabi should create a pool of talented individuals and a career path for scientists and engineers to progress in their fields and be appropriately rewarded. The program also needs to attract local female talent living outside the city of Abu Dhabi, such as in Alin and Al Dhafra, and also local talent from other emirates in the UAE.

These actions need to be implemented to ensure Abu Dhabi develops a sustainable and world-class innovation and R&D system.

Innovation in GCC

The GCC countries are not lacking in national plans or the infrastructure required for innovation. Many institutes and laboratories have been created, for example, the King Abdullah University (Saudi Arabia) and Khalifa University KUSTAR (UAE). The purpose is to create an environment that encourages innovation and entrepreneurship and leads to the creation of new industries and economic sectors.

Even though GCC countries are late-starters in pursuing innovation and R&D, the GCC has established pockets of innovation in the services and manufacturing industries. To facilitate innovation and technology transfer, the GCC has invested in education and skills enhancement, in science parks and research facilities, and in the foundations for high-tech industries. The GCC has established research facilities working closely with the higher education institutions, such as the Qatar Science and Technology Park, the Kuwait Institute for Scientific Research, the King Abdullah University of Science and Technology in Saudi Arabia, and the Knowledge Oasis Muscat in Oman. These entities are set to be leaders in conducting research and funding, acting as incubators, and facilitating the cooperation between government, industry, and academia.

The innovative output in the GCC mainly comes from government-owned enterprises. Amongst GCC states and the Arab world, Saudi Arabia leads with 664 patents filed in 2017. The GCC country rankings in the Global Innovation Index (GII) for 2021 vary, with the UAE ranked 33rd globally and 3rd regionally and Bahrain ranked 78th globally out of 132 countries. As presented in the GII report, the GCC states, with the exception of the UAE, are categorized as underperformers, relative to their GDP levels.

One of the methods for the GCC to enhance innovation and R&D activities is to attract foreign talent that can serve as a valuable mechanism for knowledge transfer from more advanced nations in different sectors. From their experience, foreign nationals can tailor their accumulated knowledge to enhance innovation and technology in the GCC countries. Nevertheless, in the GCC, because of the large presence of immigrants, the governments control the migrant status and duration of stay. Unfortunately, there is no segregation between low-skilled and high-skilled, educated migrants. The GCC is struggling to establish a knowledge-based economy as migration and labor policies create difficulties in attracting and recruiting talent, transferring technology and knowledge, involving foreign talent in knowledge creation, and encouraging innovation. These policies restrict the flow of talent and knowledge to the region.

As innovation is one of the major factors for a knowledge-based economy, the GCC states need to build their human capabilities concurrently with the infrastructure. Building local capabilities in innovation takes time, thus using foreign talent would be an appropriate solution to support innovation initiatives and to train and mentor the local talent. However, for that to occur, the immigration policy and regulations need to be changed to attract foreign talent. For example, a PhD holder could be granted a five to ten-year visa (renewable when he/she is working on research) to give them the appropriate time to work on R&D projects, without having the constant worry of renewing their residency status or being limited by the maximum visa age of 60 years, or 65 years for scientists and researchers.

Conclusion

Many countries recognize the importance of innovation for the development and diversification of the economy. Consequently, countries have created bodies such as the Ministry of Education, Culture, Sports, Science and Technology (MEXT) in Japan, the Federal Ministry of Education and Research in Germany, and the Ministry of Science and Technology in China.

All developed countries encourage and support innovation. In the last few decades, low-tech manufacturing has been transferred to less expensive regions. However, knowledge-based manufacturing and high-tech activities were kept in the advanced countries. The emerging economies are investing in R&D and high-tech value-added activities to catch up with the developed nations in creating knowledge-based economies.

Nations across the globe recognize the vital role of innovation in economic diversification and development. Many countries have developed innovative strategies to create an innovation ecosystem and work closely with different stakeholders to reach the strategic goals of the innovation efforts.

Regardless of the importance of infrastructure and financial funds, human capital is the most important part of the innovation ecosystem. Creating effective capabilities is a process that can develop appropriate human capital (scientists, engineers and technicians) and coordinate the different players to contribute to the innovation activities. The industrial policy should support innovation and technological advancement, which means the policy should be future-directed and have foresight for the nation and economy.

Singapore, in its pursuit of a knowledge-based economy, developed an ecosystem that supported developing, funding, and commercializing its technology. On the other hand, the UAE and GCC have the infrastructure and many other elements but lack the ability to develop genuine technology and commercialize it.

The innovation factor has had a considerable impact on Singapore's economic diversification and development. The Singapore case is a very good example of how a small country can diversify and develop the economy by focusing on the technological advancement of its manufacturing industries and strengthening its innovation capabilities. Singapore set a strategic goal to become a knowledge and R&D-based economy. The government stressed innovation and R&D and structured policies to support them through several means: establishing higher educational entities and research institutions to create a pool of local talents and conduct R&D activities; creating the ecosystem and environment to support innovation in the private and public sectors, and; attracting international firms to establish R&D activities and technological manufacturing.

The innovation factor has had a minimal impact on the economic diversification and development of Abu Dhabi. There were no innovation or research and development activities that led to the creation of new products or the economic sector. Abu Dhabi's weaknesses in innovation and R&D are not surprising given the fact that creating a science and R&D-based economy is a long-term process and Abu Dhabi has only recently invested in the creation of a local innovation infrastructure, including the establishment of research and technology centers and branches for several international universities. Thus, it will take time before the fruits of these investments come to bear, including the number of scientific articles and patents that are developed locally.

The innovation factor has had a negligible impact on economic diversification and development. The GCC countries have not established an effective innovation system and this is reflected in the low number of patents registered locally.

CHAPTER 9

Entrepreneurship

The heart of economic growth and diversification

"We must create economic opportunity, build a culture of entrepreneurship, get people to take responsibility for improving their lives, rather than putting them in a position where they sit back in their poverty and blame others for it."

— PAUL KAGAME, PRESIDENT OF RWANDA (1957–PRESENT)

*M*ost developing economies are under growing pressure from the global economy. Traditional assets, such as cheap land and labor, do not determine the success and failure of an economy. There are new elements that are shaping economic scenarios, such as skilled workforces, access to capital and information, lifestyle amenities, as well as entrepreneurship and environments for innovation.

The entrepreneur is the one who creates the business and promotes the ideas of the business. Entrepreneurs play a vital role in creating new sectors and businesses and are usually people willing to take risks and start first. They have insight and the ability to foresee opportunities and take action. Many countries, especially the United States, strongly encourage entrepreneurs to be active and take a prominent role in the economy. They are affected by, and in turn affect, the economy significantly. Advanced economies encourage and support entrepreneurs because of the positive impact they have on the economy. Entrepreneurs can play an influential and effective role in the development and diversification of the economy.

Based on broad research, entrepreneurship is the ability and willingness of an individual to perceive and create new economic opportunities, commercialize, industrialize, promote ideas to the market, and take risks that accompany the uncertainty of the opportunity. Entrepreneurship is a behavioral characteristic of individuals; it is not an occupation. Entrepreneurs may execute their entrepreneurial traits during a specific stage of their career.

Entrepreneurs are risk-takers, decision-makers, investors, innovators and opportunity seekers. These functions allow entrepreneurs to tackle new industries, expand the economy to new frontiers, and keep the economy evolving and growing.

The role of entrepreneurship in economic diversification

Entrepreneurship as defined above will feed into diversification, since entrepreneurs seek to create new businesses with new products and sometimes even new industries. Audretsch and Fritsch, in 2002 their study "Growth Regimes over Time and Space", found that a high startup rate in a region will lead to higher growth rates. Entrepreneurs, by their ability to distinguish and create new economic breaks, will lead to the establishment of new economic sectors. The prime involvement of entrepreneurship in the diversification of the economy would include the startup of new firms in new economic sectors and industries, and the transformation of inventions and ideas into new products. The products of entrepreneurship can be found in new or existing goods or services that are introduced to the market, either by a startup or an existing firm.

The evidence of the effects of establishing more new firms with new products, on the diversification and development of the economy, appears more clear-cut, especially in the 1980s and 1990s. In analyzing 16 European countries over the period 1988 to 1993, Thurik (1999) reported in his study "Entrepreneurship, Industrial Transformation and Growth", that the increase of small firms had a positive effect on the Gross National Product (GNP). Another study by Robbins et al., (2000), called "An Empirical Assessment of the Contribution of Small Business", performed an analysis of 48 American states for the period 1986–1995. They found that in any state with a higher amount of small new business, the productivity level increases, and new sectors evolve.

An OECD (1998) study called *Fostering Entrepreneurship*, suggests that countries with growth in entrepreneurial activity enjoy higher rates of economic growth, because entrepreneurship works as a vehicle for innovation and technology spillovers. Entrepreneurship contributes to economic diversification by creating new products, businesses and industries.

The Global Entrepreneurship Monitor (GEM) measures entrepreneurial activity among a country's labor force, who are either engaged in starting a new business or managing a business less than forty-two months old. GEM emphasizes the positive impact of the entrepreneurial activity level on economic growth as the data indicates that there is no country with a high entrepreneurial activity level and low economic growth.

Studying some of the countries that have allowed their people to be entrepreneurs and innovators and have helped them set up their businesses, shows that entrepreneurship has contributed to the economic diversification of many nations. The common trend is that the countries that have high levels of entrepreneurs are those that are going through a paradigm shift when it comes to their commercial opportunities and overall system. At the same time, countries facing higher unemployment and where economic conditions are not up to the market, are where people are starting to take things into their own hands and utilize the opportunities that are available to them.

The United States remains a beacon of entrepreneurism where an average of 534,000 small businesses are created every month in different industries. Many of those businesses grow considerably. The world's largest company, Walmart, was founded in 1962 by entrepreneurs, while multi-national and multi-billion-dollar companies such as Google, Apple, Facebook and Amazon, did not exist a few decades ago.

Entrepreneurship is heavily rooted in American history. The nation was founded and then established by risk-takers who were ready to sacrifice old certainties for new opportunities. School children in America are brought up on heroic stories of inventors such as Thomas Edison and entrepreneurs such as Andrew Carnegie and Henry Ford.

America has become a beacon of entrepreneurship due to several structural advantages:

1. It has a mature venture-capital industry, which started from the beginning of its existence through individuals and rich families. Its first venture fund, the American Research and Development Corporation, was established in 1946.
2. It has close relationships between universities and industries. The American universities act as economic engines rather than facilities for teaching theory only. All universities are connected

with science parks, technology offices, business incubators and venture funds. For example, Stanford University gained US$200 million when Google went public. In addition, almost 50% of the startups in Silicon Valley were initiated in universities.

3. It has an open immigration policy and it is noteworthy that more than half of Silicon Valley startups were founded by immigrants. In addition, a quarter of the science and technology startups in America have had somebody born outside the country, either the CEO or CTO. In 2006, foreign nationals were named as inventors or co-inventors in a quarter of American patent applications.

The diversification of the US economy is a result of the long history of entrepreneurship and risk-taking mentality. All businesses started with entrepreneurs who took the initiative and started new ideas and succeeded in all industries in manufacturing or services.

Singapore entrepreneurship

Entrepreneurs form the basis of Singapore's economy and helped the nation to become a trading hub before independence. Most of the entrepreneurs at that time were concentrating on services to support the entrepot industry and some associated manufacturing activities. When the government decided to adopt the export-orientation strategy, it did not depend on the local entrepreneurs as the government wanted the international companies that would bring manufacturing capabilities and open the doors for export.

Singapore decided that if it was to develop and diversify its economy, it had to significantly increase its manufacturing and production capacity for export, and for that, it needed to attract foreign investors. After independence, the government launched an aggressive industrialization program to attract foreign investors. However, in its rush to industrialize and attract foreign investment, the government neglected the merchant class and the small manufacturers in the country. Thus, until the 1980s, Singapore did not have policies or initiatives to support entrepreneurs.

Entrepreneurship started to receive attention after the first economic recession in 1985. The government realized that it was over-reliant on foreign firms and needed to counter that by supporting and encouraging local investors, as highlighted in the Economic Strategies Committee (ESC) report in 1986. Therefore, the government decided to use local entrepreneurs. However, this was not an easy task, and there were many programs and policies implemented to shift the employment culture and to make changes in the education system to adopt creativity, innovation, and entrepreneurship.

The Economic Strategic Committee was established in 1986 to chart new directions for Singapore's economy after the recession in 1985. It identified local entrepreneurship as being instrumental to Singapore's future economic growth. The Small and Medium Enterprise (SME) Master Plan was produced in 1989, which introduced measures and initiatives and infrastructure for entrepreneurial activities.

The 2002 Economic Review Report indirectly led to the creation of the Action Community for Entrepreneurship (ACE) in 2003, to prepare the environment in Singapore for innovators and entrepreneurs to prosper and succeed.

According to the Global Entrepreneurship Monitor, the progress of entrepreneurship in Singapore had been evolving. GEM annual reports indicate that over the years from 2001 to 2014 the Total early-stage Entrepreneurial Activity (TEA) indicator for Singapore increased from 2.1 to 11 (refer to Table 9.1). In 2013, GEM reported that 19.6% of Singaporean respondents received entrepreneurship training. The number of entrepreneurs in Singapore is rising and most of them are in one of the twenty-one accelerators or incubators funded by the National Research Foundation.

Table. 9.1. Key indicators from the Global Entrepreneurship Monitor for Singapore

Indicator	2001	2003	2005	2011	2013	2014
Nascent entrepreneurship rate	1.2	3	3.7	3.8	6.4	6.4
Total early-stage Entrepreneurial Activity	2.1	5	7.2	6.6	10.7	11
Entrepreneurial intention		11.2	17.0	15	15.2	9.4

sources: GEM reports

Entrepreneurship ecosystem in Singapore

The entrepreneurship ecosystem represents the combination of conditions and players that shape the framework in which entrepreneurial activities take place. Singapore created many funding schemes including seed grants, equity financing, loans, and tax incentives.

As part of its effort to support entrepreneurs and startups, Singapore established Block 71, a building transformed into the startup epicenter. In its special reports on entrepreneur ecosystems in 2014, *The Economist* labelled the island on which Block 71 is located as "the world's most tightly packed entrepreneurial ecosystem". As of 2014, Block 71 hosts more than 1,200 people, 260 startups and 25 incubators/accelerators. The success of Block 71 led to the creation of another two buildings – Block 73 and Block 79 – which offer space for accelerators, banks, law firms, venture capital, community, and social enterprises. These three blocks formed LaunchPad

@ one-north, Singapore's startup core. At present, LaunchPad @ one-north is a 6.5-hectare site that offers a conducive environment and nurturing ecosystem for startups and enablers in the biomedical sciences, infocomm, media, electronics, urban solutions, and engineering industries.

The 2021 World Bank report *The Evolution and State of Singapore's Start-up Ecosystem* indicates that there are 184 accelerators, incubators, and other intermediaries in the ecosystem. To be accepted into the startup programs, first-time entrepreneurs must apply through an Accredited Mentorship Partner (AMP); there are at least 27 AMPs in Singapore, several of which are listed in Table 9.2.

Table 9.2. Some of the Accredited Mentorship Partners (AMP) and related sectors

AMP	Economic sector
Action Community for Entrepreneurship (ACE)	All sectors
Advanced New Technology Incubator	Hardware, robotics, and automation
Nanyang Technological University	Advanced manufacturing and engineering, health and biomedical sciences, urban solutions and sustainability, services and digital economy
Singapore Management University	Fintech, cybersecurity, data analytics and artificial intelligence, Smart City innovations, transportation, and logistics
Startup-O	AI, fintech, consumer technology, medical technology, IoT, SaaS
ST Engineering – Innosparks	Smart cities and healthcare
Mistletoe Singapore	Preventive medicine and sustainability, lifelong learning, new city design, permaculture and token economy
Mencast Innovation Centre	Specializing in nanotech, energy technology, industrial IT, life science and agriculture science
SIFOOD	Agriculture technology, food technology, clean technology, healthcare

Singapore has created many funding schemes to support entrepreneurs. The Startup Enterprise Development Scheme (SEEDS) is a startup investment fund scheme run by SPRING, an enterprise development agency under Singapore's Ministry of Trade and Industry. Startups can receive matching funds through SEEDS of up to S$2 million to match private funds raised.

In addition, Singapore has established the Global Investor Program (GIP), an arrangement under which investors with a million dollars may earn permanent resident status if they plan to start a business or invest substantially in Singapore. The GIP is a program established to enhance the innovation ecosystem.

Various programs and initiatives were created by the government to attract international and talented entrepreneurs. For example, the EntrePass initiative, launched in 2004, is a one-year renewable work visa granted to immigrants who own a new company (less than six years) and have S$50,000 or more in capital. In addition, the proposal needs to meet one of the following criteria: (1) it holds intellectual property; (2) has funding from a venture capital entity accredited by the government; (3) has research cooperation with A*STAR or a university, and; (4) is located at an incubator supported by the state.

Extensive government efforts to develop the ecosystem have made a significant impact. Singapore's National Research Foundation undertook a holistic study in 2008 to identify gaps in the entrepreneurial landscape and develop initiatives to tackle these gaps. It established the National Framework for Innovation and Enterprise (NFIE) to facilitate initiatives and programs such as the Proof-of-Concept (POC) grants, Early Stage Venture Capital (ESVF), the University Innovation Fund (UIF), and the Technology Incubation Scheme (TIS), all of which have contributed to the establishment of many entrepreneurial activities over the years. These are accompanied by other initiatives from the Media Development Authority (MDA), SPRING Singapore, and the Infocomm Development Authority (IDA).

Data from the NRF indicates that about S$100 million in funding from schemes such as ESVF and TIS has enabled support for startups to attract capital investments from the private sector of about S$400 million, which is four times the state's funding. The TIS program has had a marked success rate in which NRF supports 85% of its funding, capped at S$500,000. By 2019, more than 3,600 tech startups were operating in Singapore.

Another initiative is the University Innovation Fund, which provides funds to universities to step up entrepreneurial schemes on campus. Startup activities were increasing in NUS, SMU, and NTU. For example, the NUS Overseas College (NOC) program has sent thousands of students for internships in entrepreneurship and startups to Silicon Valley and similar startup hotspots. The student startup fund under the UIF has created many innovative projects, expanding the pipeline for startups and funding from TIS and other funding programs is available if needed at a later stage. The creation of different accelerators and incubators has augmented the mixture and dynamics of the entrepreneurial ecosystem.

According to the 2021 World Bank report, since 2014, Singapore has accounted for well over half of the total aggregate value of deals in the ASEAN region. And in 2019, Singapore invested approximately 75% of total venture capital dollars into the region, solidifying its leadership role amongst its neighbors. At a more granular level, in 2019, approximately S$10.9 billion was invested across 592 startups.

There are 606 Venture Capital (VC) firms in Singapore, which provide a good chance for startups to get funding because most government funding schemes are offered in multiple categories of the VC fund that startups can acquire. The existence of many VC firms in Singapore and the deals they offer for startups has led to many entrepreneurs having successful exits, such as Brandtology and tenCube, which have had a positive effect on the ecosystem.

In 1999, Singapore established a program for technical entrepreneurs known as Technopreneurship 21 (T21). T21 is a cooperation between the government and private sector to establish foundations for high-tech entrepreneurial activities. The initiative covers areas that are essential for the advancement of technopreneurship, such as education, facilities, regulations and financing. Table 9.3 shows the different government entities that have schemes or programs to support entrepreneurs in Singapore.

Table 9.3. Government Entities and their Schemes to Support Entrepreneurs

Government Entity	Supporting Scheme
National Research Foundation (NRF)	1. Early Stage Venture Fund (ESVF) 2. Proof-of-Concept Grants (POC) 3. Technology Incubation Scheme (TIS) 4. Global Entrepreneur Executives (GEE)
SPRING	1. Technology Enterprise Commercialization Scheme (TECS) 2. Angel Investors Tax Deduction Scheme 3. Startup Enterprise Development Scheme 4. Business Angel Scheme 5. Sector Specific Accelerator Program (SSA) 6. Venture Debt Risk-Sharing Program
Action Community for Entrepreneurship (ACE)	ACE Startups Scheme
Community Care	1. ComCare Enterprise Fund (CEF) 2. Youth Social Entrepreneurship Program (YSEP)
National Volunteer and Philanthropy Center (NVPC)	New Initiative Grant
Environment & Water Industry Program (EWI)	Fast-Track Environment & Water Technologies Incubator Scheme (Fast-Tech)
Interactive Digital Media Program Office (IDMPO)	1. IDM (Interactive Digital Media) Jump-start 2. Mentor (i.JAM) Reload scheme
International Enterprise (IE)	Market Access Incubation Program (MAIP)

Action Community for Entrepreneurship

Following the 2002 recommendations of the Economic Review Committee, the Action Community for Entrepreneurship (ACE) was formed in May 2003 as a national program to develop and enhance the environment for innovation, entrepreneurs and enterprise in Singapore, and to strengthen the nation's competitiveness. ACE was launched to support entrepreneurs and the private sector.

The direction for ACE is to support ambitious entrepreneurs to innovate, which includes creating startups, supporting their development, providing them access to markets and networks, and supporting them in attracting local and international opportunities. The vision is to have as many as possible of these startups as international operators.

To execute and implement its strategies and initiatives, ACE established four Action Crucibles (AC) that led the implementation of ACE's initiatives.

1. The Culture AC – to help foster a more entrepreneurial culture in Singapore.
2. Research and Policy AC – to develop and enhance knowledge and technology to generate a positive effect on entrepreneurship.
3. The Rules AC – to reduce the regulatory burden through revising the government initiatives and regulations for entrepreneurs and enterprises.
4. The Internationalization AC – to advise and support companies on international markets.

ACE is led by a steering committee, which sets the strategies and direction for entrepreneurship in Singapore. Some of the steering committee members lead working groups to guide certain focus areas under ACE. There are five sub-committees and two task forces, which supervise the following working streams.

- ACE startups – aims to support entrepreneurs to establish their first venture, to enhance entrepreneurship and to create jobs for Singaporeans. ACE selected twelve partners to work with startups in evaluating applications, supporting startups in receiving funds, and in mentoring. Since its launch, the program has approved more than eighty startups.
- Mentoring – aims to assist ACE startups to develop sustainably with mentoring and support during the first years of operation. ACE created a pool of about seventy experienced entrepreneurs as mentors for startups.
- Networking – aims to provide appropriate platforms for startups to create networks with potential investors, mentors, customers, and partners. Every year ACE organizes many networking events to link startups with different players and stakeholders.
- Overseas Chapter – aims to create networks to support startups to access international markets and engage with new players and investors. The chapters created platforms for Singaporean firms to showcase their products and services. The First Chapter was launched in Beijing (ACE Beijing Chapter) in 2012 and with the assistance of the Beijing Chapter, startups such as MiuZee and Smoov expanded to China.
- Communications – aims to promote entrepreneurship and awareness of ACE and its work.
- The Tech-Connect Task Force – aims to enhance the technology of local firms and address the shortage in the current technology landscape and link firms with other innovation and technology ideas.
- The Entrepreneurship Education Task Force – aims to evaluate the education system and propose new approaches for teaching entrepreneurship in schools to nurture entrepreneurs from youth.

The impact of entrepreneurship on economic diversification and development

Table 9.5. Impact of entrepreneurship strategies/policies on diversification

Strategies/ policies	Outcome	Impact on economic diversification
Creation of ACE	• Supports entrepreneurs in their journeys • Markets the startups internationally • Supports creating partnerships with international firms	• Creates many startups in different sectors • Creates new sectors through partnering with global firms • Creates new products for the global supply chain
Funding schemes	• Different schemes to support entrepreneurs in different industries	• New startups in different industries • Local startups go international
Establishing incubators	• Hosts startups • Creates the environment for startups to develop their product and market it • Creates connections between academia and business	• Creates startups in different economic sectors • Creates new products through new businesses • Many innovative ideas are translated into profitable business

Entrepreneurship in Abu Dhabi

Entrepreneurial activity is assumed to have a strong impact on economic development and diversification through innovation and R&D activities. Entrepreneurship creates jobs, generates wealth and contributes to the development of the economy and nation as a whole. Entrepreneurs are seen to be a critical mechanism for introducing new innovations and ideas to the market.

As previously stated, Singapore pushed for innovation and entrepreneurship after the recession in 1985 and realized the importance of entrepreneurs for the future of the nation and achieving their goal to create a knowledge-based economy.

Abu Dhabi has made remarkable advancements in its economic and social development over the past few decades through the contribution of startups and entrepreneurs to the economy is not yet significant due to their limited capabilities and the lack of government support in past years. Presently, the entrepreneurial potential is not being fully utilized and further strengthening of entrepreneurship among the Emirati population will be required to nurture talent and develop the next wave of entrepreneurs and innovators.

Encouraging entrepreneurial culture and supporting startup development is at the heart of the economic strategy of Abu Dhabi. With the vision to become a competitive technological and knowledge-based economy, the government realizes that entrepreneurship and startups play a major role in diversifying and developing the economy, enhancing innovation, increasing employment and attracting investment.

Abu Dhabi is leveraging its wealth to create a diversified and sustainable economy with a strong emphasis on startups, small and medium-sized firms, as well as entrepreneurship and innovation. The government supports aims to establish a suitable legislative environment that encourages entrepreneurial activities, as well as developing and nurturing an entrepreneurial culture.

Nurturing an entrepreneurial culture is not an easy or quick process. It needs to be developed in young Emirati through the education system and, simultaneously, by creating an entrepreneurial environment that encourages and endorses independent employment as well as generating awareness and collaboration between the different players and contributors to support and encourage entrepreneurial activities.

Entrepreneurial activities and attitudes in Abu Dhabi

Abu Dhabi's DED issued the *Abu Dhabi Innovation Index* in 2014, indicating that the established business ownership rate is 5.3% and the local TEA rate is 11.1%. Of the Emirati entrepreneurs, 82.5% are not full-time business owners (i.e., they are part-time entrepreneurs), and most of the time have employment in government entities.

An analysis drawing on GEM reports, a 2014 DED study, and a 2013 Zayed University study called *Entrepreneurship: An Emirati Perspective*, the following features on entrepreneurs can be identified for the UAE.

- Emirati entrepreneurs take advice more often from family (76.7%) and friends (82.8%), than professionals, such as lawyers (10%) and bankers (10%). This means that UAE entrepreneurs are mainly involved in small-scale activities, are not really risk-takers, and are not focused fully on their startups.
- Emiratis have positive attitudes towards entrepreneurship, with four out of five viewing this avenue as a good career choice. However, only one out of twenty is participating in startups or new business activities. Therefore, a gap exists between the perception of entrepreneurship in society and the extent to which individuals are ready to engage in entrepreneurial activities.
- Society view business failure negatively, which forms a cultural barrier that affects startup rates among Emiratis; fear of failure prevents about one in three Emiratis from starting a business.
- Four per cent of fully Emirati-owned companies export 75% or more of their products, in comparison to 14% of all companies in the country. This indicates a need to tap into the international market.

- One hundred per cent of new Emirati-owned businesses are in no or low-tech industries. Because of the high risk of technological innovation, Emirati entrepreneurs have minimal or no involvement in the high-tech industries, creating a type of innovation barrier.
- Receiving a business loan from a bank is not easy for entrepreneurs in UAE. It is easier to get a personal loan rather than a business loan if a person is employed and has a stable salary. This forms a financial barrier that partially explains why most entrepreneurs in the UAE are part-time entrepreneurs.

Entrepreneurs financing programs in Abu Dhabi

Bank restrictions on financial funding were one of the issues negatively impacting entrepreneurship in Abu Dhabi, so the government created the Khalifa Fund for Enterprise Development (KFED) in 2007. KFED is the lead agency in Abu Dhabi supporting Emirati entrepreneurs. The fund's goal is to develop Emirati entrepreneurs through comprehensive programs offering counselling, training, capacity building, support services, and financing. KFED provides funds ranging from AED 100,000 to AED 10 million.

Other government programs involving grants for startups are listed below.

- Akoun Campaign, which is run by KFED and DED, promotes the "Bright Ideas Bright Futures" business ideas competition with first to third-place prizes of AED 50,000, AED 30,000, and AED 20,000, respectively.
- Flat6lab is a startup accelerator program that has an office in Abu Dhabi in cooperation with Twofour54 and provides seed

funding, office space, workshops and educational programs. The program links entrepreneurs with mentors and advisors.

- Ibtikar is a Twofour54 initiative to provide funding and support for young talent who are interested in the entertainment industry and media. The program along with funding, provides advice, guidance, and support in planning and networking.
- Ghadan 21 was launched in 2019 to support and deliver the transformation of Abu Dhabi's economy, knowledge ecosystem, and communities.

Facilitating effective commercialization in Abu Dhabi

Around the world, countries have invested heavily in R&D and innovation without necessarily benefitting directly from any financial returns on investment. This highlights the importance of establishing active processes to transfer ideas from the testing level to products for the market through both new startups and existing companies.

Developing startups or spin-out companies is necessary to the success of entrepreneurial activities. The economic ecosystem needs to support these companies in using innovative ideas and transferring them into business and products for consumers. Business incubation could be used to develop the new companies and support their efforts in commercialization. Business incubators are important in creating a supportive environment for entrepreneurs who need training, funding, support in management and marketing, and many other services. Incubators can add value to startups in four areas: analyzing and identifying business needs; monitoring, evaluating and supporting when needed; providing access to needed networks; and providing necessary support to receive capital. Incubators develop and enhance the entrepreneurial culture in a region and attract skilled individuals who can benefit from the ecosystem in the incubator.

Khalifa Fund for enterprise development

The Khalifa Fund for Enterprise Development is the main government agency of Abu Dhabi that supports entrepreneurship and startups. It was established in 2007 to provide different financing products and services.

- Bedaya: funding startups with loans of up to AED 3 million.
- Zeyada: funding the expansion of startups with loans of up to AED 5 million.
- Tasneeaa: supports startups in small-sized manufacturing with loans of up to AED 10 million.
- Microfinance: supports home-based businesses with loans of up to AED 100,000 and training on management and financial activities.
- Khutwa: supports small enterprises and targets specific social groups with loans of up to AED 250 000.
- Al Hasela: funds young fishermen with loans of up to AED 500,000 in cooperation with the Abu Dhabi Fishermen Association.

Most of KFED's funding is for programs of a social nature. Even though KFED pursues economic and social projects, the social aspect is highly important to the extent that about 40% of clients fall under this category. Viewing and analyzing KFED activities highlights some interesting points.

- Since starting its activities in 2007, and until 2019, KFED received more than 15,000 applications; 1,170 have been approved, which is an average of 97 projects per year.
- No interest rates are applied on KFED loans.
- Most KFED loans have seven years to be redeemed except for microfinance (two and a half years). Loan maturity is five years in most projects except for microfinance (two years). A grace period of two to three years is applied to all programs except microfinance which has six months.
- KFED portfolio projects are mostly service (44%), followed by manufacturing (32%), agriculture (17%), and trade (7%).

These activities demonstrate that KFED has a social as well as economic imperative. It supports both entrepreneurs and startups. KFED created different loan schemes to provide support to different groups in society including women and people with difficulties. The KFED loans scheme provides support to projects in different areas such as services and manufacturing. These loans are provided with generous terms including no interest rates, long maturity periods, and very low collection rates.

The impact of entrepreneurship on economic diversification in Abu Dhabi

Like Singapore, Abu Dhabi senses the urgency to support entrepreneurs and startups to become a knowledge-based economy. From the analysis, it can be concluded that both states have taken different approaches to boost entrepreneurship.

- In Singapore, government bodies were created to manage, coordinate and fund activities in the entrepreneurship ecosystem.

Support for startups includes regulation, finance, networking and marketing. Abu Dhabi, on the other hand, is still trying to develop ways to support the development of entrepreneurship. KFED and Ghadan21 were created in 2007 and 2019, respectively, to provide financial support, however, there is no existing entrepreneurship environment in which to develop and enhance entrepreneurship.

- Singapore created ACE to support startups inside the country and abroad. ACE coordinates between different players affecting the entrepreneurship environment. In Abu Dhabi, the role of KFED and Ghadan21 is to support startups financially and conduct some training, but their role does not go beyond that. Abu Dhabi needs to create an entrepreneurship environment and ecosystem.

- The GEM reports show fairly high levels of entrepreneurship in Abu Dhabi, however, most Emiratis work in the public sector. Financial institutes do not provide loans to startups and the social prospect of failure is holding entrepreneurs back. As well, the link between innovation and entrepreneurship is weak. In general, Abu Dhabi does not have an environment that encourages entrepreneurship and startups. Singapore overcame these problems by creating ACE, which worked to boost entrepreneurship activities, changing the culture and enhancing the elements that support entrepreneurs.

- Singapore used incubators such as OneNorth to support entrepreneurs and innovators in their journeys. Abu Dhabi just created Hub71 as an incubator in 2019. Abu Dhabi needs to create incubators to enhance and develop startups, possibly connected to the industrial sectors of Vision 2030. The incubators provide support in different areas, such as training, management, marketing, networking, and financing.

For Abu Dhabi to increase the level of entrepreneurship requires the use of different approaches. For example, the government should create an entity to manage, support, and guide entrepreneurs and startups. It must also design and implement a comprehensive strategy to enlarge and diversify the economic sectors through startups and entrepreneurs. In addition, a champion for each sector should be identified to mentor and support the newcomers. A strong candidate to champion such an effort could be Mubadala, EDGE, Tawazun, Masdar, Sinaat or ADNOC.

Abu Dhabi can capitalize on its cultural diversity and the large number of expatriates that can significantly support entrepreneurship. The mixture of talented individuals from different countries will have a positive effect on Emiratis. It will encourage cooperation with international companies and the joint activities between talented expatriates to establish the capability to enter the international markets. The new emigration laws will also be easier to attract international entrepreneurs.

Abu Dhabi still has many issues to address in order to establish the environment for entrepreneurs and startups that provides the different elements needed to initiate ideas and develop them to present to the local and international markets.

Entrepreneurship in the GCC

The GCC states have clearly identified their aim to transform their economies into diversified knowledge-based economies. These transformations will enhance entrepreneurship in the national population, through interactions with foreign technology and knowledge to absorb and develop new technologies for the region.

GCC states have recently directed initiatives to the development of startups and to nurturing entrepreneurship. Entrepreneurship improvement is critical for economic development and diversification since it leads to the creation of new industries and economic sectors. Many supporting entities for SMEs have been established across the GCC. Some examples include the Mohamed Bin Rashid Establishment for SME Development and Khalifa Fund for Enterprise Development in the UAE; Tamkeen in Bahrain; the National Fund for Small and Medium Enterprises in Kuwait; Sharakah in Oman; the Development Centre for SME in Saudi Arabia, and; Enterprise Qatar in Qatar.

While their mandates vary, most aim to enhance SME access to funding, offer counselling support, and encourage the government procurement of SME products and services. Despite these efforts, there are some difficulties facing SME growth. For example, the level of loans for SMEs is low, receiving only 2% of total lending in the GCC, compared to 8% across the Middle East[20].

Another factor restricting entrepreneurship in the GCC is the culture of no tolerance for failure. Similar to the Emiratis, entrepreneurs across the GCC mostly have government jobs and establish startups in the private sector as a part-time activity. As well, the education system does not promote entrepreneurship and risk-taking. Similar to Abu Dhabi and the UAE, the challenges facing entrepreneurs in the GCC more broadly are:

- Non-supporting culture;
- Limitations within the legal system;
- Lack of support from financing platforms;
- Lack of education opportunities for entrepreneurship and/or innovation;
- The need for qualified management to support the development of a sustainable entrepreneurship ecosystem, and;
- Shortage in factors that build entrepreneurial experience.

---

20   Rocha, Roberto, Subika Farazi, R. Khouri, and D. Pearce (2011) The Status of Bank Lending to SMEs in the Middle East and North Africa Region Results of a Joint Survey of the Union of Arab Bank and the World Bank. World Bank Policy Research Paper.

Conclusion

Entrepreneurs play a major role in the economy by creating new businesses, which in turn create jobs. The effects of entrepreneurship on economic diversification and development derive from the newness of products and services. This includes the startup of new firms in existing or new economic sectors, and the transformation of inventions and ideas into economically viable entities.

Any nation seeking economic development and diversification needs to find the mechanism to create and develop entrepreneurial behavior among its people. In addition, it needs to create the system to support entrepreneurs in all different stages of their journey.

The entrepreneurship factor has had a moderate impact on Singapore's economic diversification and development. Singapore realized the important role of entrepreneurship in the economy from the early stages of its journey. After independence, because of the lack of capabilities, funds and an entrepreneurial local private sector, the government focused on attracting international firms to develop the capabilities and grow the economy. After the 1985 recession, the government realized that it needed to develop and enhance the local private sector and entrepreneurship. Since then Singapore has created many entities, initiatives, and programs to support entrepreneurs and startups.

In Abu Dhabi, the entrepreneurship factor has had a very low impact on economic diversification and development. Abu Dhabi needs to establish and strengthen its innovation and entrepreneurship ecosystem. Entrepreneurial development needs an innovation system and R&D labs as a source of new ideas. This also requires individuals who can recognize opportunities and transfer them into products or services for the market.

The impact of the entrepreneurship factor on economic diversification within the GCC has been negligible. While there is support among individuals for entrepreneurship, the culture and government systems do not support entrepreneurship and there are many challenges that need to be addressed to create a sustainable ecosystem for innovation and entrepreneurship.

CHAPTER 10

Private Sector

How can a strong private sector protect the economy from global economic downturn?

"We must never forget that it is the private sector – not government – that is the engine of economic opportunity."

— Bill Richardson, former governor of New Mexico (1947–present)

"I believe the private sector and small businesses drive our economy, and that means the federal government should work to ensure the private sector is as robust as possible."

— Ann Kirkpatrick, US Congresswoman (1950–present)

The role of the private sector in the diversification and development of economies has been seen in both developed and developing countries. There is no country that has advanced in its economic development without the private sector having played a substantial role, such as in the newly developed countries like Singapore and South Korea, or in the already developed countries that are generally in the West. The private sector has grown in the West to include transnational companies that have expanded their business to many countries, across many continents.

The resilience of the economy depends on the strength of the private sector and the efficiency and ability in reallocating resources when economic shocks hit. The private sector has the skills and ability that allow it to be more responsive to new market trends than the public sector.

The private sector is part of the economy that is not controlled or governed by the government. However, the government sets the rules and regulations for the private sector to keep the market open for competition for everybody and to maintain fair treatment and opportunity for everyone.

Economic competitiveness is the ability to succeed in the global market under free and fair market conditions. Thus, to have a strong private firm compete internationally, it should go through strong competition in the local market and such competitiveness can be successfully encouraged through free-market-based approaches. Fair and intense competition is necessary to enhance the efficiency and productivity of the economy.

For developing nations, there is a need for policies to enhance competitiveness and strengthen private sector firms to be able to compete globally and develop the economy. The existence of strong competition between private entities is a prerequisite for a strongly developing market.

The private sector is more sensitive to changes in the market than the public sector, and is, therefore, more flexible to absorb, respond, and recover from economic downturns. In addition, the private sector is more efficient and productive whilst the public sector is burdened by over-employment and inefficiency. It is within these circumstances the private sector plays a critical role in establishing economic flexibility through the diversification of the economy.

The private sector also enhances the entrepreneurial skills that contribute to the development and diversification of the economy and strengthen its responsiveness to market trends and shocks.

The World Bank's (2005) *World Development Report* stated that private sector investments in facilities and markets enhance the infrastructure of the economy, which assists in attracting foreign investors to the nation and contributes to the development, diversification, and growth of the economy. The private sector plays a role in strengthening the competitive environment and thus enhances the efficiency and productivity of entities. Additionally, the report emphasized the importance of the private sector in creating new jobs and providing more employment opportunities.

Role of the private sector in the diversification of the economy

The private sector plays a strong role in the development and diversification efforts of the economy of any country. There are many examples from different countries in this regard. South Korea is a good example of the strong role of the private sector in building the economy. Korea's fast development and growth might not have been as effective, had it not been for the powerful free enterprise of the leading generation business front-runners. Such entities laid the groundwork for business groups such as Samsung, POSCO, Hyundai and LG. South Korea's economic growth and expansion is the result of the progression of the private sector.

The economic progress in South Korea did not happen overnight, and the private sector's contribution formed the cornerstone of this progress. The aim of the government was always to strengthen the private sector participation in economic development and diversification, and the private sector was the leading player in the high performance of exports. According to World Bank data, South Korea was the seventh-largest exporter worldwide in 2016 with a value of US$483 billion, which was the result of the private sector's high performance. The private sector in South Korea was not only concentrated on business. It also performed social duties, such as the education and training of employees by establishing schools to help workers finish their education and upskill.

The South Korean economy is characterized by conglomerates called chaebols, which are defined as diversified interconnected companies and family-owned business groups. According to a *Bloomberg* (2017) report on South Korea's chaebols, in 2015 the top five examples (Samsung, LG, SK, Hyundai and Lotte), accounted for 58% of the GDP, which is US$1.383 trillion. Through the diversification of their business, the chaebols could support the government policies for developing and diversifying the economy, and were able to compete internationally and take a large share of the international markets in many industries, such as electronics, communications, shipbuilding, and the automotive industry.

The private sector in Singapore

The private sector plays a significant role in the development and diversification efforts of the economy of a country. Singapore is one nation that has witnessed impressive economic growth over the last five decades, and the private sector has played a significant role in this progress. The economy of Singapore is one of the most diverse economies worldwide. State-owned companies play a considerable role in the economy of Singapore; however, the private sector also plays a substantial role, and the state is encouraging the private sector to become increasingly involved in economic development[21].

On gaining independence, Singapore relied on the foreign private sector to attract funds and technology, with the government preferring foreign investors compared to local investors. Through providing infrastructure and tax incentives for foreign companies to export from Singapore, the local private sector was marginalized. The government believed that MNCs would provide employment, create export products, and bring advanced technologies.

The companies in Singapore are divided into three types: local companies, foreign companies, and government-linked companies (GLCs), who act and sometimes compete in the market as private entities. The GLCs play a major role in the development of the private sector through direct public investment in new economic sectors. However, the development agencies (statutory boards) operating in the economic sectors provide support for players in specific industries, including local enterprises, GLCs and MNCs, and coordinate among them and other stakeholders and actors.

One of the mandates of the EDB is to develop and support the growth of private firms, and their expansion and entry into international markets. The EDB partners with many government entities such as Jurong Town Cooperation and Urban Redevelopment Authority, as well as with other agencies responsible for certain aspects of private sector enhancement. For example, the Central Provident Fund (CPF) has created mechanisms by which it can support and provide funds for the private sector.

Singapore created different agencies, similar to the EDB, to develop and maintain long-term visions of each sector and industry. They were also generated to attract foreign investors, create entities, and support

---

21   Siddiqui, Kalim (2010) The Political Economy of Development in Singapore. Research in Applied Economics, Vol 2(2), pp.1-31.

the economy through export mostly; invest in some firms and/or enter into joint ventures; create links and coordinate the activities between MNCs and local enterprises; and encourage the creation of production links between MNCs, GLCs and local enterprises.

Even though it functioned from the sidelines, because of a lack of trust from the government, the local private sector managed to survive through engagement in agile and adaptable technology and applications that supplied components and parts to MNCs and GLCs. However, since the end of the 1980s, a shift in the government's economic direction occurred, which permitted more substantial involvement by the local private sector.

After the recession in 1985, and as a result of the strategic committee recommendations in 1986, the support of local enterprises became important. The Small Enterprise Bureau was established in the same year to provide the support needed for local small enterprises to grow. The government created programs to assist the development and cater to the needs of local businesses. One of the earliest initiatives was the Local Industry Upgrading Program (LIUP), whose aim was to develop the efficiency, reliability, and international competitiveness of local industries by creating strong ties with international firms.

In 1976, Singapore established the Small Industry Finance Scheme (SIFS) to offer low-cost funding to local SMEs in manufacturing and related support services. In 1985, the SIFS program was expanded to cover the non-manufacturing sectors. In addition, the Small Industry Technical Assistance Scheme, established in 1982, offered funds to cover part of the cost of in-service training for workers.

The government in Singapore supported the private sector in different ways such as through incentives, funding, education and training, and infrastructure. The government managed its support for the private sector to focus on targeted industries for a specific time and to encourage local and international investors to participate in that industry.

Reason for a new focus on the private sector

There are many reasons that led Singapore to groom the local private sector. One reason is that Singapore learnt from the crises it had been through. After the 1980 recession, the government developed a new strategic direction for the economy. The urgency for economic reform was further motivated by the financial crisis that hit Asia in 1998. It was also motivated by the rise of low-cost labor in nations of East Asia. As a result of the intensive regional competition in Asia, Singapore could not keep competing in low-cost manufacturing, because of the high cost of workers in the country.

To further advance the economy, and to manufacture high-tech and develop its own technology in the future, Singapore supported and encouraged local firms to take a role in the industrial structure. The local firms were supported in playing the role of suppliers of small components and services, connecting with foreign technological partners to enhance Singapore's technological capabilities. The idea was that the MNCs would transfer technology and manufacturing capabilities, but only talented firms could develop these technologies and capabilities further and convert them into permanent local operations.

A further reason is globalization, which creates interconnections between international business and is not contained by boundaries. This has created the need for quick responsiveness from enterprises and the ability to adapt to technologies from abroad.

To increase incentives for foreign investors, Singapore created a network of strong and reliable local suppliers (clusters). The goal was to grow strong and capable SMEs through operating in relationships with the MNCs and supplying them with products and services.

Supporting SMEs

Singapore developed the SME Master Plan in 1988 to shape the partnership between the government and private sector. The five main themes of the SME Master Plan were:

1. Technology adoption
2. Business planning and finance
3. Human resource management
4. Productivity improvement and training
5. Marketing and business partnership

The *Singapore Competitiveness Report* (1998) stressed the need to develop SMEs and to coordinate the link between these and international companies to consolidate and combine resources to achieve competitiveness and create clusters for industries.

In 2000, another strategic plan was released, titled *SME 21*. The vision of *SME 21* was to develop the local firms to contribute to the potential knowledge-based economy. The Singapore Productivity and Standards Board (SPRING) was directed to coordinate with the EDB and other government bodies to develop and enhance the capabilities of local enterprises and support them to have their own technology and innovation.

Singapore created the Trade Development Board (TDB) in 1983 to support the local private sector. However, it was not optimized because local enterprises had no role in industrial policy. The TDB was brought to life in 1986, as the new strategy for the economy took shape and new industrial policies required the involvement of local enterprises and the development of the private sector. The EDB provided different schemes and support to the local private sector companies on different stages of their maturity as shown in Table 10.1.

Table 10.1. Assistance schemes and programs instituted by the Economic Development Board

Startup	Growth	Expansion	Going Overseas
Local Enterprise Computerization Program	ISO 9000 Certification	Automation Leasing Scheme	Business Development Scheme
Local Enterprise Finance Scheme	Local Enterprise Finance Scheme	Brand Development Assistance Scheme	Double Deduction for Overseas Investment Development Expenditure
Product Development Assistance Scheme	Local Enterprise Technical Assistance Scheme	Franchise Development Assistance Scheme	
R&D Incubator Program		ISO 9000 Certification	Franchise Development Assistance Scheme
Skills Development Fund	Local Industry Upgrading Program	Local Enterprise Computerization Program	Local Enterprise Finance Scheme (Overseas)
Venture Capital	Market & Investment Development Assistance Scheme	Local Enterprise Finance Scheme	Local Industry Upgrading Program
		Local Enterprise Technical Assistance Scheme	Market & Investment Development Assistance Scheme
	Product Development Assistance Scheme	Local Industry Upgrading Program	
		Market & Investment Development Assistance Scheme	Overseas Enterprise Incentive/Overseas Investment Incentive
	Pioneer Status/ Investment Allowance	Pioneer Status/ Investment Allowance	
	Skills Development Fund	Product Development Assistance Scheme	
		Skills Development Fund	
	Software Development Assistance Scheme	Software Development Assistance Scheme	
		Total Business Plan	
	Venture Capital	Venture Capital	

source: Economic Development Board

Multi-national companies in Singapore

When Singapore gained independence, there was a requirement to create jobs and to develop the economy and the nation. However, the government did not have the money necessary to support its initiatives, it did not have strong local enterprises to rely on, and it did not have the proper infrastructure to serve social and economic aspects. The government needed a different approach to develop, sustain, and grow the economy. Subsequently, the government decided to partner with two kinds of enterprises, MNCs and GLCs, and viewed the local private sector, at that time, as weak and lacking capabilities. This was a pragmatic way of isolating the local private sector and involving them in tackling the challenges facing the new nation. Export was the cornerstone of the strategy of Singapore; however, local enterprises did not have the manufacturing capabilities or access to the international market and had no motive to enter a new business and support the government's initiatives. Thus, the government had to turn to international companies to bring their manufacturing facilities to the nation and sell abroad. To keep controlling the strategic sectors, the government created government-linked companies (GLCs) to invest in these sectors. In addition, in the 1960s, the government did not have sufficient capital to support investment in the infrastructure and the economy. It was, therefore, practical to invite foreign investors to bridge the gap.

Since independence, many MNCs have opened manufacturing facilities in the nation. In 2013, MNCs accounted for 75% of the output of manufacturing and about 85 % of manufactured exports in Singapore. Two-thirds of the equity capital invested in manufacturing came from foreign regions. MNCs were the major player in technological transfer. As a result of the 1985 recession, the government endorsed the diversification of the economy and encouraged investment in high value-added manufacturing and service sectors. To diversify the economy and increase the sources of revenues, the government encouraged the local enterprises to expand internationally and explore new markets.

Impact of the private sector on economic diversification

Table 10.2. Impact of private sector strategies/policies on diversification

Strategies/ policies	Outcome	Impact on economic diversification
EDB support to the private sector	• Attracts MNCs • Facilitates cooperation between local and MNCs • Supports local business at different levels of maturity	• MNCs create businesses in existing and emerging economic sectors • SMEs become suppliers to MNCs
Statutory board support	• Each statutory board is responsible for developing its industry, including local private sector industry • Sets the regulations and prepares the environment for companies to operate efficiently • Creates cooperation between different players in the industry	• Creates more SMEs to cover different parts of the industries • Creates cluster base activities to have economies of scale • Generates the ability for the private sector to sell in the global market
SME plans	• Administrative and finance support • Training and productivity improvement • Marketing • Facilitates relationship with international partners	• Creates SMEs in different sectors • Increases productivity and competitiveness of SMEs • Creates new partners in new sectors

The private sector in Abu Dhabi

Abu Dhabi's economic development and diversification strategies rely on the contribution of the private sector. The Abu Dhabi Economic Vision 2030 depends on the role of the private sector as the employer, receiver and adapter of foreign technologies, and driver of diversification and advancement in the quest for a knowledge-based economy.

Although the private sector in Abu Dhabi has grown to play an increasing role in the economy, it is still dependent upon government financial and economic support. Its contributions to economic development and diversification have been modest in international comparison. While the private sector has made huge steps since the 1960s, most of the activities are connected to government-funded activities rather than autonomous diversification and many of them work as agents to international companies.

The government is the driver of demand in Abu Dhabi, with its expenditure and incentives stimulating the economy. The efforts to diversify the economy into new industries has been led by government companies, with the private sector contributing little to the diversification by moving to new economic sectors, or the employment of locals.

The data on SMEs are not solid in the UAE in general. Some unofficial estimates indicate that 32% of SMEs operate from Abu Dhabi, whereas Dubai has 45%. According to the Statistics Centre Abu Dhabi, in 2017, 76% of firms were small enterprises, and 20% were medium enterprises. In the Abu Dhabi Chamber of Commerce (2019) report *Small and Medium-sized Enterprises in Abu Dhabi*, also in 2017, 29% of SMEs shared in the Abu Dhabi economy, and 44% in the non-oil economy.

Abu Dhabi's emphasis on SMEs

As mentioned above, the private sector was instrumental in Singapore's economic development and diversification. However, in Abu Dhabi private firms needed to be active in real business and not just work as agents; they needed to be involved in manufacturing and value-adding production. Some international studies emphasize the importance of high growth companies in inspiring and encouraging economic development and diversification. An OECD (1997) analysis *Small Businesses, Job Creation and Growth: Facts, Obstacles and Best Practices*, which looked at different countries in the 1990s, points out that high-growth firms create around 50% to 75% of all new jobs.

The potential for such firms to contribute to the development and diversification of Abu Dhabi is therefore substantial. These firms are spread across all industries and are mostly not technology-based companies. A large portion of them operate in the services industry. Since most of these firms are small, young, and spread across many industries, they can play a major role in the diversification of the economy of Abu Dhabi.

How does the Abu Dhabi government support the private sector?

With Vision 2030, the Abu Dhabi government is committed to diversifying the economy. Strengthening the role of the private sector is one of the nine pillars of the vision. Abu Dhabi has gone through a range of economic restructuring and liberalization phases since the start of the millennium. The creation of new sectors and the transfer of some functions from the state to private has benefited local firms more than international players. Local private firms are now involved in many sectors such as health, education, manufacturing, and banking, which until the 1990s were partly or completely government-owned.

Similar to the other GCC governments, Abu Dhabi has a pro-capital economic system, and the merchant class did not experience the nationalization waves that hit the region in the 1970s, which eliminated old business classes in Arab countries including Algeria, Egypt, and Syria. In the 1970s and 1980s, Abu Dhabi business owners operated as mediators and brokers for international companies to provide goods and services to the demands of the local economy and consumers.

The operations of some of the local businesses are more substantial now, covering different sectors of the economy, such as manufacturing plants, private schools, universities, banks, clinics, hotel chains, and construction businesses. The private sector employs a large number of expatriate workers in Abu Dhabi, and more than 50% of the jobs in Abu Dhabi are provided by private businesses, albeit those jobs are mainly held by foreign workers.

Steffen Hertog, in his 2013 study *The Private Sector and Reform in the Gulf Cooperation Council* highlighted that some businesses in the GCC have expanded to the international market and accumulated international assets over decades of investments, which gives the local private sector some form of independence from governments. However, Abu Dhabi is a different case, and the private sector is still heavily dependent on the government for contracts and funds. In addition, many of the public servants have their own businesses and compete with the businesses over the contracts for the government. Besides a potential conflict of interests, the involvement of key figures in the public service is irritating the private sector, which is left with the choice to either team up with public servants in high positions or close their business in Abu Dhabi.

Hertog (2013) also points out that the government in Abu Dhabi is still a strong player in the economy and the private sector is more dependent on government than almost anywhere else. Business activities are increasing and growing with the state spending and would suffer in its absence. However, the private sector has not created new products or services and is not trying to sell them to the global market. Similar to private sectors in other GCC states, public procurement is very important for Abu Dhabi private sector, since government expenditure is substantial.

Abu Dhabi needs to strengthen the private sector as stated in Vision 2030. The government aim is to become a "regulator" of services, whereas the private sector is set to be the "provider" of services. The SOEs that were created to provide the services have failed to act as a genuine private sector and work in a hybrid (government-private) system.

Challenges facing the private sector in Abu Dhabi

The private sector in Abu Dhabi faces many challenges that need to be tackled and resolved. These challenges include government bureaucracy where companies are spending significant time and resources interacting with different government departments to resolve administrative issues such as registration, licensing, and certification and documentation requirements. Some of these challenges are:

1. Lending and financing: banks in Abu Dhabi are hesitant to lend to the private sector, especially to SMEs. In 2008, 50% to 70% of credit applications were rejected by banks in the UAE, due to the failure of applicants to fulfill loan conditions and the high risk. Fifty-five per cent of SMEs could not get the credit they required. Much SME lending is through personal loans, as reported by Dun and Bradstreet (2008) in their study "SME Lending in the UAE".

2. Ownership and accounting practices: most of the private sector companies in Abu Dhabi are similar to the rest of the GCC, and are single-owner entities without distinction between private and company assets. Most of the time, the business owners treat the company accounts as a private affair and are reluctant to report activities to the lenders. Even when auditors are used, they write down what the owners give them, and their job is to justify it. This occurs even in companies that are formally owned by nationals but run by expatriates.

3. Lack of innovation: most private companies have a line of business that creates income with low-margin activities and very low effort from the owner's side. This leads to an unwillingness to innovate and take risks. The business of most private sector companies is either construction, buying and selling of goods, or standard services. This limits the creativity to come up with new products, which negatively affects the diversification of the economy.

4. Lack of cooperation: in Abu Dhabi and other GCC countries the behavior of the private sector tends to be individualistic and non-cooperative. There is a lack of cooperation between different companies (private and public) on supply chains principles. The cooperation between companies within a nation is very important to build competitive clusters. Because of this, the operation costs in Abu Dhabi are high and there are no economies of scale in production that connect different operators.

5. Competition from SOEs: state-owned enterprises are drifting from their primary role of not competing with the local private sector. Many SOEs get involved in businesses that should be left to the private sector, such as maintenance, construction, hotels, etc.

6. Competition from companies connected with high-level figures: these companies are private but owned by high-level public figures, which means they can be favored for contracts with governments or SOEs.
7. Dependence on government: the private sector has been selected by the government to be the main job provider and promoter of diversification as set out in Vision 2030. However, it is still extremely dependent on direct and indirect state expenditure and contracts.

Private sectors in Abu Dhabi and the GCC nations operate in isolation from the citizenry. They provide little employment opportunities and pay no taxes. Without taxes, no income flows from the private sector to the state, which means that there is no benefit to the general population. Nevertheless, the private sector benefits largely from the government expenditure and from the subsidized and unexpansive inputs such as power and land, which can create an uneven distribution of wealth in the society. This should not be unexpected given the imbalance of resources between the private sector and state and the short history of the private sector in Abu Dhabi. Regardless of the growth in the private sector since the 1960s, it is still dependent on the state as its client and customer. A new class of business owners working in the government are starting to more closely link the relationship between the private sector and the state.

Impact of the private sector on economic diversification in Abu Dhabi

The private sector is a major player in the economy; a fact realized by Abu Dhabi and Singapore. Even though the importance of Singapore's local private sector was not realized until the economic crises in the middle of the 1980s, since then the government has worked to support and enhance its capabilities. In Abu Dhabi, while Vision 2030 has realized the importance of the private sector, there is no strategy to develop it. From the analysis comparing both states, the following can be noted.

- Government support for entities: in Singapore, the statutory board in each sector is responsible for developing the SMEs in that sector and creating a development plan focused on SMEs and supporting private sector activity. In Abu Dhabi, there is no such entity in general, or for specific industries. The SMEs and private sector are left to navigate the business landscape by themselves.
- Government bureaucracy: Singapore reduced and minimized the government bureaucracy that companies were required to deal with. Also, Singapore eliminated the need for personal connections and favoritism to execute tasks with government administrative entities. Abu Dhabi, by contrast, is still working on reducing the bureaucracy layers for businesses to operate.
- Area of business: Singapore did not view the local private sector as a strong partner to develop new industries until the late 1980s. After that, it started to support local companies to be recipients of the new technologies and play an effective role in the present and future plans. Abu Dhabi realized the importance of the private sector but still did not create a plan to develop the private sector in different industries.

- MNCs: Singapore depends on foreign companies to create manufacturing capabilities and bring technologies to the nation. It allowed 100% ownership, facilitated activities for MNCs and created cooperation between local and foreign companies. Abu Dhabi still does not utilize the capabilities of international companies, and there is no plan to attract certain technologies and no entity to facilitate the transfer of technology to local companies.

- SOEs: GLCs in Singapore operate on a commercial basis, so their relationship with the private sector can involve competing and cooperating with each other. Statutory boards make sure that the GLCs do not overrun the private companies and do not destroy the industry. In Abu Dhabi, there is mistrust between SOEs and private sector companies. SOEs believe that they can operate in all phases of the supply chain. This is very hard to achieve and increases the cost of operations, pushes prices upwards and prevents competition in the global market. It is rare for SOEs in Abu Dhabi to show a willingness to share their business with another company. On the other hand, companies in the private sector have the same idea that they can operate without the need for local partners, and this results in not being able to sustain their business over the long run.

To create a strong and productive private sector, SOEs need to be pushed to play fairly with the private sector and compete according to robust economic standards. To achieve this, the government could treat the private sector and SOEs as equals; have anti-corruption regulations and standards that are strongly enforced in enterprises (public or private); have a separation between the government and private sector and not allow any government officials to participate in any private or state enterprises; have the private sector independent of the state; drive the private sector to have products for customers other than government, and; encourage and support the private sector to produce for consumers and sell abroad.

Abu Dhabi needs to create schemes, processes and policies to support the involvement of the private sector. The support needs to operate on different levels and in different ways and include financial support, training, marketing, infrastructure, and managerial advice. Abu Dhabi needs to create different schemes and entities to support the development and enhancement of the private sector. Importantly, there needs to be a central entity to coordinate and evaluate the results of the initiatives, especially the many initiatives that start but do not continue. The best candidate for that is the Department of Economic Development.

Abu Dhabi's private sector lacks the capabilities to support its strategic economic plans and participate in creating new industries. The private firms in Abu Dhabi need more support from the government to become autonomous firms. For each industry and economic sector, Abu Dhabi could create anchor firms around which private firms can be developed as suppliers or contractors. Each anchor firm could be the first or lead customer for the new small suppliers, and these suppliers can be encouraged to grow and expand internationally. This would drive development and growth in both targeted industries and secondary industries.

Creating an environment to maximize the potential growth of the private sector will require support from the government in marketing and export activities. Creating a cohort of local firms in different industries, especially those that have the potential and motivation to advance and grow, would support the diversification ambitions of Abu Dhabi.

The private sector in the GCC

The GCC states are creating national development strategies intended to diversify economies, enhance human capabilities and promote strong private sectors that generate employment and competitive products and services. However, as indicated by Hertog (2013)[22], the private sector performance has been declining over time, losing its historical role in the pre-oil era when it was more autonomous and had a greater influence on the economic process.

The GCC private sector has become a client of the states and is coupled with the political elites. Over the past decades, it has created business empires that profit from government spending and depend on protective regulations to build barriers to entry in many business activities. These business empires are also taking advantage of the availability and low price of energy and other inputs.

The private sector does not like to take risks and prefers instead low-risk roles, such as agents or brokers to international companies that sell into the local market. The GCC private sector needs to play an effective role in the diversification and development efforts, and the governments need to tackle two main issues in particular: the governments need to disassemble the monopoly (agency) system, which would lead to building a dynamic and competitive private sector, and; they need to develop regulations to separate power (politicians and public servants) from wealth (private sector and SOEs). As long as politicians and public servants are allowed to either own or work in a profit-oriented enterprise, then corruption can occur, and this would erode the competition between companies in the country.

---

22   Hertog, Steffan (2013) The Private Sector and Reform in the Gulf Cooperation Council. Research papers, 30. London: LSE Kuwait Programme.

The 2017 IMF report *The Economic Outlook and Policy Challenges in the GCC Countries* indicated that GCC countries had improved in some areas to ease doing business. An example is setting up one-stop windows to support businesses in meeting government requirements and accelerating licensing and registration processes (e.g., Kuwait, Oman, Qatar, and Saudi Arabia), and customs (Bahrain, Oman, and Saudi Arabia). Also, some governments support the development of SMEs (Oman and Saudi Arabia). Other governments, such as Saudi Arabia and the UAE are working to enhance the efficiency of public service through outsourcing services. Saudi Arabia launched a program to improve the business environment called "Removing Obstacles to the Private Sector".

The IMF[23] has recommended that GCC countries need to take further actions to grow the private sector through several approaches.

- Publicly funded projects should be financially and commercially feasible.
- Legal and regulatory frameworks should ensure the proper management of fiscal risks.
- The business environment should ensure minority investor protections, trading across borders and easy access to credit.

The GCC private sector as a whole is similar to that in Abu Dhabi, connected to the government and facing the same challenges highlighted in the Abu Dhabi section. The GCC governments need to create strategies to support and groom the private sector in different industries and motivate it to contribute to the economic diversification and development goals.

---

23   IMF (2017) 'The Economic Outlook and Policy Challenges in the GCC Countrie'.

Conclusion

The role of the private sector in the development and diversification of the economy of a nation cannot be overlooked either in developed or developing countries. The participation of the private sector in the growth of the country involves enhancing the competitiveness of the economy through improving efficiency and productivity, as well as supporting innovation activities. A strong private sector has a significant impact on the quality of life and economic wellbeing of a nation. Governments in many countries are relying to a large extent on the performance of the private sector for growth and economic progress.

On the other hand, governments in many nations serve an authority and regulatory role and provide a level of regulation encouraging the development of the private sector as well as developing adequate competition law in different markets to support the private sector to compete on the global level. Government policy should be directed towards developing effective governance, reducing bureaucracy, developing an entrepreneurial environment to support the private sector, and providing adequate infrastructure and a skilled workforce that contribute collectively to developing the private sector.

The existence of a robust private sector is highly important these days with globalization and has become the way that economies can survive and progress. The magnitude of economic shocks has increased such that a country's survival depends on the resilience of the economy and the ability of its private sector to respond to the economic shocks and recover from them. South Korea is a very good example of the strong role of the private sector in developing the nation and the economy and transferring the nation from an agricultural economy to high-tech manufacturing.

The private sector factor has had a significant impact on Singapore's economic diversification and development. The private sector, especially the foreign component, has played a critical role in the economic development and diversification of Singapore since independence. Because of the need for foreign funds and manufacturing capabilities, the government attracted the foreign private sector in the form of MNCs. The government used the local private sector to receive foreign technologies and supported it in creating indigenous products to sell globally.

In Abu Dhabi, however, the private sector factor has achieved minimal impact on economic diversification and development. It focuses mostly on construction and represents international companies and services, and does not take risks to explore the under-represented industries. A comprehensive policy to make the private sector the engine of economic development and diversification is necessary. Abu Dhabi could achieve its goals by creating a business-friendly environment that encourages the development of enterprises, creating new companies and expanding the existing businesses.

The private sector has had some impact on economic diversification and development in GCC countries. GCC countries have used SOEs rather than the private sector to drive economic development. The private sector operates as either SMEs in the services and retail sector, or as agents for MNCs. The private sector still has a long way to go to support the strategies for diversifying the economy, and currently lacks the capabilities and funds required to develop export industries.

CHAPTER 11

State-Owned Enterprises

The government's arm in the economy, if not supervised, will cripple the nation

"State-owned enterprises (SOEs) appear to be an enduring feature of the economic landscape and will remain an influential force globally for some years to come."

— PRICEWATERHOUSECOOPERS[24]

growing and sustainable economy is the aim of every country. The growth of the economy contributes to the development of the nation and improves the standard of living for the people. As part of a system, state-owned enterprises (SOEs) support the development of the nation in various ways. State-owned enterprises provide the infrastructure and services, which are essential for economic and social advancement. They also serve the strategy of economic diversification by entering a new industry and

---

24 PricewaterhouseCoopers (2015) State-Owned Enterprises Catalysts for Public Value Creation? accessed at https://www.pwc.com/gr/en/publications/government/state-owned-enterprises-catalysts-for-public-value-creation.html

bearing the associated risks, and by paving the way for the private sector and entrepreneurs to establish businesses in the new sector and industry.

State-owned enterprises exist in almost all countries. More than 2000 SOEs exist in the OECD countries, with most operating in sectors considered strategically important, such as power generation, transportation, finance, and telecommunications.

The influence of SOEs on the global economy has increased over the past two decades. For example, the share of SOEs in the *Fortune Global 500* grew from 9% in 2005 to 20% in 2017. This augmented presence has been determined mainly by the growth of Chinese companies. In fact, three Chinese SOEs (Sinopec Group, China National Petroleum, and State Grid) are in the *Fortune Global 500* list of top five SOEs for 2021, with 82 out of the 143 Chinese companies in the overall list.

State-owned enterprises are created for different purposes in different countries. Sometimes, it is for social reasons, such as establishing infrastructure, creating jobs, developing remote or undeveloped areas, providing services and goods at low prices, and participating in healthcare and education. At other times, it is to support economic growth through diversifying the economy, encouraging industrialization, supporting innovation through developing or acquiring advanced technologies, and enhancing the competitiveness of the country internationally. Sometimes the reasons are political, such as protecting some strategic industries or assets from the control of foreign companies.

The 2011 World Bank study *Overview of State Ownership on the Global Minerals Industry* concluded that the economic sectors that experience changes in technology, face decline, or pose a high risk for investment, take advantage of the SOEs' appetite to take risks and invest in such sectors. Governments in many nations, especially in developing nations, use SOEs to control strategic resources.

The thirteen largest oil companies worldwide, which control most of the global oil production and reserves, are SOEs.

State-owned enterprises have many names – government corporations, government-linked companies, public enterprises, the public sector, and so on. But all of them serve the same purpose; they are controlled by the government and focus on developing and delivering services to specific sectors of the economy. As a broadly accepted definition, SOEs are enterprises in which the state has substantial control through owning equity in the entity – which can be full, majority, or even minority ownership – and has a strong influence on the decision-making.

State-owned enterprises are entities created by the state to participate in commercial activities. They are wholly or partially owned by the government, and their unique characteristic is executing government objectives through commercial activities and methods. Most of the time SOEs take advantage of their connection with the government and gain monopoly control over many economic sectors such as natural resources, telecommunications, energy, healthcare, and sectors that have a political or social impact, such as media. In many cases, the government-nationalized economic sectors and industries are converted into state-owned enterprises.

How SOEs support economic diversification

State-owned enterprises are highly influential and are a growing force in many countries. They are an effective player in diversifying and developing the economy of the country. Many SOEs are engaged in manufacturing and services, and are active internationally. In many nations, SOEs become the driver of technological advancement. They become global players because of the competition for resources and talent. Some governments use SOEs to fund and enhance innovation and R&D, equipping the nation for a better position in the global economy. China, for example, declared in the 2013 release of the *Made in China 2025* strategic plan, to assist Chinese companies to compete more successfully in the global markets, to improve the quality of products and strengthen the high-tech export capability.

State-owned enterprises should not be a threat or be threatened by the private sector, and a collaboration between both parties should exist. SOEs should use the private sector as part of the supply chain of an industry. The 2014 World Bank report *Corporate governance of state-owned enterprises* highlighted the important role that SOEs play in providing infrastructure and sustainability across the supply chain and by not competing with the private sector. This strategy has proved worthy as it ensures sustainable economic diversification.

A 2013 study by Kowalski and colleagues called "State-Owned Enterprises: Trade Effects and Policy Implications", found that 204 (10.2%) of the largest *Fortune 2000* companies were SOEs owned by 37 countries. China had the largest share of enterprises, with 70 SOEs, followed by India (n=30), Russia (n=9), the United Arab Emirates (n=9) and Malaysia (n=8). In addition, the authors noticed that these countries are also significant traders. For example, the top eight nations (China, the United Arab Emirates, Russia, Indonesia, Malaysia, Saudi Arabia, India and Brazil) jointly amounted to more than 20% of world trade, with China alone accounting for about 10% of the world trade in 2010. Thus, SOEs have played a significant role in the economic diversification in these countries. SOEs are active in Europe and the United States but on a smaller scale than in other countries. The OECD's 2017 report *Size and Sectoral Distribution of State-Owned Enterprises* indicated that SOEs in OECD countries employ 2% to 3% of the workers, and in some countries, such as Norway, more than 12%.

The role of state-owned enterprises is more suitable when the private sector is unwilling to invest in industries and businesses with high risk or a long maturity period. In many instances, SOEs are used in sectors where social gains are more important than financial gains. SOEs are used to ensure access to global services for all citizens and provide services and goods to all citizens, even for the poor or those living in remote areas. As cited in the OECD (2017) report, 51% of SOEs in OECD countries are in utilities. Many SOEs were created to establish infrastructure and provide services to support the human and economic development of a nation.

Many countries are implementing policies for economic development and diversification. SOEs play significant roles in the diversification efforts through establishing good infrastructure, innovation, and technology transfer, and by providing financial support, among other things. SOEs support the private sector to play an effective role in diversification efforts because in most cases SOEs cannot deliver this themselves. As such, SOEs should work as a regulator for industry and create a market for competition between the entities of the private sector and encourage them to improve their capabilities to contribute to economic diversification. Governments need to enhance efficiency and enforce good corporate governance of SOEs because increasing the efficiency and effectiveness of SOEs can enhance the efficiency and profitability of the industries in which they are involved.

However, in many countries, the private sector is weak and cannot provide the support needed for diversification and long-term economic strategies, and instead concentrates on short-term, quick-profit investments. As a result, many nations use SOEs to lead the efforts for economic diversification and development. State-owned enterprises sometimes have the responsibility to develop an industry or a sector, and act as incubators for the private sector and entrepreneurial companies in the value chain of the industry.

Inefficient state-owned enterprises

Even though there are many advantages to having SOEs, in many countries poor management has become a serious problem with SOEs, resulting in corrupt and inefficient entities. Large SOEs face problems similar to those of large private sector firms when they grow into substantive and complex companies, with many overlapping layers of hierarchy that cripple the company. This is particularly the case when they have a monopoly.

In his study "State-Owned Enterprise Reform", Chang (2007) presented two causes for corruption and underperformance by SOEs:

1. The principal-agent problem: SOEs are not managed by their owners (citizens). Unable to supervise management, the owners (citizens) cannot judge the performance of the managers accurately. Subsequently, managers put in suboptimal efforts.
2. The soft budget constraint: as part of the government, SOEs can secure financial assistance when the performance drops. This support relaxes the SOE managers and negatively affects their performance.

These two causes explain poor performance among SOEs. The lack of supervising management will lead to bad performance and inefficiency within the firm. If managers know they will be punished for poor management and bad performance, for example, through a salary cut or job loss, they will gain the incentive to manage the firm effectively and ensure good performance. Underperforming and/or corrupt managers of SOEs are more concerned about their personal gain and welfare than the organization and rely on government assistance and bailouts. As an old Arabic saying states, "The one who is guaranteed forgiveness, will misbehave".

State-owned enterprises play a direct and important role in enhancing the economic diversification of the country through investment in infrastructure and strengthening the base needed to establish and enhance different sectors. In addition, SOEs are used as outward FDI for income revenue, and for economic and sometimes political reasons.

East Asian countries such as South Korea, China and Singapore, have effectively used SOEs to force industrialization and support the development, diversification, and growth of the economy. There are many examples of successful SOEs such as Singapore Airlines, which is 57% government owned through Temasek Holdings; the French carmaker Renault; the Brazilian jet manufacturer EMBRAER; and the Korean steelmaker POSCO.

Governments have been using SOEs to lay the foundations for different economic sectors to attract international companies as a way of drawing in financial capital, technologies, manufacturing processes, and quality assurance practices. This strategy has been utilized by China to develop the economy (China used inward and outward FDI to diversify its economy). It is evident that multinational state-owned enterprises became the main player for the stability of the economy, and its development and diversification.

State-owned enterprises in Singapore

Since its independence, Singapore's government provided initial investment and support to spark and encourage the establishment of industries. This policy was to overcome the concern that there were insufficient incentives to establish and sustain strong industries in a small-sized market such as Singapore.

As the private sector was weak and lacked funds or expertise, to jump-start industries and economic sectors, the Singaporean government created Government-Linked Companies (GLC) and statutory boards. The government played an entrepreneurial role and created state-owned enterprises in different sectors such as manufacturing, finance, trading, transportation, and services. Some of these companies have joint ventures with international investors. For example, the Singapore Refining Company is a joint venture with Caltex and British Petroleum, while the Petrochemical Corporation of Singapore is a joint venture with Shell and a Japanese consortium. Some of Singapore's GLCs have grown to become well-recognized names internationally, such as Singapore Airlines.

Singapore created SOEs in most sectors out of necessity as it emerged from colonialism with major social and economic problems. Goh Keng Swee, the deputy prime minister in the mid-1970s, stated in 1972 that "The government has to be the planner and the mobilizer of the economic effort". The leaders were convinced that the government had to maintain control over the economic and social activities, yet there was a commitment to let the market set the prices.

The government's belief was that industrialization was necessary for development and advancement. In addition, industrialization would create more jobs and factories that were able to accommodate large numbers of workers quickly. As the local private sector lacked capabilities and motivation to move from trade or port services to manufacturing and new economic sectors, the government, when it was planning to establish a sector or invest in strategic projects, used the SOEs or international investors.

For example, the maritime and logistics industry started in the 1960s when Keppel Shipyard and Sembawang Shipyard were created to take over the British-deserted facilities in Keppel and Sembawang, and to keep the port active for the workers to keep their jobs. Then Neptune Orient Lines (shipping) was established to keep the flow of ship traffic through Singapore port. The Port of Singapore Authority (PSA) was established in 1964 to operate, manage, and coordinate the different activities in the port. This motivated many companies to work in different areas of the maritime and logistic industry, and by the second decade of the new millennium there were 7,000 logistic companies in Singapore, contributing around 9% of the GDP annually.

Government-linked companies

Numerous government-linked companies were created either directly by ministries or through government holding companies, such as Temasek Holdings, which provided a wide range of goods and services. In addition, many other government entities created their own companies, such as the National Trades Union Congress (NTUC), which created many cooperative businesses, including supermarkets, taxis, and a travel agency. The statutory boards also formed subsidiary companies and entities, for example, A*STAR formed many laboratories and institutes.

The paper by Ramirez and Tan (2004) "Singapore Inc Versus the Private Sector" reported that the government claimed that GLCs functioned on a commercial basis as for-profit entities, similar to private sector companies, and that they are assumed to provide financial profits and returns. They work under the same principles and market forces as private entities and do not receive any aid or special treatment from the state. The authors point out that government domination is lenient, and that the state usually does not intervene with the management of GLCs directly. However, GLCs seem to receive some privileges because of government ownership.

Kirkpatrick's (2014) study "Managing State Assets to Achieve Developmental Goals" suggested that Singapore encouraged its

GLCs to function on a commercial basis and compete on an equal level with private businesses, with both local and foreign entities. For example, GLCs under Temasek Holdings are applying corporate governance policies developed by the company, however, Temasek does not control or manage the decisions or operations of the GLCs under it. To enhance the international corporate governance, GLC board members are not allocated to government officials, though there are international people with the right experience who are board members of some GLCs.

The government aims to invest in strategic sectors and business, but not to be involved in the management beyond the point at which the enterprise becomes self-sustaining. The government does not hesitate to pull out its support or close down unprofitable companies as GLCs were not created for social or employment-generating purposes. They should compete on a commercial basis with private firms and multinational companies and even with each other. However, the government of Singapore is unwilling to relinquish total control over the GLCs. In 1987, the Public Sector Divestment Committee recommended that the government should sell the shares in many of the GLCs.

The Heritage Foundation, which ranks Singapore as the second freest economy in the world, states that GLCs dominate Singapore's economy. The enterprises under Temasek Holdings alone accounted for 10% of the GDP and about 27% of the stock market in 2000. Many researchers pointed out that it was hard to create a complete list of GLCs in Singapore since the influence of the government is not exposed through direct ownership (fully or partially) of GLCs. There are other means that government can influence entities, such as controlling resources and having the ability to allocate them when the government considers them suitable.

Temasek Holdings

In 1974, the government established Temasek Holdings to re-organize its investments and channel them to benefit the economy in Singapore. It is wholly owned by the government and has considerable holdings in most economic sectors, including transportation, energy, banking, shipping, real estate, and communications. As of 2020, Temasek holds about S$306 billion in assets. Despite the privatization efforts in the 1980s and 1990s, through Temasek Holdings the government still owns majority shares in many companies that cover all areas of public life, such as rail transport and Singapore Power.

The government established Temasek Holdings under the Ministry of Finance to manage its investments in GLCs. At that time, thirty-six companies were transferred to Temasek's control. Since then, these companies and newer ones have been given opportunities to expand and diversify their operations, and the total number of GLCs is now estimated to be in the hundreds. These GLCs are divided between first-tier, subsidiaries, or associate's companies, which often have third-tier subsidiaries, and so on. Table 11.1 shows some of the companies under Temasek Holdings and the sectors they are involved in, including finance, property, telecommunications, transport and logistics, infrastructure and engineering, and utilities.

Table 11.1. Some of Temasek Business Groups

Name of Group	Total Assets (S$ billion) (S$B)	No of subsidiaries	No of associated companies	Sector
Development Bank of Singapore	646	88	17	Finance
Singapore Telecom (SingTel)	43	139	36	Communications
Singapore Airlines (SIA)	23,369	24	32	Aviation
Keppel Corporation	13,816	144	39	Multi-industry
Capital Land	193	102	30	Real Estate
Semb Corp Marine	8.9	33	12	Transportation & Logistics

source: https://www.temasek.com.sg (2017).

The impact of state-owned enterprises on Singapore's economic diversification and development

Table 11.2. Impact of Public Sector Strategies/Policies on Diversification

Strategies/ Policies	Outcome	Impact on Economic diversification
Creation of Temasek	• The government created business firms • Partnering with MNC to create manufacturing • Invest in emerging sectors	• Temasek subsidiaries in every economic sector • Created companies to start new sectors • Attract MNC to partner to start new economic sectors • Invest globally to import technology and open market for products
Create GLCs	• Strong companies (GLCs) in different industries • Created a strong local partner for MNCs • Pave the way in the new industries where the Private sector is hesitated to inter.	• Create new economic sectors starting with GLCs • Attract private sector (local and international) to new industries • Support local companies by creating a supply chain opportunities

State-owned enterprise in Abu Dhabi

State-owned enterprises are a major element of Abu Dhabi's economic structure. Some SOEs, such as the Abu Dhabi National Oil Company (ADNOC) manage strategic sectors and are major providers of income. Mubadala established Masdar in 2006 to create and develop a renewable energy sector. A number of SOEs in Abu Dhabi, such as Etihad Airways, Mubadala, ADIA, and Abu Dhabi Holding (ADQ), have emerged as globally known brands. The SOEs are the motor of economic diversification and are present in almost all sectors, including petrochemicals, tourism, hospitality, transport, banking and manufacturing, see Table 11.3.

The government has long-term social and economic strategies and objectives. It invests in commercial objectives as well as social objectives with a long-term return on investment, aligned with the strategic long-term objectives. To support the strategy to diversify the economy away from petroleum, Abu Dhabi created SOEs such as Emirates Aluminum, Borouge, and Emirates Steel, taking advantage of the petroleum feedstock. The 2016 IMF country report indicates that the assets of SOEs in Abu Dhabi reached US$458 billion, about 214.7% of the national GDP, however, this excludes SOEs such as ADIA, Mubadala, and ADNOC.

The role of SOEs in the economic diversification of Abu Dhabi

The success of SOEs in terms of productivity and efficiency leads to the development, growth, and sustainability of the economy and country. A 2014 OECD report on the effects of SOEs on the economy, stated that an improvement in SOE productivity of about 5% could enhance financial resources by 5% of a nation's GDP, particularly when SOEs dominate the economy. On the other hand, if they are inefficient and underperform, they waste resources and take them from other priorities. According to the OECD, with good corporate governance in state companies, SOEs can significantly improve productivity, job creation, and economic growth.

There are many reasons for Abu Dhabi to create SOEs. Examples such as ADNOC, Etisalat, and the Abu Dhabi Water and Electricity Authority (ADWEA), are distinguished players in the strategic sectors, where the state can play the role of driver. In addition, Abu

Dhabi created enterprises to develop new sectors to support its strategy to diversify the economy. For example, Masdar is intended to start the renewable energy sector, since this sector is not economically attractive to private companies and needs more investment to become attractive to the private sector.

SOEs are in a large number of sectors, including financial services, real estate, utilities, transportation, tourism, health, and education, among others. Table 11.3 shows some of the companies that are owned either fully or partially by Abu Dhabi. This table was created using IMF and Bloomberg data on the status of SOEs in Abu Dhabi in 2015. Since then, many changes have transpired, such as Mubadala controlling IPIC, the creation of ADQ to control many of the government's commercial assets in Abu Dhabi, the creation of the EDGE group in the defense sector, and the creation of G42 in advanced technologies.

Table 11.3. Some of Abu Dhabi's SOEs, sector and total assets

Name	Sector	AD Ownership	Total asset, US$ million 2015
Mubadala Investment	Multi-sectors	100	125,000
Senaat	Manufacturing	100	7,510
Tawazun	Defense	100	-
Etihad Airways	Aviation	100	15,900
Abu Dhabi Ship Building Co.	Defense & Marine	50	372
Abu Dhabi Aviation Co.	Air Freight & Logistics	100	1,272
Union Cement Co.	Construction Materials	54.3	373
Fujairah Building Industries	Construction Materials	77.4	113
National Bank of Abu Dhabi	Financial	98.4	110,699
Abu Dhabi Commercial Bank	Financial	83.9	62,152
Union National Bank PJSC	Financial	93.1	27,742
National Bank of Ras Al-Khaimah PSC	Financial	88.3	11,042
Tourism Development & Investment	Tourism & Real Estate	100	11,779
Agthia Group PJSC	Food and Beverage	51	645
Abu Dhabi National Hotels	Hotels & Resorts	72.2	2,657
National Marine Dredging Co.	Marine Ports & Services	54.1	1,370
Abu Dhabi National Insurance Co. PSC	Insurance	53.7	1,526
Al Ain Ahlia Insurance Co.	Insurance	55.6	551
Al Fujairah National Insurance Co. PSC	Insurance	84.6	114
Abu Dhabi National Energy Co.	Utilities	71.7	30,461
Gulf Pharmaceutical Industries	Pharmaceuticals	22.6	954
Emirates Telecommunications Group Co	Telecommunication	99.4	34,924

sources: Bloomberg and IMF

EDGE group

EDGE was launched in November 2019 to form the technology arm of Abu Dhabi's defense sector. Since the beginning of the millennium, Abu Dhabi has been investing in defense and creating many manufacturing companies for different products. But there has been a lack of communication between different players, which has sometimes become unhealthy competition. In 2017, the Emirates Defence Industries Company (EDIC) was created and a foreign expert was brought in to restructure the defense sector. But he was a disaster and almost destroyed everything that had been built in the defense sector at that point. In 2019, the government of Abu Dhabi got rid of the foreign expert and even disassembled his company EDIC. A new company called EDGE was created under Faisal Al-Bannai, an Emirati who had experience in private business, who created and managed Axiom and then founded DarkMatter. Both companies were successful, which led the government of Abu Dhabi to trust him in leading the EDGE group and creating a strong defense industry.

EDGE was a merger of 25 companies drawing from EDIC, Emirates Advanced Investments Group (EAIG), Tawazun Holding, and other independent organizations. EDGE has combined annual revenue of over US$5 billion and has more than 12,000 employees working across its five core clusters: Platforms & Systems, Missiles & Weapons, Cyber Defence, Electronic Warfare & Intelligence, and Mission Support.

EDGE's priority is to be part of efforts to transform the country's advanced technology capabilities to make it fit for an evolving digital era. EDGE's forward-looking strategy will continue to focus on addressing national security threats that are adapting through new technological means, strengthening current capabilities and industry R&D, and developing technology for export growth.

In 2020, EDGE was ranked among the top 25 military suppliers in the world by the Stockholm International Peace Research Institute (SIPRI). With this being the first time that a Middle East company has been named among the largest exporters of original equipment manufacturers (OEMs) for defense and security, EDGE's presence is a notable ranking for the UAE.

So far, Faisal Al-Bannai is on the right path to advancing the defense industry in the UAE and making it competitive with global players. At the same time, EDGE is guiding the other UAE entities involved in the defense industry to groom them and support them in their journey. Will he be able to continue his journey?

Corporate governance and performance

In 2016 the IMF reported that 92% of total debt in Abu Dhabi is generated from the SOEs. The IMF stressed that the main factor for the high debt was corporate governance. Hence, corporate governance is very significant not only for the performance of SOEs, but more critically to the performance of the economy as a whole.

Since the financial crisis and the decline of the oil price, the government in Abu Dhabi has been applying stricter terms on the funding of projects for SOEs, especially given the accumulation of high debt as a result of poorly managed SOEs.

With the lower oil prices and resultant lower revenues to the government, the state will not continue financing non-performing SOEs or offering support to those that are not successful and that keep demanding money. The government has started to prioritize its funding to more successful and useful projects. As these projects are increasing in number and scope, the funds are being directed to those with a higher potential of success or serving a strategic purpose.

In a 2014 paper on SOEs, the OECD suggested that corporate governance was a key reason that enabled some nations to advance and achieve remarkable growth. Norway, for example, has high standards of corporate governance. Abu Dhabi, in its Vision 2030, cites Norway as a model to follow. The Norwegian government uses the value at entry process to prioritize and select projects. The value at entry process builds on the United Kingdom's Gateway Review process. Both processes ensure that projects are aligned with government strategy, deliver value for money returns, and have an acceptable risk profile.

As suggested by the OECD, one of the decisions that can guarantee good corporate governance is the separation between the state and SOEs. In Norway, ministers, active politicians and government officials are not allowed to be on the boards of SOEs to avoid conflicts of interest. However, in Abu Dhabi, the selection of the board members remains an issue, and it struggles to apply guidelines compatible with the OECD's framework for SOEs. There is no centralized entity to supervise and evaluate these companies, and no formal processes to monitor the performance of the SOEs and their management.

The SOEs in Abu Dhabi have complex structures of ownership with multiple UAE sovereign wealth fund investors, and the absence of a centralized or coordinated ownership entity. State ownership is executed through investment vehicles, including Mubadala, Senaat, TDIC, ADNOC, and ADQ, among many others. The status of non-centralized ownership and the lack of coordination can allow the SOEs and executives to avoid scrutiny for poor management and performance.

Most OECD countries have created entities to centralize ownership, such as Finland and New Zealand, whereas others have created a dual-ownership model, as in Germany and Switzerland. In this latter case, a central ministry (generally the Ministry of Finance, or Treasury) shares the ownership with a sectoral ministry.

Corruption in SOEs is a global issue and the only way to fight it is by having a high standard of corporate governance and having qualified management to lead these entities. A global survey by OECD related to bribery of foreign officials found that the employees in SOEs were the largest targeted group and 57% of all bribes occurred during procurement activities.

Privatization and SOEs

In the past two decades, the Abu Dhabi government wanted to ease its control over the utilities and services with the idea that privatization would be better for the government and the citizens. Abu Dhabi privatized many of its utilities and services while keeping a high percentage of the ownership with the government. In addition, many SOEs were created in different economic sectors to lead economic development and diversification.

Although the privatization idea was good in principle as a way of providing a better outcome, when applied it did not serve its objectives of greater efficiency, less cost, and better-quality outcomes. In their paper, "Strategic Policy Choices on Privatization in an International Mixed Duopoly", Xu and Lee (2012) presented many reasons for not achieving the objectives of privatization. The main reasons are listed.

- The chairperson and board members are government officials, and the CEO is either an official in the government or reports to a government official. While the entity appears as an independent company with a board and structure, its culture and mentality remain similar to a government department.

- The selection of the chairperson, board members and executives is based on personal relationships and friendship ties, not on capability.
- These SOEs do not operate on a commercial basis. Their operating costs are very high and their investments are costly and provide either limited or no returns. The SOEs depend on the government to cover them for poor performance.
- The SOEs take their direction from the government for investment actions and no decisions are taken unless they are approved by a high level in the government. This delays timely project execution.
- As the government is in control of the decisions in these SOEs, the SOEs do not hold responsibility for their actions.

It is crucial for Abu Dhabi to implement good governance standards, such as the OECD corporate governance guidelines on SOEs. These guidelines contain recommendations relevant to Abu Dhabi. For example, the management of the playing field between private and state-controlled firms, the commercialization of the SOEs, and the professionalization of boards of directors and assigning them greater powers and autonomy.

There is a need for a centralized entity for ownership and coordination under the executive council. The role of this entity could include but is not restricted to:

- Coordination between the SOEs;
- Training and certifying executives for high-level positions in these companies;
- Selection of competent chairpersons, executive officers and board members;
- Monitoring of performance;
- Evaluation of the performance of the company, chairperson, board, and executives;

- Replacement of those who are underperforming, and;
- Preventing new leaders from repeating the same mistakes of previous leaders.

Abu Dhabi uses the SOEs to support the diversification of the economy with state-owned companies in almost all sectors. The performance of these companies does not meet the expectations for the many reasons discussed in this chapter.

A comparison of the impact of SOEs on economic diversification

Both states (Abu Dhabi and Singapore) are using state-owned enterprises in each field and sector, but the ways they manage their SOEs differ.

- Singapore strongly pushes its GLCs to operate on a commercial basis and to be efficient and allow competition between each other. Abu Dhabi, on the other hand, does not push its SOEs strongly for this purpose, and the government protects the SOEs and always provides support for them.
- Singapore used GLCs as anchors and leaders in each sector to pave the way, support SMEs, and host developers of new technologies in different manufacturing sectors, such as Neptune Orient lines for transportation and ST Engineering group. Abu Dhabi is not using its SOEs as anchors for different economic sectors which creates hurdles for smaller companies who need a big brother entity to support them and make manufacturing more efficient on the national level.
- Singapore used GLCs to create new economic sectors when needed, such as steel mills in the 1960s, electronics in the 1970s,

computers in the 1980s, and biomedicine in the 1990s. In Abu Dhabi, there is no direction to do that. Furthermore, in some sectors where SOEs were created to elevate those sectors, it did not succeed because the SOEs worked alone and did not support small companies to take a share of the industry. Also, there is no higher entity that can manage and coordinate the activities between the different public and private players.

- In Singapore, most of the time the GLCs support SMEs and do not compete with them or try to get rid of them. In Abu Dhabi, SOEs are not always supporting SMEs and sometimes try to take over their business and push them out of the industry, which affects the strength and continuity of the industry.

State-owned enterprises in the GCC countries

State-owned enterprises have played a very significant role in the development and diversification of the economy, as evident in the East Asian economies. SOEs can invest and operate manufacturing industries, tourism facilities, strategic sectors, and service industries. They can be part of the creation of a non-oil economy, non-oil revenue sources and non-oil exports.

In the GCC countries, SOEs play a bigger role and are in every industry and sector. This mixed role between private and public sectors, however, allows the management to take advantage of poor governance for personal benefit. As SOEs depend on the government for funding, few are profitable because the compensation for the employees and top management is very high and sometimes are not covered by the regular operations of the company. These companies are not efficient and cost the governments billions of dollars.

Steffen Hertog has produced a few publications on the GCC, one of which is "How the GCC Did It: Formal and Informal

Governance of Successful Public Enterprise". In this paper, Hertog explains that the corporate governance standard in the GCC is a unique one, unlike international standards where the board is independent of the management. The boards are always selected by the government and board members come from the government ranks. This blurs the line between government as the manager of the SOE and as a board member, leading to situations where management actions of an SOE may not be questioned by the board.

Even though SOEs are state-owned, sometimes these entities become a family inheritance, with the father staying in the leadership position for ten to fifteen years and when he steps down, he brings his son in as the new leader.

For the GCC to have strong and effective SOEs, one option is to run these entities according to best practice standards and as private sector companies, and to not assign any government-connected person to lead the companies and enforce strong OECD corporate governance standards.

SOEs in the GCC in many ways are similar to those in Abu Dhabi and have the same issues with performance, governance, and culture. SOEs are using the protection of governments to survive. This should be stopped and SOEs should go through major restructuring to create strong, efficient, and capable companies to compete globally.

Conclusion

State-owned enterprises are an effective tool for governments when the private sector hesitates to invest in a new sector or business area with high risk and uncertainty, or if there are political and social causes of investments.

In many nations, especially in East Asia, SOEs have played a very effective role in the success of economic development and diversification. China is the best example to observe how SOEs assist in the diversification and development of the economy and advancement of the whole nation since the end of the 1970s.

There are many successful SOEs across the world and many others suffer from bad management and performance, because managers rely on the government's bailout for assistance. The management of SOEs, as it occurs in private sector firms, must be supervised and punished for failure or rewarded for success.

The state-owned enterprise factor has had a major impact on Singapore's economic diversification and development. Singapore's SOEs have played a vital role in the development and diversification of the economy. As Singapore was going in the direction of diversifying the economy, it needed companies to lead the way in the new sectors. Because the new sectors would need substantial startup investment and the returns were not guaranteed and would take time to recover, the private sector was hesitant to take the initiative. As a result, the government of Singapore created its own companies to lead the way in the new sectors, such as Singapore Airlines, SignTel, Singapore Technologies and MCS Group (MediaCorp). As shown in Table 11.1, Singapore has SOEs operating in different sectors of the economy that support the strategy to diversify the economy.

The state-owned enterprise factor has had a limited impact on the economic diversification and development in Abu Dhabi, it was not as expected. State-owned enterprises in Abu Dhabi are similar to those elsewhere in the GCC and the Middle East and North Africa (MENA) regions, where the government is a generous customer and protector. Even though the SOEs act like independent corporations and apply corporate governance, in reality, they operate as units under the government to do a certain job, even if it costs twice as much.

The state-owned enterprise factor has had an impact on economic diversification and development in the GCC countries. GCC countries have made extensive use of SOEs with poor leadership, which have delivered poor outcomes and have failed to deliver innovation or exports. They even sometimes have negative effects on diversification with high-cost overruns for their projects, forcing the government to change its plans and strategies.

CHAPTER 12

Final Thoughts and Recommendations

How can the wheel of diversification and development lead to a journey of success?

"We must not rely on oil alone as the main source of our national income. We have to diversify the sources of our revenue and construct economic projects that will ensure a free, stable and dignified life for the people."

— Shaikh Zayed, founding father of the UAE (1918–2004)

This study has analyzed the key factors for economic diversification and drawing on the existing literature and research has created the diversification framework (wheel of diversification). Using the methodologies of secondary data analysis and impact evaluation, the factors of the model that support economic diversification were tested by applying them to the case of Singapore's successful diversification. Subsequently, the model was used to evaluate Abu Dhabi's and the GCC countries' progress in diversification, which showed areas for improvement to achieve a successful diversification of the economy.

Developing the wheel of diversification model

As discussed in previous chapters, there are many economic development models that have been created to guide nations in pursuing the goal of economic growth and development. Examples include the linear stages of growth and structural change models, the neo-Marxist and Neoclassical Revival of the 1980s models, and Porter's Diamond, Double Diamond, and General Double Diamond models. Many, if not all, of these models have been used by many countries around the world. However, they were not successful, especially in the developing countries, because the models were designed for European countries, whose context is different from developing and GGC countries. Accordingly, none of these models is fit to solve the economic development issues of nations such as those in the GCC, which have limited capabilities except for one natural resource. In addition, there is no model designed for economic diversification. All of the models are designed for economic development instead.

The model in this study (the wheel of economic diversification) is designed to guide developing nations to success in economic development and diversification. The model focuses on factors that are critical to developing economic diversification and maintaining and enhancing growth over time. Creating these factors and enhancing their capability to ensure high-quality outcomes will lead to successful diversification, which in turn leads to economic development and growth.

The GCC countries have tried many economic models over the past few decades, however, none of them has been successful, because no model was designed to guide a nation with one natural resource on the path to diversifying its economy. The model used in this study (the wheel of diversification) bridges this gap and many gaps that developing countries face, such as education, training, infrastructure, technology, a weak private sector, and so on. The wheel of diversification is a framework designed to guide and direct governments along their journey to economic development and diversification.

Measuring the effectiveness of factors in driving economic diversification

As the purpose of the framework was to guide successful economic diversification, it was necessary to evaluate the impact of the factors on the economic diversification and development of the country. To facilitate this, the research developed an assessment tool highlighting the impact element within each factor and measuring the impact on a scale of 1 to 7, where 1 is "No Impact" and 7 is "Transformational Impact". Based on the impact assessment of elements within a factor, an overall impact score for each factor driving economic diversification was developed.

As the benchmark for the successful economic diversification of a country, Singapore was analyzed for how strategies were designed and implemented to achieve the highest impact of factors towards supporting economic diversification. Subsequently, the framework was applied to Abu Dhabi and the GCC countries to evaluate the impact of factors on their ability to achieve economic diversification. Table 12.1 shows the impact comparison of factors in the wheel model in driving economic diversification and development in Singapore, Abu Dhabi, and the GCC countries. It can be noted that the strength and quality of the outcome of these factors in Singapore had the greatest effect, however, in the GCC states some of these factors had a low impact because the quality of the outcome was low.

Table 12.1. Factor Effectiveness[25]

Factor effectiveness in driving Economic Diversification and Development				
Scale 1 = No Impact, 4 = Moderate Impact , 7 = Transformational Impact				
		Singapore	Abu Dhabi	GCC
Outer Circle	National Resources/ Financial Fund	5.9	5.35	4.85
Middle Circle	Human Development	6.8	2.65	2.5
	Governance, Institutions, and Policies	6.5	3.4	2.6
	Infrastructure	6.45	5.35	4.9
Inner Circle	Export Orientation	6.6	2.65	2.2
	Innovation	6.45	2.05	1.95
	Entrepreneurship	5.4	1.95	1.95
	Private Sector	6	3.2	3.5
	State-Owned Enterprises	6.5	2.8	2.8

Figure 12.1 is a radar diagram that shows diagrammatically the impact of factors in driving economic diversification and development in Singapore, Abu Dhabi, and the GCC countries. The radar diagram highlights the significant difference in the impact of factors between Singapore, Abu Dhabi and the GCC countries.

Each of the factors is seen to have a significant impact on economic development and diversification in Singapore. However, in Abu Dhabi and the GCC countries, only the natural resources/ financial fund and the infrastructure factors can be seen to have a significant impact on economic development and diversification.

25 Al-Shamsi, A. (2020) 'Strategies to Diversify and Develop the Economy of Abu Dhabi and GCC Countries: Application of "Wheel of Diversification" model", Thesis submitted in partial fulfillment of the requirements for Doctorate in Business Administration (DBA), University Of Wollongong, Dubai.

Effectiveness of Factors on Economic Diversification and Development

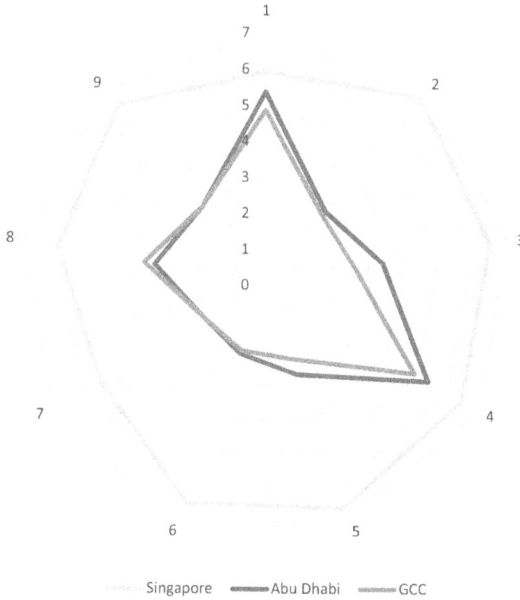

Figure 12.1. Radar Diagram showing the impact of the Factors in the Wheel Model[26]

Table 12.2 shows a comparison of the factor impact assessments for Singapore, Abu Dhabi, and the GCC countries, and provides an overview of the strategies that were employed in each case to achieve the desired factor impact. This comparison helps to identify the missing and/or weak links in strategies that prevented Abu Dhabi and the GCC countries from achieving the high-quality impact of factors towards supporting economic diversification.

---

26   Ibid

Table 12.2. Overview of factors

Factor	Singapore	Abu Dhabi	GCC	Overview and gaps in strategy
Natural Resources/ Financial Fund	**Impact = 5.9.** Despite having no natural resources, Singapore created a sovereign wealth fund that has played a vital role. Singapore overcame the shortage in natural resources income by creating an internal saving system.	**Impact =5.35.** Abu Dhabi has established sovereign wealth funds that are primarily used to supplement oil income in periods of low oil pricing.	**Impact = 4.85.** Most GCC countries have significant oil reserves that have funded their development. While most GCC countries have established sovereign wealth funds, they have not used them effectively to drive economic diversification and development.	• While Singapore has no natural resources, it has overcome this weakness through the establishment and management of an internal saving system and sovereign wealth fund as well as attracting FDI. • Even though petroleum dominates the GCC economy, there is no industry or supporting industries established in relation to the petroleum industry. Most of the GCC countries still rely on international companies in the petroleum industries in the different stages.
Human Development	**Impact = 6.8.** Singapore has proactively developed its leaders and systemically developed the competencies that the country needs to both deliver efficiently in	**Impact = 2.65.** Abu Dhabi has applied a lot of effort in human development, but there has been no synergy between the efforts and their continuation.	**Impact = 2.5.** The GCC states have not developed leaders with the competencies required to develop and implement complex policies and programs, nor have they developed competencies in the	• Since its establishment, Singapore has focused on developing its leaders and providing its people with both quality of life and the competencies needed to deliver its strategy. The GCC countries have relied on tribal models to select leaders based on relationships, not competency.

Factor	Singapore	Abu Dhabi	GCC	Overview and gaps in strategy
	the current markets and to prepare for future market changes.	There is an effort to match the outcome of the education system with industry requirements, but this is very slow.	workforce required by industry, and have failed to attract and retain competent expatriates.	• Singapore has used foresight to proactively develop the new competencies required to support the new industries. • The GCC countries have not been successful in matching capability development to meet industry needs and there remains a cultural barrier to vocational professions. • Singapore decided early in its development to target high-caliber expatriates to help drive innovation and R&D. The GCC countries have failed to provide an environment that is attractive to retain high-caliber expatriates. Singapore has progressively built its own local high-quality technical experts (researchers, engineers and scientists), while the GCC countries are lacking in students studying in high-tech areas.

Factor	Singapore	Abu Dhabi	GCC	Overview and gaps in strategy
Governance, Institutions, and Policies	**Impact = 6.5.** The government has played a vital and positive role in developing the nation and the success of the economy. The government and administration in Singapore are one of the most effective and non-corrupt worldwide.	**Impact = 3.4.** Abu Dhabi is lacking in competent leaders in institutions and has not been effective in enforcing policies.	**Impact = 2.6.** While GCC governments have developed vision statements they have failed to develop and properly implement programs to deliver the visions. In a similar way, governments have initiated laws, but have failed to have them effectively enforced.	• Singapore has established a robust system of governance that is transparent and mandates teamwork and accountability. • In GCC countries, while there are laws for governance that are not mandated, there is no accountability, a significant lack of teamwork and integration across institutions, and a significant shortage of suitably competent local staff. • In Singapore, institutions have been established to drive sector development, while in the GCC countries there is no system for sectoral development.
Infrastructure	**Impact = 6.45.** Infrastructure played a vital role in the development of Singapore and in the diversification of the economy. Infrastructure was used as a way to attract foreign	**Impact = 5.35.** Abu Dhabi's infrastructure is capable of supporting the efforts to grow and diversify the economy. The existing and future infrastructure projects all	**Impact = 4.9.** Most GCC countries have used funds from oil exports to develop their infrastructure. There are many major projects in the GCC countries to establish the infrastructure needed for economic	• Both Singapore and the GCC countries have been effective in developing extensive infrastructure. The key difference is that Singapore has delivered value-for-money in infrastructure, while GCC countries have experienced very large cost and schedule overruns and often had low-quality outcomes.

Factor	Singapore	Abu Dhabi	GCC	Overview and gaps in strategy
	companies to invest in certain sectors, and it provided incentives to local companies to expand their business to different sectors.	support the social and economic development of Abu Dhabi.	development and diversification.	• In the GCC there is no system for evaluating, selecting and monitoring infrastructure projects.
Export Orientation	**Impact = 6.6.** Export orientation drove Singapore's economic diversification and development. This factor was the reason for Singapore being what it is today. Because of this factor, Singapore's products have become globally competitive.	**Impact = 2.65.** Abu Dhabi is trying to develop strong industries for export, but it did not create the right schemes for that from policies and incentives. Abu Dhabi is pushing for industries that are using petroleum feedstock, which is not sustainable because it depends on subsidies and support from the government. There are no incentives for export even though Abu Dhabi has enhanced market access for its	**Impact = 2.2.** While many GCC countries export oil, they have failed to establish manufacturing sectors that can compete on the international market and contribute to GDP growth.	• Singapore realized early in its development that exports were essential if the country was to grow economically. It established a robust capability to develop exports and through a proactive transformation strategy, such as creating clusters and allowing MNCs to create manufacturing for export, has been able to maintain strong export growth that has, in turn, contributed very strongly to economic diversification and development. • The GCC countries have had very significant income from oil exports and have not had the same pressure as Singapore to enhance exports to develop and diversify the economy (the economy is not export-oriented).

299

Factor	Singapore	Abu Dhabi	GCC	Overview and gaps in strategy
		products within the UAE through regional and bilateral trade agreements.		• GCC countries have policies to grow exports, but because of inefficiencies and subsidies, the outcomes have been minimal. There are no entities responsible for the success of this approach similar to the EDB in Singapore. There are no incentives system for exports.
Innovation	**Impact = 6.45.** Singapore is a good example of how a small country can diversify and develop the economy by focusing on technological advancement in manufacturing industries and strengthening its innovation capabilities. Singapore set a strategic goal to become a knowledge and R&D-based economy.	**Impact = 2.05.** The weakness of Abu Dhabi in innovation and R&D is not surprising given the fact that creating a science and R&D-based economy is a long-term process and Abu Dhabi has only recently invested in the creation of a local innovation infrastructure, including the establishment of research and technology centers	**Impact = 1.95.** There are different approaches among the GCC states. Most GCC countries did not set strategies for innovation but created institutes instead. Innovation and R&D activities are still new to the GCC region and will take time to create knowledge-based economies in the countries that are pursuing this goal. The GCC states need to use foreign talent to jump-start innovation.	• Singapore has placed innovation as central to its strategy, providing substantial funding for R&D, and proactively developing a robust system to drive innovation. Singapore has used innovation to establish viable products and services for export that are internationally competitive. Singapore has used foresight to continually change its innovation focus to ensure that it remains internationally competitive. • GCC countries do not have an innovation ecosystem that supports innovators to take their ideas further by developing and creating products from them.

Factor	Singapore	Abu Dhabi	GCC	Overview and gaps in strategy
	The government structured policies to support this goal by establishing higher educational entities and research institutions to create a pool of local talent and conduct R&D activities; creating the ecosystem and environment to support innovations in the private and public sectors, and; attracting international firms to establish R&D activities and technological manufacturing in Singapore.	and branches for several international universities. Thus, it will take time before the fruits of these investments come to bear. Abu Dhabi needs to think of attracting foreign talent, since its population remains small.	Some of the GCC states apply face value to innovation policies, but have not significantly funded R&D, and have not established a system to support or drive innovation.	• GCC countries do not have entities or strategies to develop innovation capabilities such as labs, engineers and scientists, or to build and monitor an innovation ecosystem. • The GCC has failed to identify areas where it can develop and innovate. When this does occur, it is unstructured and it is not linked to a clear strategy, or developed or supported systemically. • GCC countries failed to identify technology areas where they can own the patents and use their knowledge to export value-added products to the international market. • Create a system to facilitate the relationship between local and international companies for technology transfer and spillover.

Factor	Singapore	Abu Dhabi	GCC	Overview and gaps in strategy
Entrepreneurship	**Impact = 5.4.** After independence, because of the lack of capabilities, funds and an entrepreneurial local private sector, the government focused on attracting international firms to develop the capabilities and grow the economy. After the 1985 recession, the government realized that it needed to develop and enhance the local private sector and entrepreneurship. Since then, Singapore has created many entities, initiatives and programs to support entrepreneurs and startups.	**Impact = 1.95.** In general, entrepreneurial activities need an innovation system and R&D labs as a source of germination. This involves individuals who can recognize opportunities and transfer them into products or services for the market. Abu Dhabi does not have an ecosystem to support such entrepreneurial activities (local and/or foreign).	**Impact = 1.95.** Similar to Abu Dhabi, there is no ecosystem to support entrepreneurs in the GCC countries.	• Singapore has an ecosystem that supports entrepreneurship. • GCC countries do not have an ecosystem to support entrepreneurship and startups • GCC countries too often rely on: • SOE monopolies to drive innovation – these SOEs have resisted change and have not provided innovation; • MNCs to provide technology transfer – this strategy has not been successful. MNCs enter the GCC market to sell their existing products. They establish local facilities for simple and low-value activities but do not transfer technology to local companies. • GCC states need to have entities to facilitate the transfer of technology and spillover technology to local startups and companies.

Factor	Singapore	Abu Dhabi	GCC	Overview and gaps in strategy
Private Sector	**Impact = 6.0.** The private sector has played a critical role in the economic diversification and development of Singapore since independence. Because of the need for foreign funds and manufacturing capabilities, the government attracted the foreign private sector in the form of MNCs.	**Impact = 3.2.** The private sector is not playing a strong role in the diversification efforts even though it was mentioned in Vision 2030 that it should be a major player in realizing the vision. There is no entity or policy to develop the private sector.	**Impact = 3.5.** GCC countries have used SOEs rather than the private sector to drive economic development. The private sector is formed by either SMEs in the services and retail sectors, or agents for MNCs. The private sector lacks the capability and funds required to develop export industries.	• Singapore initially relied on MNCs to establish an export-based manufacturing sector, however, in its second transformation it changed its strategy to establishing and growing the local private sector. • Singapore has established many sector-focused statutory boards. One of the mandates of these boards is to develop and support private companies in that sector. • GCC governments still rely extensively on SOEs • Singapore coordinates the technology spillover from MNCs to local companies. GCC countries do not do this. • In GCC countries, the private sector plays a very minor role, providing low technology services and acting as agents for MNCs. The GCC countries have entities that are supposed to be equivalent to Singapore's EDB and can contribute to the private sector development, but in reality these are not as effective as the EDB.

Factor	Singapore	Abu Dhabi	GCC	Overview and gaps in strategy
State-Owned Enterprises	**Impact = 6.5.** As Singapore was going in the direction of diversifying its economy, it needed companies to lead the way in the new sectors. Because the new sectors would need substantial startup investment and the returns were not guaranteed and would take time to recover, the private sector was hesitant to take the initiative in the new sectors. As a result, the government of Singapore created its	**Impact = 2.8.** SOEs in Abu Dhabi are similar to those elsewhere in the GCC and MENA regions, where the government is the generous customer and protector. Even though the SOEs act like independent corporations and apply corporate governance, the reality is that SOEs are considered to be units operating under the government and performing a certain job, even if it costs twice as much.	**Impact = 2.8.** The GCC countries have made extensive use of SOEs. These SOEs have poor leadership, delivered poor outcomes, and failed to deliver innovation or exports.	• Singapore uses SOEs as key drivers in innovation and targeted sector development. The SOEs are required to partner closely with the private sector • The Singapore SOEs operate under robust governance and have their outcomes consistently measured. Failure to deliver the required outcomes results in the removal of the SOE leadership or its closure. Singapore enforces robust anti-corruption processes. • In GCC countries, SOEs dominate the market with effectively no transparency, efficiency, innovation, or accountability. Through having government bureaucrats lead SOEs, corruption and conflicts of interest are significant concerns.

Factor	Singapore	Abu Dhabi	GCC	Overview and gaps in strategy
	own companies to lead the way in the new sectors such as Singapore Airlines, SingTel, Singapore Technologies and MCS Group (MediaCorp). Singapore has SOEs operating in different sectors of the economy that are supporting the strategy to diversify the economy.			• The GCC lacks a system to monitor and evaluate the outcome of SOEs' activities. The GCC needs to create strong and independent entities to monitor and evaluate SOEs.

Strategy Formulation and Implementation

In addition to the factors in the wheel model, this research has found that Singapore's economic development and diversification has been impacted significantly due to four components. These components played a strong role for each factor in the model to have the efficiency and quality outcome required to be effective and have a positive impact on the diversification efforts. The four components, listed below, form the overall environment (process and philosophy) that should guide the implementation of the model and its factors:

- Systemic approach – the factors are established and managed as a robust system that has redundancy within it and the components in the system work cooperatively together. An example is the development of high-quality teachers, who enter a constructed system of selection, training, evaluation, and career staging to ensure professional growth.
- Foresight – the country has established an effective system that provides foresight. The country uses foresight to develop the strategy for future transformational change. The government of Singapore and different agencies depend on foresight to plan their strategies and anticipate global trends. Each agency and department has its foresight team which works closely with the Center for Strategic Future (CSF) under the Prime Minister's Office.
- System of systems – the factors operate independently but work together in an acknowledged system of systems. The system of systems is driven by the country's overarching strategy and vision and creates synergy between the components of the factors. The system of systems architecture enables the removal and replacement of components. For example, each statutory

board works to develop and enhance its area as an independent system and at the same time works in cooperation with the other statutory boards to meet the goals of the national strategy.

- Implementation in a complex and emergent world – Singapore created its systems with the ability to adapt to external change. The country uses robust implementation plans and processes with clear accountabilities for delivering outcomes.

Strategy formulation and implementation have been essential to Singapore's success while weakness in this element has had considerably adverse effects on the success of the GCC countries in using their oil wealth to deliver non-oil economic development and diversification.

Singapore has established the model factors as robust systems, established a capability in foresight, connected all the factors together as a system of systems, and used a formal and robust implementation process to deliver transformational change. However, Abu Dhabi and the GCC countries do not have, and did not apply, the four components as Singapore did, and their efforts to diversify their economies have not been successful:

- Systemic approach – Abu Dhabi and the GCC countries have not established each of the factors as an effective and robust system. As the proverb states, 'You are only as strong as your weakest link'. Unfortunately, for Abu Dhabi and the GCC states, most of the factors are weak and do not provide the building blocks required to support economic development and diversification.
- Foresight all GCC countries are too dependent on external consultants and external institutional advice. The advice given by these consultants and institutions is often generic and, as such, provides the country with no genuine advantage. So, Abu Dhabi and the GCC countries need to become more trusting

and reliant on their own local capabilities and local expertise to develop better foresight and strategic plans.

- <u>System of systems</u> – Abu Dhabi and the GCC countries do not use a system of systems approach to gain synergy from the factors. The system of systems enables multiple independent/semi-independent systems to effectively work together to deliver high-order strategic outcomes. However, the effectiveness of the system of systems is dependent upon:

  1. having robust and effective systems as its components;
  2. each of the component systems having the capability to work effectively as part of a system of systems, and;
  3. having the capability to establish and manage the overall system of systems.

  Unfortunately, neither Abu Dhabi nor any of the GCC countries have these three foundations to establish and utilize a system of systems approach to achieve a competitive advantage.

- <u>Implementation in a complex and emergent world</u> – Abu Dhabi and the GCC countries do not use formal and robust implementation processes, and do not use a structured transformational approach. Western countries such as the United States, UK, and Australia have recognized that the design and implementation of both policy and programs is complex and requires specialized competencies that are fundamentally different to traditional policy and strategy formulation and project management. Australia, the UK, and the US each have a 90% shortfall in leaders with the competencies required to lead and manage complex programs. Singapore established a dedicated program to develop its future leaders with competencies in managing complexity more than thirty years ago under the leadership of its Chief Scientist. Australia declared complex program management as a critical skills shortage in 2007 and established a dedicated program to develop its future leaders. The Australian program uses a methodology to select its potential future leaders based on them possessing the special attributes as defined in the Australian Government's Complex Project Management Competency Standard. Abu Dhabi and the GCC countries need to establish a dedicated program to select, develop, and mentor a cohort of future leaders who can support the government in developing and implementing the complex policies and transformation programs required to drive economic diversification and development.

Recommendations

A way forward to implement the GCC economic visions

For Abu Dhabi and the GCC to diversify their economies requires the strategy and implementation plans to strengthen the factors and to fulfill their visions. The implementation plans need to be structured and instituted as a complex program that is delivered in a complex and emergent environment. From the analyses of Singapore's experience, the following steps need to be taken.

1. Establish a system for each factor to raise the quality of its outcome with clearly defined roles and responsibilities.
2. Make all factors part of a system of systems.
3. Create entities similar to the statutory boards in Singapore for each factor, to build robustness and resilience into each factor's system.
   - Each entity should create a strategic plan for the factors to develop and set regulations affecting that factor as well as manage and coordinate the relationships within the factor and outside partners.
   - It should set the standards and KPIs for the factor to guarantee the outcome quality.
4. Create a council for economic development to fulfill the vision.
   - The members need to be competent and have formal qualifications such as a doctorate, a lengthy period of industry working experience (outside of academia) and have no members from government departments or SOEs.
   - The council needs to have foresight, strategy and implementation responsibilities.
   - The council needs to coordinate with each entity to create a development roadmap, regulation, and standards for each

factor and make sure it is complementary with the other factors.

- The council needs to develop a realistic strategy and implementation plan to execute the vision in each sector and make the necessary changes to the vision to make it successful (the implementation will be complex as a system of systems, which exists within a complex and emergent world).
- One or more anchor champion companies need to be at the center of development for that sector (for example, Masdar for renewable energy; ADNOC for petroleum, etc.);
- The development plan should include technology, human capital, and companies.
- The council needs to be strong and authoritative, and able to force the players to do their tasks.
5. The leader of the entity (SOE or public department) should be concentrating their efforts into that entity and should not have executive responsibility in another entity.
6. GCC countries need to introduce a process that integrates Norway's value at entry process, and the United Kingdom's Gateway Review and treasury five-case models.

Many developing countries similar to Abu Dhabi and the GCC states are capable of diversifying the economy and can build a resilient economy. From reviewing the gaps that Abu Dhabi and the GCC countries have in each factor (Table 12.2), and to maximize its economic growth and diversification potential, the GCC states will benefit through implementing the following recommendations, as listed in Table 12.3, which can serve any developing country.

Table 12.3. Recommendations for developing nations using the wheel of economic diversification

Factor	Recommendation for developing nations
Outer Circle (Base Factors)	
Natural Resources/ Financial Fund	• Create local companies with strong capabilities (upstream and downstream) for working with natural resources, that can compete and expand globally. • Enhance the efficiency of the management of the sovereign wealth funds, pension funds, natural resources and SOEs • Create policies to tap into the internal savings of citizens

Middle Circle (Enabler Factors)	
Human Development	• Establish a robust competency framework for the selection, development, mentoring and promotion of leaders, management, and technical positions in government and state-owned enterprises • Establish a new immigration visa model specifically to attract and retain high-caliber engineers, scientists, managers, and entrepreneurs • Create entities responsible for developing local researchers, engineers and scientists. The GCC states need to have strategies to increase the capabilities of the leaders and workforce, and groom researchers, engineers and scientists • Create entities responsible for skills development by coordinating with education entities to develop curricula connected to industries, guiding the companies to seek the right training for their employees, and preparing a skilled workforce for potential industries • Create job structures and hierarchies for specialists that differ from management • Establish an incentive system to attract and retain high-caliber engineers and scientists in this field

Governance, Institutions, and Policies	<ul><li>Hold top/key managers in government ministries, institutions and SOEs accountable for performance</li><li>Appoint leaders based on merit and make them accountable for outcomes</li><li>Create policies that promote a fair-play environment for business</li><li>Establish entities similar to statutory boards for different economic sectors to lead the development and growth of the sector and create a mechanism to monitor and coordinate the activities and develop sector-specific plans</li><li>Sector-focused strategic development plan – create a plan for each industry including a definition of critical success factors, value chain mapping, cluster development for business linkages, and sector-specific strategies</li><li>Be more diligent in fighting corruption, IP protection, contract enforcement, etc.</li><li>Create a system to enforce high-quality standards for production and services</li></ul>
Infrastructure	<ul><li>Establish a systems-based model to define future infrastructure needs and align the strategic project with economic strategy</li><li>Create an evaluation and selection process for infrastructure projects with an internationally recognized best-practice system that is transparent, reliable, and efficient. It should cover project complexity and include operational systems and asset management</li><li>Create the infrastructure required to attract international partners such as specialized parks</li></ul>

Inner Circle (Driver Factors)	
Export Orientation	• Support local companies to develop capabilities and markets in target areas or be part of the global supply chain in their industry • Create a system (or entity) to push for more exports and monitor the quality of the export products • Allow international firms to open their manufacturing for export • Create a system to connect local companies with international companies to be part of the global supply chain, for example, clusters for different industries • Support local entities to manufacture and export • Coordinate between labs and international and local entities for R&D and spillover technology • Support the development of technologies for export to markets in target areas or be part of the global supply chain
Innovation	• Establish an organisation similar to A*STAR to drive innovation and support engineers and scientists to remain focused on R&D • Create an innovation strategy that is aligned with the economic vision and works towards creating new economic sectors for the future • Create funding schemes to support innovation activities • Co-fund innovation with international companies • Create a system to support engineers and scientists to remain focused on R&D • Attract international talent and experts to provide innovation • Create labs in focus areas to attract international companies, alongside international talent and experts to provide innovation • Facilitate the technology spillover from international to local companies by creating networks between local and international entities

Entrepreneurship	• Establish incubators in focus areas to support the generation of new ideas by entrepreneurs • Create a system to support startups and spillover, and allow international entrepreneurs to work in the country • Create an ecosystem supporting entrepreneurs that includes financing, reducing bureaucratic/government administrative activities, and supporting operations, marketing and sales
Private Sector	• Revise the government procurement process to enhance private sector capabilities and apply competitive process for selection • Force big contractors to sub-contract local SMEs • Force big contractors and SOEs to outsource some operations to the SMEs • Coordinate and monitor relationships between local and international companies to enhance technology spillover and be a manufacturing supplier for OEM • Create a framework to support the connection between labs, local companies and the international companies • Create a strategy to support the development of SMEs in each economic sector, and ensure its proper execution
State-Owned Enterprises	• Remove SOE monopolies and enforce commercial base operation • Require SOEs to deliver innovation as a measurable outcome • Hold SOE leadership and management fully responsible for performance • Require business plans to include a detailed and executable implementation strategy, budget plan, performance measures, and measurable outcomes • Create an entity to monitor and evaluate the performance of SOEs, also to select, evaluate, and monitor senior managers and leaders of the SOEs

Conclusion

The objective of this book was to identify the strategies and factors used by nations to diversify their economy away from single commodity-based systems or nations with no natural resources, and to assess the potential effectiveness of applying these strategies. The research achieves this as follows.

- By developing the wheel of diversification model to identify the factors that countries should address to achieve diversification of their economy.
- By evaluating the model against the successful economic diversification of Singapore to identify the strategies that need to be implemented in developing each factor to support economic diversification.
- By examining Abu Dhabi and GCC countries against the model to assess their current strategies within each model factor and identify the requisite areas of improvement. The GCC states and Abu Dhabi have deficiencies in similar areas, although Abu Dhabi is slightly better than the others in its diversification efforts.

The GCC governments have invested heavily in each of the factors, however, the outcomes have been disappointing. The governments need to review the factors and adjust them to develop robust factor systems. To facilitate the process, this research highlights the areas that policymakers in the GCC countries need to address.

Leadership

Leadership and governance will determine which path a nation will take in the future. For states to reach their vision(s), they need to develop the skills and capabilities of the leaders of their organizations, departments, and entities. They need to have formal systems to select, evaluate, monitor, and mentor the leaders to ensure effective outcomes of the entities they lead. The selection process should be merit-based with leaders chosen for their competencies. This is particularly important in the selection of the heads of public entities, SOEs, and departments, for when incompetent people are given leadership roles in important entities, this can cripple the organization, which can be a significant contributor to the economy.

Export and open economy

Export orientation is not just a process, it needs to be a doctrine that everyone in government and the economic environment believes in and follows. The GCC countries are pushing for exports, however, these are not genuinely rewarding. For example, although Dubai has a high rate of export, it is not adding significant value to the emirate especially in areas of technology and human capabilities. The GCC could learn from Singapore by creating industries for export that are globally competitive and increase the local GDP.

Governments in the GCC are creating industries that are dependent on the feedstock of petroleum, that need cheap (subsidized) energy, and that require subsidies to be internationally competitive. However, this is an ineffective approach. The GCC governments need to open the doors to allow international companies to establish manufacturing in the region. They also need to create clusters around this process led by the local private sector, and not create clusters that isolate foreign firms from the rest of the economy. The GCC countries need to use the private sector in the clusters to harness foreign technology to develop new export products. Working with international companies can make the local private sector more efficient and competitive globally.

Exporting will benefit the GCC economies when they enhance the capabilities of local firms (private or public) and make them competitive in the international market. However, if the export is dependent on subsidies from the government to compete in the global market, this is not efficient practice and will have no impact on the factors that promote economic growth and diversity.

The GCC states, except for Saudi Arabia, have small workforces and domestic markets. Therefore, it is difficult to sustain large-scale manufacturing activities. The GCC states need to unify their markets and coordinate their economic strategies, as it is not financially viable for GCC states to invest in the same economic activities, such as aluminum and petrochemical products. For example, in a range of less than 200 nautical miles, there are three major ports acting as logistic hubs: Jabal Ali in Dubai, which is the oldest, Khalifa Port in Abu Dhabi, and Hamad Port in Qatar.

Human capabilities

For innovation and entrepreneurship, the GCC states need to work on cultural change to embed innovation and entrepreneurship in the minds of the people. The GCC countries, except for Saudi Arabia, have a relatively small number of nationals which means that they cannot be involved in all activities and cannot produce a significant number of scientists, engineers and entrepreneurs. The GCC countries need to learn from Singapore and other countries by creating an immigration system that attracts talented people from across the world. The current system does not segregate between highly skilled and educated people and low-skilled workers. The system works against attracting talented people as they do not feel secure in their status and are continuously faced with the possibility of expulsion from the country. The GCC governments need to rethink how they can create innovation and entrepreneurial activities in their nations, so these fields are not solely in the hands of nationals. When intellectual property is created in a country it belongs to that country only if it is used, otherwise it will go to other countries where it can be used, irrespective of the nationality of the innovator. The same thing applies to entrepreneurs. When they create a venture and succeed the wealth will be for the region in which they are working – nationality has nothing to do with it. The GCC states need to create systems to attract and retain talented people from across the world.

Transparency

The private sector needs to be enhanced and supported to be effective in growing and diversifying the economy. In addition, there needs to be a separation between power and wealth. However, in the GCC states, the private sector is often forced to build alliances with high officials due to their common involvement in business and directing government contracts in their favor. While some of the GCC governments are trying to impose anti-corruption regulations and processes, as long as government officials can own or work in private entities, corruption will continue to exist, and the private sector will continue to depend on the money from the government contracts provided by partnered officials and will not be forced to be efficient.

In the GCC countries, SOEs play a major role in the government activities, however, it is generally accepted that the costs are at least double or triple what it costs in the private sector. The idea of SOEs is good, but GCC governments need to evaluate the way it is running these entities. The relationship between SOEs and governments needs to be transparent with the former managed to corporate governance standards. However, there is no point in having a policy of governance if it is not enforced. The selection of the heads of the SOEs is instrumental to the effectiveness of the outcomes of the factors, and it is imperative that they have the necessary capabilities to lead that specific organization.

The GCC countries do not lack strategies and plans to transform their economies. Their visions and strategies encourage economic diversification and development. The difficulty that GCC states confront is in implementing these plans. As a general rule, in complex policies and programs, the vision and strategy accounts for about 20% of the effort, while the implementation accounts for the remaining 80%. The GCC countries need to focus on leadership, developing robust factor systems within an overarching system of systems, and implementation in a complex and emergent environment.

Conclusion

Beyond the Wheel

*I*f all goes well applying the wheel, a nation will become economically diversified and it will advance. It will find its place among the advanced nations, with its products having global reach. To keep advancing, a nation should adopt a culture of learning and improvement.

The journey of advancing a nation is dependent often on doing things without knowing they will work and leaders will face unknown issues that need to be tackled. But successful leadership will manage the issues properly and mitigate uncertainties, and this should become the process to continue national progress.

Leadership should not be concentrated on one person; it should be a process that can handle any issue, especially the unknowns. Creating and grooming leaders should be one of the priorities of all entities in any nation seeking advancement. Leaders don't grow on trees, they are cultivated, refined with experience in different levels, and trained to make smart judgments. Not all people are brought up to be leaders but become one; only a few tend to become great leaders.

Building strong leaders in different entities will lead to smart decisions. Leaders should demand data before making decisions, so that they can analyze the material and then make decisions. This process should be applied at all levels to lead to smart decision-making and efficiency in entities and within the nation as a whole.

The delegation of authority and decision-making processes is very important for advancement. It allows people at different levels to contribute positively, reduces workflow bottlenecks, defines clearly the roles and responsibilities, and enhances leadership capabilities.

Cluster boards vs factor boards

To have a successful journey using the wheel, someone must take responsibility to implement plans and reach goals (short, medium, and long-term). Creating boards to be responsible for each factor and cluster will serve that purpose. It will also create a balance or check between boards to make sure that each is taking the right action, otherwise, they will have a negative effect on other boards, and vice versa.

The relationship between boards should be cooperative and non-competitive. They should all contribute to the strategic goals of the wheel: that is, to become a diversified and developed economy, and to enhance the capabilities of the nation to compete on a global level. Each board cannot work on its own, and must work with other boards to contribute to a broader goal and culture of working collectively and altruistically.

Low hanging fruit

"Low hanging fruit" is a term used by many entities to get fast wins in order to reach the ultimate goal. But most of the time the "low hanging fruit" become the only winning point of the project or strategy.

A quick win is not the ultimate goal. But in some entities, it becomes part of the culture to jump from one project to another to keep the attention on new projects and ideas instead of finishing what is at hand. A quick-win culture hurtles the economic visions of most nations, because politicians are looking for point-scoring to present as business success and to use this to achieve media exposure and become part of an inner circle of leadership.

If anyone talks about "low hanging fruit" and "quick wins" then you should know that this person is opportunistic, will not finish what is at hand, and will jump the ship when it starts to sink.

Set good factors

The success of the wheel of economic diversification and development is dependent on the success of each factor. The success should be measured by the quality of the outcome and not by how much the government spends to have shiny and glamorous factors. For example, a government can spend a lot of money promoting innovation and entrepreneurship, but if it does not have the ecosystem to take innovation from being an idea to a commercial product, then this factor becomes a failure. Success in this factor relies on contributions from other factors and the support of clusters using the innovations. In other words, success can only be achieved through a system of systems approach, whereby no factor can work individually and the result of one factor (good or bad) affects all other factors.

An altruistic culture is the key to success. Many strategies have failed because of the struggle between different groups. Patriotism is not thinking you are the only one who knows what is best for the nation, it is how you can help others to present their strengths for the good of the nation. Success in each factor is about the quality of the outcome and how this contributes positively to the other factors, clusters, and the nation as a whole.

It is not an easy task to achieve a successful journey of economic advancement, especially now in a time of individualism, where self-success is often considered more important than group success. But with good processes and systems in place, individuals can achieve their success and contribute to the success of the country.

Dr. Ahmed Saeed Al-Nayeli Al-Shamsi

Dr. Ahmed Saeed Al-Nayeli Al-Shamsi is the Special Advisor to the Chief Executive Officer/ Group Managing Director of EDGE, an advanced technology group for defense and beyond.

He took up this role after retiring from the UAE Armed Forces as a Staff Colonel.

Dr. Al-Shamsi helped establish Tawazun, the industry enabler responsible for the creation and development of a sustainable defense and security industry in the UAE, as well as its subsidiaries, and was a member of Tawazun's Economic Council for nine years.

He represented Tawazun in governing boards of organizations such as the International Golden Group (IGG), which specializes in providing high-end defense and security solutions; ADASI, an end-to-end solution provider in the autonomous systems industry; Remaya, a key player in shooting training and ranges management; NIMR-Algerie, a producer of Nimr vehicles in Algeria, and; Tawazun Industrial Park.

He also represented the organization in various committees such as the Organising Committee of Global Manufacturing and Industrialisation Summit (GMIS), the Joint Committee with the Republic of Russia for Industrial Defence Capabilities, as well as panels managed by the Ministry of Foreign Affairs with partner nations.

Dr. Al-Shamsi holds a doctorate in business administration from the University of Wollongong – Dubai. The research focuses on the strategies of economic diversification in Abu Dhabi and the GCC.

He completed his bachelor's degree in aeronautical engineering from Embry–Riddle Aeronautical University, United States, and has attended various specialized courses at military schools and colleges.

Notes